KU-495-690

THE POLITICS OF QUASI-GOVERNMENT
Hybrid Organizations and the Dynamics of Bureaucratic Control

Hybrid organizations, governmental entities that mix characteristics of private and public sector organizations, are increasingly popular mechanisms for implementing public policy. Koppell assesses the performance of the growing quasi-government in terms of accountability and control. Comparing hybrids to traditional government agencies in three policy domains – export promotion, housing and international development – Koppell argues that hybrid organizations are more difficult to control, largely due to the fact that hybrids behave like regulated organizations rather than extensions of administrative agencies. Providing a rich conception of the bureaucratic control problem, Koppell also argues that hybrid organizations are intrinsically less responsive to the political preferences of their political masters and suggests that as policy tools they are inappropriate for some tasks. This book provides a timely study of an important administrative and political phenomenon.

JONATHAN G S KOPPELL is Assistant Professor of Politics, Policy and Organization at the Yale School of Management, Yale University.

THEORIES OF INSTITUTIONAL DESIGN

Series Editor
Robert E. Goodin
Research School of Social Sciences
Australian National University

Advisory Editors
Brian Barry, Russell Hardin, Carole Pateman, Barry Weingast,
Stephen Elkin, Claus Offe, Susan Rose-Ackerman

Social scientists have rediscovered institutions. They have been increasingly concerned with the myriad ways in which social and political institutions shape the patterns of individual interactions which produce social phenomena. They are equally concerned with the ways in which those institutions emerge from such interactions.

This series is devoted to the exploration of the more normative aspects of these issues. What makes one set of institutions better than another? How, if at all, might we move from a less desirable set of institutions to a more desirable set? Alongside the questions of what institutions we would design, if we were designing them afresh, are pragmatic questions of how we can best get from here to there: from our present institutions to new revitalized ones.

Theories of institutional design is insistently multidisciplinary and interdisciplinary, both in the institutions on which it focuses, and in the methodologies used to study them. There are interesting sociological questions to be asked about legal institutions, interesting legal questions to be asked about economic institutions, and interesting social, economic and legal questions to be asked about political institutions. By juxtaposing these approaches in print, this series aims to enrich normative discourse surrounding important issues of designing and redesigning, shaping and reshaping the social, political and economic institutions of contemporary society.

THE POLITICS OF QUASI-GOVERNMENT

Hybrid Organizations and the Dynamics of Bureaucratic Control

JONATHAN G S KOPPELL
Yale School of Management

CAMBRIDGE
UNIVERSITY PRESS

PUBLISHED BY THE PRESS SYNDICATE OF THE UNIVERSITY OF CAMBRIDGE
The Pitt Building, Trumpington Street, Cambridge CB2 1RP, United Kingdom

CAMBRIDGE UNIVERSITY PRESS
The Edinburgh Building, Cambridge, CB2 2RU, UK
40 West 20th Street, New York, NY 10011–4211, USA
477 Williamstown Road, Port Melbourne, VIC 3207, Australia
Ruiz de Alarcón 13, 28014 Madrid, Spain
Dock House, The Waterfront, Cape Town 8001, South Africa

http://www.cambridge.org

© Jonathan G S Koppell 2003

This book is in copyright. Subject to statutory exception and
to the provisions of relevant collective licensing agreements,
no reproduction of any part may take place without
the written permission of Cambridge University Press.

First published 2003

Printed in the United Kingdom at the University Press, Cambridge

Typeface Minion 10.5/12 pt.   *System* LᴬTEX 2$_\varepsilon$ [TB]

A catalogue record for this book is available from the British Library

ISBN 0 521 81956 3 hardback

23019 433

The publisher has used its best endeavours to ensure that the URLs for external websites
referred to in this book are correct and active at the time of going to press. However, the
publisher has no responsibility for the websites and can make no guarantee that a site will
remain live or that the content is or will remain appropriate.

In Memory of
Harold Seidman,
scholar and public servant

Contents

Figures

Tables

Acknowledgments

In the summer of 1993, I didn't know the difference between Fannie Mae, the government-sponsored enterprise, and Fannie May, the purveyor of chocolates. Nevertheless, Aida Alvarez, director of a new, obscure federal agency called the Office of Federal Housing Enterprise Oversight (OFHEO), hired me as employee no. 8. For that, I am grateful.

The experience opened my eyes to the peculiar world of quasi-government. OFHEO is a government agency created to ensure that other governmental organizations are doing what they are supposed to do. Very odd. More surprising, I found this type of arrangement is actually quite common. Intrigued, I took my newfound interest in "quasi-government" with me to the University of California.

Many people in the Berkeley Department of Political Science deserve my gratitude. In particular, Judy Gruber was a marvelous advisor. Her careful reading, thoughtful comments and encouragement were invaluable. The Institute of Governmental Studies (IGS) provided my campus home and family. IGS directors Nelson Polsby and Bruce Cain have been vital as critics and advisors. Thanks also to Todd LaPorte, John Ellwood and the IGS Library staff, a group united by their helpfulness.

Much of the research and writing was carried out in Washington, DC, where Tom Mann and the Governmental Studies department graciously provided me with a base of operations at the Brookings Institution. Later I moved to the New America Foundation at the generous invitation of its president and founder, Ted Halstead. New America was the perfect place to finish the doctoral project; it offered the quiet and resources needed to get work done and the intellectual distraction necessary to stave off madness.

The transformation of my doctoral dissertation into this spellbinding volume was accomplished at my current institutional home, the Yale School of Management. My colleagues, in particular Doug Rae and Ted Marmor, have been incredibly supportive, offering advice and encouragement. Series editor Bob Goodin was a reliable source of sound suggestions and good cheer.

Finally, the most significant contributor to this project has been Professor Jennifer Steen, who happens to be my wife. She read countless versions of every sentence in this book (including this one) and offered innumerable suggestions, criticisms, edits and bits of needed positive feedback. Like it or not, she acquired detailed knowledge of hybrid organizations, and reciprocated by sharing her unparalleled insight into self-financing candidates. I cannot thank her enough.

Acronyms

CBO	Congressional Budget Office
DAI	Development Alternatives, Inc.
EEOC	Equal Employment Opportunity Commission
EF	Enterprise Fund
EPA	Environmental Protection Agency
ExIm	Export-Import Bank of the United States
FCA	Farm Credit Administration
FDIC	Federal Deposit Insurance Corporation
FEC	Federal Election Commission
FHA	Federal Housing Administration
FHEFSSA	Federal Housing Enterprises Financial Safety and Soundness Act
FHFB	Federal Housing Finance Board
FHLMC	Federal Home Loan Mortgage Corporation (also known as "Freddie Mac")
FNMA	Federal National Mortgage Association (also known as "Fannie Mae")
FOIA	Freedom of Information Act
GAO	General Accounting Office
GCCA	Government Corporation Control Act
GNMA	Government National Mortgage Association (also known as "Ginnie Mae")
GPRA	Government Performance Results Act
GSE	Government-Sponsored Enterprise
HAEF	Hungarian American Enterprise Fund
HUD	US Department of Housing and Urban Development

IF	Investment Fund
ITA	International Trade Administration
NAFTA	North American Free Trade Area
OFHEO	Office of Federal Housing Enterprise Oversight
OMB	Office of Management and Budget
OPIC	Overseas Private Investment Corporation
OSHA	Occupational Safety and Health Administration
PAEF	Polish American Enterprise Fund
PTO	Patent and Trademark Office
RFP	Request for Proposals
SBA	Small Business Administration
SEC	Securities and Exchange Commission
SEED	Support Eastern European Democracy Act
TDA	Trade and Development Agency
TPCC	Trade Promotion Coordinating Committee
TVA	Tennessee Valley Authority
USAID	United States Agency for International Development
USDA	United States Department of Agriculture
USTR	United States Trade Representative
VA	Department of Veterans Affairs

1

Introduction

In the aftermath of the attacks on the World Trade Center and the Pentagon, attention was focused on the failings of the private firms charged with securing America's aviation system. The low quality of airport security – a fact long known to frequent travelers in the United States – was suddenly an urgent concern. The Bush Administration quickly suggested that the government might assume responsibility for screening passengers and baggage, a function then performed by low-paid employees of private security firms hired by individual airlines (Schneider and Nakashima 2001).

This development was quite striking inasmuch as President George W. Bush followed in the tradition of Ronald Reagan, calling for a smaller federal government and increased responsibility for the private sector. What was not surprising, however, was that the general suggestion was soon followed by the proposal that a government corporation be created to handle the weighty task of hiring, training and managing the personnel charged with preventing another September 11.

Government corporations are a type of "hybrid" organization. The appeal of hybrids, entities that combine characteristics of public- and private-sector organizations, lies in the belief that they combine the best of both worlds: public accountability and private efficiency. Indeed, the General Accounting Office (GAO) expert testifying before Congress regarding his agency's survey of possible structures of the new security agency noted the general view "that the screening performance and accountability would improve under a government corporation" and such an entity would be "more flexible and less bureaucratic than a federal agency" (GAO 2001).

For reasons too numerous to catalog here, the Transportation Security Administration was not created as a government corporation (Schneider

2002). Still, the episode gives an indication of the prominence of hybrid organizations in contemporary governance and the need to better understand these peculiar entities frequently called upon to carry out public functions.

Created by governments to address public policy needs, hybrids resemble private companies in form and function. Many hybrids are privately owned, profit-seeking businesses. They generally charge fees for the services they provide, allowing them to cover the cost of their operations. And they are exempt from many of the laws and regulations that apply to government agencies, giving them flexibility as they pursue organizational objectives.

Hybrids are not commonly referred to as a *class* of institutions because each is unique in terms of history, purpose and organization. Still, many are familiar fixtures. In the United States, for example, the Federal Deposit Insurance Corporation (FDIC), the Port Authority of New York and New Jersey, and the Tennessee Valley Authority (TVA) are known to many people. At the very least, their names are familiar.

Hybrids are perhaps more common outside the United States. In Commonwealth countries, the peculiar class of organizations dubbed "quangos" perform a dizzying array of functions. Public enterprises, companies that are owned all or in part by government, are relatives of American hybrids that are common around the globe. There is even a mysterious class of transnational hybrid organizations such as the World Bank and International Monetary Fund that are publicly financed by multiple nations yet run as semi-private entities.

For every hybrid that is somewhat familiar, there are many more that operate in the shadows, carrying out mundane functions such as power generation, school construction and the management of our railroads. If the obscurity of most hybrids creates the impression that these institutions are marginal in the scheme of US government, that impression is misleading:

- Hybrids are big; the combined liability of federal hybrids (i.e., the amount of money guaranteed by hybrid organizations) exceeds $2 trillion, more than the entire federal budget for this (or any) year.
- Hybrids are numerous; there are more than fifty federal hybrids and hundreds more in state and local government.
- Hybrids are vital; hybrids perform critical functions, ranging from financing home purchases to operating metropolitan transit systems to disposing of weapons-grade uranium.

In short, hybrids touch the lives of virtually every American. Despite the lack of popular or scholarly attention quasi-government is critical, and in the coming years it is likely to grow in importance. To borrow the words Arthur Miller penned for Linda Loman, attention must be paid.

Why are hybrids of interest?

Although hybrid organizations are not new, they are increasingly common features of the governmental landscape. Their proliferation can be explained by several factors. First, proponents of quasi-government promise greater effectiveness than traditional government agencies at lower cost to taxpayers. Second, at a time when all things governmental are regarded with suspicion and the triumph of capitalism is widely celebrated, hybrids are appealing precisely because they seem more "businesslike" than a typical government program. Third, the desire to trim the budgets of government at all levels has led policy-makers to seek out alternatives that will ease the burden on public appropriations.

There are legitimate reasons for concern that the growth of this "quasi-government" is continuing unchecked. Collectively, hybrids embody an alternative relationship between elected officials and public bureaucracies – or, to use the language of economics, principals and agents. Many tools traditionally utilized by principals to control their agents are not part of quasi-government (Smith 1975, Musolf and Seidman 1980, Moe and Stanton 1989). For example, the leaders of many federal hybrids are not appointed by the President but elected by stockholders. Other hybrids are exempt from the yearly appropriations process through which Congress exercises its oversight function. These constraints on government agencies often were put in place, however, to ensure due process, fairness, equity and other values related to proper public administration in democratic regimes (Kaufman 1977).

As a result, critics of quasi-government claim that hybrids are simply beyond the control of elected officials, and, by extension, the public. In the rush to move government expenditures off-budget and bring "market efficiency" into the public sector, policy responsibilities have been delegated to hybrids with little consideration of the potential *political* costs. Thus critical questions have gone unanswered – even unasked.

Do we sacrifice popular sovereignty by granting public authority to semi-private institutions? Is the quasi-government accountable to the public? Are hybrids beyond the control of our elected representatives? These are the central questions of this book.

Accountability and control are core considerations of political science. An "unaccountable" government, insulated from the public and their elected representatives, threatens the very legitimacy of a democratic political system (Krislov and Rosenbloom 1981, Gruber 1987). In light of the swelling ranks of hybrid organizations – and their latent threat to democratic accountability – this study is long overdue.

It is crucial to note that this book is not based upon the assumption that hybrid organizations are inherently more difficult to control or less accountable than government agencies. On the contrary, the purpose of this volume is to determine if, when and why that is the case. Proponents of the hybrid model argue that freedom from the bureaucratic "red tape" that ensnares government agencies endows hybrid organizations with the flexibility necessary for success. The purpose of this book is to fill in the other side of the ledger.

Learning from hybrids

There is an additional benefit to studying political control of hybrid organizations. It yields tremendous insight into the nature of control over traditional government agencies. Like Oliver Sacks' studies of abnormal psychology that provide understanding of normal brain physiology (Sacks 1987), this book highlights the function of structural features of government agencies by revealing the consequences of their absence from hybrid organizations. This study of hybrids revealed that the absence of some features does result in loss of control. However, the absence of other features seems *not* to diminish organizational accountability.

Thus attention is focused on an aspect of the "principal-agent" relationship frequently overlooked in the bureaucratic control literature. Typically studies of bureaucratic control evaluate the relative influence of various principals: Congress, the President, the courts, interest groups. Rarely are variations in the structure of *agents* even considered. By comparing hybrids and traditional agencies in three policy domains, this study is designed to accomplish just that objective.

To understand the dynamics of quasi-government and evaluate the consequences of variation in agent structure for bureaucratic control, American federal hybrids and traditional government agencies were compared in three policy areas: export promotion, housing and international market development. In each area, explicit principal preferences were identified and the performance of the organizations was examined to determine the extent to which the different types of agents satisfied these preferences. The design and theoretical implications of this research are addressed at greater length in the second chapter.

The strange world of the federal quasi-government

The United States Constitution is quite vague regarding the structure of the executive branch of the federal government. Article I, section 8 states simply that Congress has the power "To make all laws which shall be necessary and proper for carrying into execution the foregoing powers, and all other powers vested by this Constitution in the government of the United

States, or in any department or officer thereof." This vagueness has permitted the executive branch to adapt to changing demands with countless innovations, variations and mutations. Indeed, experiments in administrative structure are an American tradition. *McCulloch* v. *Maryland*, one of the cornerstone cases that defined the Supreme Court's power, considered the legitimacy of a novel organization, the Bank of the United States (Stanton 1994). The Bank was just the first in a line of seemingly unprecedented public institutions.

The most familiar bureaucratic form is the executive department. In the early days of the Republic, departments were few and small. The Departments of State, Treasury and War conducted the business of the federal government until 1849. The spirit of experimentation with organizational form was alive and well at this time. One of the most peculiar American governmental entities, the Smithsonian Institution, was created in 1846 following years of congressional deliberation. Established with the gift of James Smithson, the Institution is governed by a committee that includes the Vice-President, the Chief Justice of the Supreme Court, and Members of Congress appointed by the Speaker. Not only is this structure likely unconstitutional, it remains unique even by today's standards.

The Civil War and territorial expansion prompted more conventional government growth. Offices and personnel were added and new departments created (Interior in 1849, Justice in 1870, Agriculture in 1889). Even with this major expansion, the size of the federal government did not approach the current scale until well into the twentieth century.

World War I prompted the next wave of expansion. Mobilization led to the creation of a set of institutions intended to prepare the United States quickly for war. The Emergency Fleet Corporation, US Grain Corporation and War Finance Corporation were set up as government corporations to allow them to act more quickly than government agencies (Pritchett 1946a). After the war they were phased out, their assets sold, their operations halted. These organizations were ancestors of modern American hybrids in the sense that they operated as independent entities carrying out functions that resembled private-sector organizations (e.g., overseeing the construction of vessels and housing for workers).

This set the pattern for government expansion during the New Deal and World War II. Faced with the Depression and a need for military mobilization, Roosevelt and Congress created a familiar alphabet soup of entities, including several hybrids that still operate today – the Export-Import Bank (ExIm), Tennessee Valley Authority and Federal Crop Insurance Corporation – as well as several agencies that were later "hybridized," partially or completely sold to private parties. The government did not shrink following World War II as it did in the wake of World War I. Fear of a renewed Depression kept agencies in place; sustained economic expansion through the 1950s tempered the need to cut government spending.

Indeed, the growth of the federal government in this period nearly kept pace with that of the previous decade. This expansion slowed dramatically by the end of the 1960s. Debt from the "Great Society" programs and the Vietnam War as well as the financial crises of the 1970s limited the federal government's ability to address policy problems with direct expenditures. This helps account for the creation of numerous hybrids in the late 1970s and 1980s, including the Rural Telephone Bank, the Pension Benefit Guaranty Corporation, the Legal Services Corporation and others.

Budget constraints and rules have always been a significant factor in the explanation for the growth of American quasi-government. The transformation of the Federal National Mortgage Association ("Fannie Mae") from a government agency to a government corporation to a privately-owned government-sponsored enterprise, for example, can be directly attributed to revisions in budget rules. Designated a government corporation to escape inclusion in the budget, Fannie Mae was restructured again when government corporations went from "off-budget" to "on-budget" status. This necessitated another change in Fannie Mae – this time it became a government-sponsored enterprise – to get it back off-budget (interview 112, Tierney 1984, 79).

In recent years, efforts to trim the federal budget sustained the appeal of the hybrid form generally and increased interest in selling government-owned organizations to investors. For example, the Student Loan Marketing Association – an entity that performs a function for student loans similar to that performed by Fannie Mae for home loans – is being "fully privatized" (Crenshaw 1997). This will raise money for the Treasury and move debt off-budget. It has been suggested that other agencies should be "hybridized" or sold for similar reasons.

There are other rationales for creating hybrids. At the state and local levels, hybrids are utilized as instruments to overcome a wide range of obstacles faced by traditional public bureaucracies. New York State's public authorities, for example, are known for pioneering the "moral obligation" bond as a means of circumventing limitations on state government borrowing. This created not a legal obligation of payment, as prohibited by the borrowing limits applied to government agencies, but a moral obligation that investors accepted with a wink (Sharkansky 1979). Other authorities have been designed to straddle multiple jurisdictions (e.g., the Port Authority of New York and New Jersey) or enable their leaders to operate free of constraints created by state laws and regulations.

Outside the United States, there are hybrid organizations with origins similar to those of American quasi-governmental entities. The most commonly

utilized label for such organizations is "quangos." Quangos (which are discussed at greater length later in this chapter) are generally associated with
Commonwealth nations. Many quangos began their existence as government bureaus but underwent a transformation at some point for fiscal or
ideological reasons.

There are also large numbers of hybrids with histories quite different
from their American cousins. These organizations are often referred to as
"state enterprises," "public enterprises" or "state-owned enterprises." Unlike
American hybrids, these enterprises generally were founded as private companies. At some point, for reasons of market failure, national interest or
political movement, the company or an entire industry was nationalized.
That is, the government assumed ownership of all or part of a profit-seeking
business. In developing countries, many public enterprises were founded
with public capital and thus have been hybrid from their inception. These
types of hybrids are quite different from those that have been discussed in
the American context. They were not created – or hybridized – to deliver
some public good in place of a government agency. As a result, the expectations for such entities, and the standards by which they are judged, are often
quite different. The findings of this book are least relevant for this type of
hybrid organization, as shall become clear in the ensuing pages.

There is an additional emerging class of hybrid that looms large on
the horizon. These hybrids serve multiple nations and have literally global
"jurisdictions." This diverse group of entities includes prominent institutions such as the World Bank and the International Monetary Fund. These
organizations are financed by the governments of the world and/or returns
on loans made to borrowing nations. Smaller, and far less visible, is the growing population of entities created to govern specific areas of international
activity. Examples include the World Intellectual Property Organization and
the Internet Corporation for Assigned Names and Numbers, and there are
many other bodies with relatively narrow purposes. These entities look more
like government agencies than many hybrids in that they perform traditional
governmental functions rather than providing services for customers. Their
transnational character and reliance on fees paid by client organizations
(including governments) distinguish them from traditional agencies.

The ranks of all types of hybrid organizations are sure to continue swelling.
Suggestions for new hybrids at all levels of government around the globe
emerge frequently. In the United States, hybrid structures are deemed superior by some because the hybrid, unlike the government agency, must
maintain financial discipline to survive in the market place. Thus traditional
agencies are sometimes targeted for conversion into hybrids. Congress has
considered, for example, "hybridization" (usually labeled "privatization" for
its political appeal) of the Social Security Administration and the Air Traffic

Services of the Department of Transportation. These organizations could fund their own operations with fees paid by users for services and would provide a one-time boost to the Treasury with their sale.

In addition to the recent proposals for security-related hybrids, multiple new hybrid suggestions emerged from the Clinton Administration. "America's Private Investment Corporations" would have been a set of funds created to stimulate investment in underdeveloped American communities; the proposal was dropped by Clinton's successor (Markoff 1999). "Kiddie Mac," a proposed government-sponsored enterprise, would have financed construction of childcare facilities (Scherer 1999). One hybrid that *was* created under Clinton was In-Q-It (later renamed In-Q-Tee), a CIA-backed technology venture capital fund (Henry 2002).

In search of an analytic framework

Despite their popularity and importance, hybrids have not received much attention. Improbable as it may seem, in fact, no one knows just how many federal hybrids exist. This is a function of ambiguity, not secrecy. A General Accounting Office report on government corporations, a subset of hybrid organizations, relied upon organizations to characterize themselves (1995). That is, organizations were included in the report only if they considered themselves government corporations! The labels Congress attaches to organizations reveal little regarding the nature of the institution. Corporations are called agencies. Agencies are called foundations. Foundations are called corporations. The slipperiness of the labels calls to mind the conversation of Alice and Humpty-Dumpty in Lewis Carroll's *Through the Looking Glass:*

> "When *I* use a word," Humpty-Dumpty said, in rather a scornful tone, "it means just what I choose it to mean – neither more nor less."
>
> "The question is," said Alice, "whether you *can* make words mean so many different things."

The world of quasi-government would make Humpty-Dumpty beam. As a result, establishing order is an imposing task. Even the simple objective of determining what organizations to consider hybrids can be elusive.

One way to identify hybrids is to sort the entire universe of governmental institutions. Harold Seidman offers a system that, by his own admission, "makes no claim to scientific exactness" (Seidman and Gilmour 1986, 254). At the core of the federal government lie the *executive departments.* Those mentioned already have been joined by Commerce, Labor, Health and Human Services, Housing and Urban Development (HUD), Transportation, Energy, Education and Veterans Affairs (VA). The Executive Office of the President has grown to resemble a department encompassing several large agencies, most notably the Office of Management and Budget (OMB).

Closest to this core are a host of *independent agencies*, including the Environmental Protection Agency (EPA), the National Aeronautics and Space Administration, the Peace Corps and the Small Business Administration (SBA). Seidman cautions that *independence* means only that the agency is not part of an executive department, not that it is independent of the President or executive branch (1986, 254). There are numerous *institutes* (e.g., National Institute of Health) and *foundations* (e.g., National Science Foundation) associated with executive departments. *Commissions*, often created to perform regulatory functions, *are* independent and insulated from executive branch influence by virtue of statutorily required partisan balance in membership and lengthy terms not coinciding with presidential administration.

All of the entities mentioned so far are solidly governmental. They receive federal appropriations, are governed by presidential appointees, and are subject to federal rules and regulations. Seidman proposes three more categories for entities that are less traditional in character. *Government corporations*, such as the Federal Deposit Insurance Corporation and TVA, have a business-related purpose, produce revenue and conduct a large number of transactions with the public (GAO 1995). *Private institutions organized by the federal government to provide contractual services* include well-known research establishments like the Los Alamos National Laboratory and the Rand Corporation.

Then there are the leftovers. Seidman dubs this final category "*the Twilight Zone.*" This remainder bin includes well-known organizations such as the Federal Reserve Banks, Fannie Mae and Amtrak. These entities were created by Congress but are privately owned (or partially owned by private parties). They are tied to the federal government by unique privileges, distinctive regulation and unusual appointment schemes.

The problem with Seidman's typology is its lack of an organizing principle. Many of the organizations in one category have much in common with institutions in other categories. For example, almost all the denizens of the Twilight Zone are as independent as, say, the Nuclear Regulatory Commission. No dominant characteristic orders the population. This implies a definition of hybrid organizations that would focus on what the organizations *are not* rather than what they *are*.

Perry and Rainey propose a typology incorporating *three* characteristics: ownership, funding and mode of control (1988). With three variables, this approach yields eight categories. One could consider organizations in categories two through eight (as numbered in table 1.1) to be hybrid organizations – although that is not indisputable.

Table 1.1 *Perry and Rainey's typology of institutions*

Category	Ownership	Funding	Control	Example
1. Bureau	Public	Public	Polyarchy	Bureau of Labor Statistics
2. Government corporation	Public	Private	Polyarchy	Pension Benefit Guaranty Corporation
3. Government-sponsored enterprise	Private	Public	Polyarchy	Fannie Mae
4. Regulated enterprise	Private	Private	Polyarchy	Private utilities
5. Governmental enterprise	Public	Public	Market	No known examples
6. State-owned enterprise	Public	Private	Market	Amtrak, Airbus
7. Government contractor	Private	Public	Market	Grumman
8. Private enterprise	Private	Private	Market	IBM

Note: This table is copied exactly as presented by Perry and Rainey (1988, table 2, 196) and does not reflect the author's view regarding proper characterizations of these institutions.

There are problems with this system. First, there are mixed ownership corporations in which the federal government shares ownership with private investors (e.g., Federal Home Loan Banks, Rural Telephone Bank). It is unclear how such institutions should be classified in Perry and Rainey's scheme. Second, many organizations receive funding from both appropriations and revenue income. Again it is unclear how such organizations should be classified.

A more serious concern, particularly with respect to the questions at the center of this book, is the "mode of social control" variable. The polyarchy/market distinction is quite slippery, as Perry and Rainey's examples reveal. Amtrak is offered as a "market" control entity while Fannie Mae is in the "polyarchy" category, meaning that it is subject to political control. While this may be true in some senses, it is far from straightforward. The requirement that Congress approve any labor agreement for Amtrak employees, for example, clearly conflicts with Perry and Rainey's classification of Amtrak as a market control organization (Woodward 1997). The executives of Fannie Mae, an organization classified as "polyarchy" in the control column, would blanch at the thought of such congressional intervention.

Even if one could definitively categorize every institution as "market" or "polyarchy" based on some structural feature, this approach would still not be satisfactory. This typology provides the answer to the "control question" without the empirical research that is the core of this book. Perry and Rainey rely upon the formal structure to formulate their characterization. This book is based on an investigation of the link between structure and actual control.

The Perry and Rainey approach does, however, offer a promising lead. A simplified version of their framework is proposed for the purpose of defining the population of hybrid organizations. The "mixed institution" problem is solved by making a default assignment of "public" and shifting to "private" at the first sign of deviation (i.e., mixed ownership is typologically equivalent to private ownership). For example, the Federal Home Loan Bank system would be coded as "private" in the ownership column.

A similar solution applies to the "funding" variable. Organizations are considered publicly funded unless they effectively cover all or most of their operating expenses with their generated revenue in most years. Funding is a more tricky matter because many entities that meet this criterion do not retain per se their earnings for subsequent use. Rather their income is funneled into the general revenues of the government and their budget is funded out of general appropriations. The appropriations level in year $t + 1$ is, however, a function of earnings in year t. Thus such entities are effectively "paying their own way."

In contrast, there are many so-called government corporations that, despite their name, are funded entirely (or mostly) through appropriations and thus would not be classified as hybrids (e.g., Corporation for National Service). Only government corporations that typically generate annual revenues nearly equal to their annual outlays are included in the hybrid category.

Finally, the "mode of control" problem is avoided by simply excluding this variable from the typology. Thus the population of federal hybrids is identified on the basis of private funding and/or ownership in the simplified version of the Perry and Rainey typology (see table 1.2).

Table 1.2 *Simplified typology of institutions*

Category	Ownership		Funding
Government agency	Public		Public
Hybrid organization	Private (or mixed)	OR	Private[a]
Private entity	Private		Private

[a] Organizations that generate revenue that effectively covers most of their operating expenses are considered "privately" funded.

This simplified version of the Perry and Rainey approach is employed to formulate a definition of hybrid organization that is used in this book:

A hybrid organization is an entity created by the federal government (either by act of Congress or executive action) to address a specific public policy purpose. It is owned in whole or part by private individuals or corporations and/or generates revenue to cover its operating costs.

This definition excludes government bureaus, including independent agencies and "government corporations," that operate on appropriated funds, regulatory commissions, institutes and some foundations that are not distinguished in organizational form from executive agencies.

This definition also does not include private firms brought into governmental orbit through contractual relationships with government agencies. Although some argue that such organizations are indistinguishable from governmental institutions (Kettl 1993, Bozeman 1987), they differ from hybrids in at least two pertinent respects: (a) the contracting agency typically bears responsibility for delivery of some service or good by contractors; (b) as a consequence, expectations for accountability and public control do not apply to contractors as they do to mixed institutions. For example, the Department of Transportation is responsible for the quality of roadway construction carried out by private contractors. This is not to suggest that concerns regarding the accountability of such organizations are misplaced or invalid. Increased reliance on contractors is a serious matter related to but not at the heart of the hybrid discussion and beyond the scope of this project.

Establishing a working definition of hybrid organizations is an important step. The population of hybrids from which the entities studied were drawn was identified according to this definition. In the pages to follow, conclusions are drawn based on the organizations studied that are offered as applicable to a more general population of hybrids.

Hybrid literature

There are considerable barriers to systematic study of hybrid organizations. First, the heterogeneity of this class of organizations makes generalization quite difficult. Every hybrid is structured somewhat differently with permutations including governance structure, funding mechanisms and relationships with elected officials. Second, the substantive complexity of the activities carried out by each organization requires the researcher to devote considerable energy to learning about the nature of the organization's operations. Third, the relative obscurity of any single hybrid organization limits the audience for work that is not broad. Nevertheless, a handful of scholars have examined hybrids and raised issues related to their structural distinctiveness.

Seidman points out the problems created by the vague legal status of government-sponsored enterprises and other hybrids. Lines of authority have been blurred and constitutional questions raised as "degovernmentalization" has continued (Seidman 1988, 25). Musolf studied several hybrids including Comsat, Amtrak and Fannie Mae and raised similar questions concerning organizational accountability (1983, 1984).

Neither of these authors offered empirical assessments of the *relative* accountability of hybrids and traditional agencies. Rather they note the extra-constitutional nature of these organizations, the alarming absence of structural controls that exist for traditional government agencies, and the apparent shortcomings in terms of accountability. Like Leazes, in his excellent study of the development of the federal government corporation (1987), they assume the connection between structures designed to achieve control and actual control over government agencies.

Of all hybrids, government corporations have been subject to the most empirical investigation, usually in the form of case studies. Perhaps the most examined institution is the Tennessee Valley Authority. Studies by Selznick (1953), Lillienthal (1944), Finer (1944) and Pritchett (1943) have made the organization's extensive powers and broad mandate familiar to students of public administration. Although these authors note the substantive structural independence of the TVA, there is little effort to compare empirically presidential and congressional influence over the TVA as opposed to government agencies.

A few authors have studied the implications of government corporation structure for management and accountability. Pritchett argues that the deviation from a standard form for government corporations reduces their functionality as alternatives to traditional government agencies (1946a, 1946b). Demonstrating that many government corporations operate and are treated in a manner similar to agencies, Pritchett warns, "It serves no useful purpose to keep the original label on a bottle when its contents have been changed, and it may cause trouble" (1946a, 383). His words obviously were not heeded, for Dimock echoed these arguments in a two-part article that urged a return to genuine government corporations, companies that operate truly free of political oversight and direction (1949).

Seidman presents an opposing view, that government corporations are instruments of government that must be subject to controls (1952, 1954). Although he is willing to acknowledge that the corporate form is appropriate for the performance of certain functions, Seidman does not accept the contention that government corporations should be placed beyond the reach of Congress or the President. In making this argument, Seidman refers to the

Cherry Cotton Mills case, in which the Supreme Court essentially concluded the same.

The subsequent literature on government corporations reflects the shifting expectations for hybrid organizations, demonstrating that the debate between Pritchett/Dimock and Seidman has never been resolved. Tierney, for example, describes the conditions under which government corporations are created and warns that expectations placed upon these entities are unrealistically high and political "interference" is inevitable (1984). Calls for reduced political influence over government corporations faded and have been replaced by critiques of the government corporation form based on their shortcomings in terms of control and dedication to public purposes. Khademian, utilizing a study of the Federal Deposit Insurance Corporation, explores the ways in which a government corporation's interest in revenue affects its management (1995). She argues that government corporations' concern for the "bottom line" clearly affects management and decision-making, a point that is bolstered by this study. Froomkin offers a set of structural reforms intended to increase accountability of government corporations and reduce risk to taxpayers, including clearer statement of legal status and public receipt of profits from corporate activities (1996).

In recent years, government-sponsored enterprises have received more attention than other hybrid organizations. Government-sponsored enterprises (GSEs) are a type of hybrid distinguished by private ownership, profitability and advantages derived from the organization's special relationship with the federal government. The most well-known GSEs are "Fannie Mae" and "Freddie Mac," two mortgage finance corporations that are traded on the New York Stock Exchange and are among the largest companies in the United States (in terms of assets). Both are discussed in detail in this book. There are other GSEs in the areas of housing, agriculture and education.

Harold Seidman – who coined the term "government-sponsored enterprise" – was the dean of a small community of authors who are responsible for the bulk of work on these entities. Seidman maintains that the GSE form is inherently problematic due to the lack of clarity regarding their purpose and responsibilities (1975). Thomas Stanton, formerly employed by Fannie Mae, has written two books and several articles explaining the relationship of GSEs to the government, the risks presented by the implicit governmental support of these businesses and the inadequacy of the regulatory mechanisms currently in place (2002, 1991). Ronald Moe was joined by Stanton (1989) in expressing concerns regarding the constitutionality of the government-sponsored enterprise structure and the implications for accountability. Seiler likens GSEs to public utilities and argues that they must be better regulated to ensure that they perform their public functions (1999).

All of these authors have discussed the political ramifications of the GSE structure, pointing out that much may be lost with the transfer of authority to quasi-governmental bodies. There is also scholarly literature devoted to the economics of government-sponsored enterprises. A central question, for instance, is the precise value of the government's support for these highly profitable companies (e.g., Kane 1999, Calomiris 1999). Because the support is implicit and based on the assumption of risk, it is an extremely thorny problem.

The greater part of the attention to GSEs is not academic but journalistic. Both Fannie Mae and Freddie Mac are important businesses, cornerstones of the American mortgage industry, and thus receive prominent attention in the business press. Moreover, they are influential participants in the policy-making process and thus receive attention in Washington as well as Wall Street. The particular subjects range from the potential expansion of Fannie Mae and Freddie Mac's business activities (Kopecki 2002, Barta 2001a) to the regulation of GSE securities (Fernandez 2002a) to the performance of Farmer Mac's board of directors (Cowan 2002). Much of the news coverage of GSEs touches on matters that are considered in this book. For example, there are individuals and organizations that criticize GSEs for their political tactics, their profitability and their accountability (e.g., Wallison 2001, Wilke and Barta 2001).

What is missing from the discussion of GSEs, like the discussion of government corporations, is any comparative assessment in terms of accountability or control. In the scholarly and the journalistic analyses of GSEs, the organizations are implicitly judged against an ideal standard that may not be met by any type of organization, public or hybrid. Moreover, discussions of GSEs are never broadened to include other types of hybrids.

Of course, there are many hybrid organizations outside the Beltway. Quasi-government has a history at the state and local level stretching back to the colonial era (Goodrich 1949, Willoughby 1917, McDiarmid 1940, Guild 1920). It is not surprising then that there is literature devoted to American sub-national hybrids (e.g., Brilliant 1975, Hawkins 1976, Betnun 1976, Hamilton and Hamilton 1981). Perhaps the most cited book related to a common type of hybrid, the public authority, is Robert Caro's engaging biography of Robert Moses (1974). The so-called "Master Builder" pioneered the use of public authorities as head of the Triborough Bridge and Tunnel Authority New York State Power Authority and several other authorities. Caro points out how Moses manipulated aspects of the authority structure (particularly bond covenants) to concentrate power. Indeed, the stories of Moses' arrogance and willingness to frustrate elected officials are legendary. Accounts of Austin Tobin and the Port Authority of New York and New Jersey also demonstrate the independence of this type of hybrid – albeit with less megalomaniacal leadership (Doig 1993, 2001).

A broader approach is used by Annmarie Hauck Walsh in her excellent study of public authorities in New York (1978). She expresses misgivings regarding the potential for public authorities to act independently but notes their potential as policy tools. Walsh acknowledges that public authorities certainly pose a control challenge – she, of course, also cites Robert Moses – but also points out the manner in which New York Governor Nelson Rockefeller was able to control the many authorities in the state and use them as instruments to get around the legislature and state constitution. She also observes that the authority structure shifts the focus of organizational management, creating a bias towards revenue-enhancing activity (1978, 337– 338), a point that is emphasized in this book. Finally, Walsh offers structural adjustments that might reduce the autonomy of public authorities, including greater integration into state government, more transparency and more fiscal controls (1978, 343–346).

There are multiple studies of "special districts" and other types of local hybrids that provide municipal services like water and waste. These entities are more common in the western United States but their popularity is growing. McDiarmid profiles California's use of entities modeled on government corporations, for example (1940). Mitchell evaluates the advantages and disadvantages of government corporations – focusing primarily on state and local authorities – and is ultimately ambivalent regarding their desirability in his summary of other studies (1999).

Foster has produced a broad study that examines the special district phenomenon (1997). She finds that "special-purpose government" often spends more money than traditional agencies to carry out the same tasks and that the same tasks consume a larger proportion of the overall budget when they are the responsibility of special districts. It is important to note that, although some special districts would meet the definition of hybrid organizations established above, many others are simply independent agencies (to use one of Seidman's categories) – governmental bodies with unique taxing authority and governance structure and limited purposes.

In addition to the literature devoted to American hybrid organizations, briefly reviewed here, there is a significant body of research related to quasi-government outside the United States. Not surprisingly, the preponderance of English-language literature devoted to hybrid organizations concerns Commonwealth nations. As discussed above, the most frequent subjects of analysis are "quangos." Much of the description of the literature on American hybrids applies to the quango literature.

First, there is no universal understanding of just what constitutes a quango. Even the derivation of the term "quango" is explained as shorthand for "quasi-non-governmental organizations" *or* "quasi-autonomous non-governmental organization" *or* "quasi-autonomous national government organization." Quangos have been described as synonomous with – or a subset of – non-departmental public bodies (NDPBs).

Second, and more troublesome, it is quite difficult to pin down a definition of this strangely named type of organization. As Flinders writes, "The number and range of bodies referred to under the acronym 'quango' is already so wide as to render the term both priceless and worthless . . ." (1999, 4). In general, quangos are organizations created by governments to pursue public policy objectives with publicly appropriated funds. What distinguishes them from traditional government agencies is their separateness from traditional ministries or departments, their appointed leadership, and their exemption from many rules and regulations applicable to public bureaucracies; hence the designation as NDPBs. In Great Britain and Australia, most quangos operate at the local or regional level rather than on a national scale.

As this general description suggests, most quangos are unlike the American hybrids of principal interest in this volume because they do not incorporate market-based mechanisms into their operations. That is, they are not in any sense a blend of the public and private sectors. Thus, while many of the accountability issues raised with respect to quangos are related to hybrid organizations because both sets of organizations are independent, they are not directly comparable. Nevertheless, the quango experience and analysis is instructive. Analysts of quangos find that the absence of structures that constrain traditional agencies does create accountability concerns for quangos similar to those observed by critics of quasi-government in the United States. Skelcher refers to this shortcoming of quangos as "a democratic deficit" (1988). Additionally, it has been suggested that, in the absence of hierarchical structures put in place to assure organizational accountability, the contractual relationships into which quangos enter take on this function (Wilson 1995). A related argument is made with respect to American hybrid organizations in chapter 3.

There are hybrids that bear a closer resemblance to the American, federal hybrids that are the subject of this book. Musolf studies Canadian (1956) and Vietnamese (1963) public enterprises in addition to American hybrids. Wettenhall utilizes a comparative approach to argue that hybrids are increasingly private in character (1987). A volume by Thynne provides descriptive overviews of quasi-government in New Zealand, Finland, Ghana, the Netherlands and China (1998).

More common than quangos or American-style hybrids around the world are state-owned enterprises, businesses owned entirely or in part by governments. These are often referred to as public enterprises or crown corporations. These entities *are* like the American hybrids that are the subject of this book in the important sense that they blend public and private. They are participants in markets, they charge for goods and services, and they generally fund their own operations. Many were created to perform some public function similar to that performed by the government (or the government in other countries).

Many other state-owned enterprises are *unlike* American hybrid organizations in that the final observation above is not true. They are not substitutes for traditional government agencies as deliverers of public programs. It is more accurate to regard most public enterprises as substitutes for private firms. Indeed, many state-owned enterprises were started as private companies and later nationalized for a variety of reasons. Public enterprises are often created in developing countries precisely because no private, profit-seeking company exists to serve the country's market (Nellis 1994).

As this statement suggests, state-owned enterprises are clearly products and instruments of public policy. However, the expectations and demands of control are quite different for many state-owned enterprises from what they are for American hybrids. For example, in their interesting study of Greek state-owned enterprises, Lioukas, Bourantas and Papadakis are concerned with managerial autonomy over "pricing decisions" and "resource acquisition" rather than matters one might deem closer to public policy (1993). That is not to say such studies are not relevant. The authors' findings regarding the conditions under which one would expect greater autonomy are likely applicable to many types of hybrids.

There are a great many articles about individual public enterprises that cannot be summarized collectively. It would consume many pages and the readers' attention to review them all, but what follows gives a flavor of the existing research. It also provides an indication of the universality of quasi-government.

Shrivastava examined public enterprises in India and focused on the distinctive tools of control over hybrid organizations available in parliamentary systems (1992). Many of these structural instruments, including the right to question and investigate enterprises, parliamentary debate practices and various committees charged with general oversight, are similar to those available to the Congress and the President in the United States. In a brief comparative section, Shrivastava compares the accountability of Indian public enterprises to those in Tanzania, Thailand, New Zealand, Australia and Nigeria (among others). Mihyo focuses entirely on "non-market controls" of public enterprises in Tanzania (1994), concluding that public enterprises are a superior alternative to government-run corporations – an observation that is consistent with the American analysts who, forty years earlier, bemoaned the erosion of true government corporations.

Also looking at state enterprises in Africa, Tangri observes that these companies provide no relief from the debilitating politics of patronage that stunts development in the nations he considered, including Uganda, Zimbabwe, Ghana and Nigeria (1999). Grosh and Mukanda have collected several essays describing the varying experiences with state-owned enterprises around Africa (1994). Only one of these argues that political influence over "parastatal" entities is actually *good.*

Friedmann and Garner have collected articles regarding "government enterprises" in Europe (1970) that provide observations from France, Germany, Sweden and Italy (among others). The various authors suggest that Europeans are more comfortable with the government being kept at some distance from the management of public enterprises. Treves notes, for example, that the Italian government retains a supervisory role with respect to corporations in which it is a shareholder (1970, 151). Closer to the United States, Stevens analyzes Canadian crown corporations and their ongoing struggle for the optimum balance between autonomy and control (1993). He uses a "game analogy" to assess the different designs of crown corporations in various Canadian provinces. Allan collects works related to the transformation (i.e., privatization) of public enterprises in Canada (1998).

With few exceptions the significant body of research devoted to the dynamics of public enterprise all over the world has a different focus from this volume. In general, studies of public enterprises are not concerned with the bureaucratic control problem per se. A great deal of research concerns the efficiency of these companies and their effects on economic development (e.g., Lott 1995, DeBorger 1993, Vogelsang 1990, Ware 1986, Foreman-Peck and Waterson 1985, Rees 1984, Fleming 1950, Meade 1944). In recent years, the privatization of public enterprises is the dominant concern driving research.

Many of the economic analyses of public enterprises argue that the organizational form is less efficient than private firms. Critics of public enterprises also argue that they are used for purposes of patronage, that the requisite mechanisms for transparency do not exist and that they operate substantially unencumbered by the prerogatives of the executive and legislative branches. All of these criticisms echo those leveled at American hybrids.

Indeed, quasi-government around the globe has generated a small population of work that could best be described as screeds (e.g., Howard 1985, Axelrod 1992, Schaefer 1996, Hendrie 1998). Many of these analyses appear in more popular journals. In general, they offer analysis of particular organizations that is colored to varying extents by an agenda. For example, common critiques of hybrids include charges that hybrid organizations exist merely to function as patronage mills for elected officials (Burstein and Shields 1997, McTague 1996), that hybrids' leaders use their positions to line their pockets at public expense (Henriques 1986, Savage 1987), and that hybrids have too much power and function beyond the influence of elected officials and the public (Axelrod 1992, Bennett and DiLorenzo 1983). There are elements of truth in many of these articles. The pertinent arguments that apply to the organizations discussed in this book are addressed. Moreover, the existence of this popular literature demonstrates the lingering suspicion many have towards quasi-government and the need for more objective scholars to pay attention.

The brief literature review presented in the preceding pages is not comprehensive. It is offered to give a flavor of existing work and establish the place of this book amidst this field. These books and articles offer rich descriptive analysis of particular types of hybrids. They offer warnings regarding the lack of accountability and the structural shortcomings of hybrid organizations in multiple contexts.

The notable shortcoming common to most of this work is the absence of any empirical comparison with traditional government agencies. Hybrids may not be perfect but that does not mean they are less accountable than government agencies. One cannot view diminished accountability as a political "cost" of quasi-government without analyzing its relative performance. Presented in the pages that follow is an attempt to better estimate that cost based on a more nuanced understanding of quasi-government in the United States.

2

Building a better model of bureaucratic control

At its core, this book concerns the relationship between bureaucrats and elected public servants: a central topic of political science. This relationship has been a subject of analysis for as long as people have elected leaders to administer public functions. Invariably, those elected must rely upon numerous individuals that the vast majority of citizens have no role in selecting. This leads to tension between these civil servants' need for latitude to perform their functions effectively and the citizenry's right to determine the course of public policy in a democracy. What is the proper balance between administrative discretion and indirect popular control of government?

Woodrow Wilson posited a politics/administration dichotomy as an ideal to which governments should aspire (1887). The elected representatives determine public policy; the appointed bureaucrats implement it. This separates the politics of policy-making from the administration. But this separation – even in Wilson's account – was possible only when all parties were in agreement on the ends of government. This condition rarely comes about. Thus the ability of elected officials – in the federal context, Members of Congress or the President of the United States – to compel bureaucrats to carry out their will is constantly strained.

In recent years, discussion of the "bureaucratic control" problem has been strongly influenced by work in the field of economics. Starting with the seminal work of William Niskanen (1971), studies of so-called principal-agent problems in the public realm started to resemble analysis of principal-agent issues in private firms (e.g., Alchian and Demsetz 1972). Even those who do not adopt the economists' methodology employ the language of principals and agents in discussions of bureaucratic control. There are principals (elected officials) that seek outcomes and agents (bureaucrats) upon whom the principals rely to deliver said outcomes.

Although few users of the terms adhere to their formal meaning as defined in the economics context, principal-agent theory has become the metaphor of choice for political scientists studying bureaucratic control. Thus the problem of political control of the bureaucracy as typically studied can be expressed as the following question:

Can Principal A secure Preference P from Agent X?

This expression of the bureaucratic control problem is useful as a starting point. Unfortunately, the full range of questions suggested even by this radically simplified formulation has not been explored. Research has focused almost single-mindedly on the first element of the expression: the Principal.

Until recently, scholars who asserted "congressional dominance" of federal agencies held sway in the field now known as "bureaucratic control" (Fiorina 1981, Weingast and Moran 1983, McCubbins, Noll and Weingast 1987, Ferejohn and Shipan 1990).

Most discussions of control deal with an explicit or implicit competition among principals for control (e.g., Eisner and Meier 1990). While congressional dominance adherents maintain "their principal" controls the bureaucracy, others have argued for alternative principals. The President, courts, interest groups, and bureaucracies themselves have been offered as equal, if not greater, influences on bureaucratic behavior (Moe 1982, Melnick 1983, Rourke 1984, Meier, Stewart and England 1991, Golden 1992, Krause 1994, Mashaw 1994). Thus they have substituted a Principal B as an alternative source of control in the same system.

The new formulation can be expressed with the following modification of the question:

$$\text{Can} \quad \begin{matrix} \text{Principal A}_{or} \\ \text{Principal B}_{or} \\ \text{Principal C} \end{matrix} \quad \text{secure Preference P from Agent X?}$$

This too is a useful question. By examining the relative strength of influences on bureaucratic behavior, such studies help clarify the opportunities enjoyed by each player in the political system to influence bureaucratic outcomes. Some more sophisticated accounts incorporate multiple principals in the explanation of bureaucratic behavior (Moe 1985, Moe and Bendor 1985, Wood and Waterman 1994). Still, there is a danger of using such findings to over-explain results. That is, without exploring the other elements in the equation, it would be premature to attribute all variation in outcome to variance on the "principal" variable.

Consider the important distinctions embodied in the term "Agent X." Organizations vary greatly in their internal structures, types of tasks they undertake and substantive policy domains. Yet almost every study of bureaucratic control has examined regulatory agencies. This is due to the relative ease in analyzing data regarding their outputs (Wood and Waterman 1991, 832, Wood and Waterman 1994). The consequences of this methodological bias for external validity have been minimized. Wood and Waterman, for example, "can think of no reason why the reported results should not be generalizable to the entire federal bureaucracy" (1991, 806).

Yet several reasons *do* come to mind. First, the very availability of readily interpretable data may make such entities more conducive to control. This idea is frequently raised with respect to the bureaucratic power derived from informational asymmetries (Arrow 1985, Miller 1992). Agents can frustrate principals by denying them information needed to evaluate performance. Ergo, where information is readily available, control may be easier. Second, levels of interest on the parts of some competing principals may vary with agency type; presidential indifference towards regulatory policy, for example, has been documented (Wilson 1980, Weingast 1981). Thus, finding congressional control of regulatory agencies may not be applicable to the entire population of agencies. Third, it may be easier for regulatory organizations to alter behavior in response to the preferences of principals than other types of organizations. For example, inspectors from the Occupational Safety and Health Administration (OSHA) may be able to cite more violations per inspection without increasing the number of inspections; in contrast, service delivery organizations may require additional resources to build more highways, say.

Thus it is vitally important that studies of bureaucratic control examine a range of agency types. This book enriches the field of bureaucratic control by examining the implications of variation in agent structure by comparing hybrid organizations and government agencies as they undertake similar tasks. The added dimension can be expressed as follows:

	Principal A_{or}		Agent X_{or}
Can	Principal B_{or}	secure Preference P from	Agent Y_{or}
	Principal C		Agent Z?

Research that purportedly studies this variation in reality *assumes* that differences in structure relate to the principal's control. For example, studies of congressional decision-making regarding bureaucratic control often treat organizational structure as the dependent variable (McCubbins 1985, Macey 1992, Bawn 1995, 1997). This provides insight into congressional decision-making and congressional beliefs regarding the effectiveness of various control mechanisms. However, empirical inquiry into implications of organizational structure for control must treat structural features as the independent variables (with "control" the dependent variable). Scholars are beginning to undertake this important line of inquiry (e.g., Lowry 2001).

The empirical research upon which this book is based essentially treated agent structure as a dichotomous independent variable. That is, in three different policy areas, organizations were classified in a binary fashion as hybrid organizations or traditional government agencies. As discussed at some length in the previous chapter, there is tremendous variation among the population of hybrid organizations.

Although this book and other works that incorporate differences in agent structure add needed complexity to the bureaucratic control model, there are many other elements that can and should be incorporated as well. Referring back to the question formulation above, we can see that the "preference" term also merits consideration.

There are logical and empirical reasons to hypothesize that a principal might have an easier time securing some preferences than others. For example, a preference consistent with the interests of an organization would surely be more attainable than one that is not. There are broader possibilities to explore. Is it easier to constrain a bureaucracy than to motivate action? Are procedural dictates more readily followed than substantive commands?

Rather than address such questions, much bureaucratic control research radically simplifies principal-agent tensions. For example, Bendor points out that many formal models of bureaucracy simplify the tension with the legislature as a battle over money (as opposed to policy) for computational and conceptual reasons (1988). Such studies measure one type of control but leave other variations unexplored and, perhaps more importantly, mask the significance of variables excluded from the model.

In chapter 4, variation in preference type is added to the bureaucratic control equation, transforming the operative questions as follows:

	Principal A_{or}		Preference P_{or}		Agent X_{or}
Can	Principal B_{or}	secure	Preference Q_{or}	from	Agent Y_{or}
	Principal C		Preference R		Agent Z?

Studying variation in preferences introduces additional complexity into the research design. Research on political control of bureaucracy generally uses institutional change as a proxy for changes in specific policy preferences held by principals. For example, changes in presidential administration or variation in the partisan composition of Congress are employed as interruptions in a time series. It is *assumed* that the institutional change is accompanied by a change in preferences.

However, in many policy areas, preferences do not change as a function of party affiliation. For example, when President Clinton was lobbying for congressional passage of the NAFTA treaty, his position was endorsed by ex-Presidents Bush, Reagan, Carter, Ford and Nixon (Agence France Presse 1993). Scholars have ignored the reality of constant preferences despite changing principals. They thus risk serious misinterpretation of the data.

Consider a recent work on bureaucratic control. Meier, Wrinkle and Polinard sought to gauge the responsiveness of the Farm Credit Administration (FCA) to the agriculture committee's preferences regarding the allocation of federal credit to farmers (1999). The authors used congressional partisanship as the independent variable, found that changes in congressional composition had no effect on Farm Credit Administration policy and interpreted this as evidence of no control. But their assumption that a change in party leadership of the agriculture committee represents a change in the committee's preference is shaky. Most members who choose to sit on the agriculture committee have a significant number of constituents whose livelihood depends on agriculture. Thus the committee members' preference, guided by the interests of their constituents, would be for greater availability of agricultural credit whether they are Republican or Democrat. It is quite possible that the FCA's failure to change its policies reflects the stable preferences of a principal, not lack of control.

As this example suggests, relying on institutional change as a proxy for preference change may yield "false negatives" – the impression that a principal lacks control when, in fact, the principal is satisfied with the agent's performance. This problem is avoided by the identification of specific articulations of policy preferences that represent a clear departure from the status quo. This is done using statements from principals (through public statements or interviews), press accounts and formal expressions (including legislation and executive orders).

In order to capture the consequences of variation in preference type, some typology of preferences is required. In this book, principal preferences are differentiated on two dimensions. "Positive" and "negative" preferences are distinguished by separating those demands that require an agent to undertake a new action from those that require an agent to cease or refrain from some activity. The second dimension on which preferences are differentiated is substantive. "Mission-related preferences" are culled from "non-mission-related preferences." This separates preferences that require the agent to alter its organizational objectives from preferences that are essentially procedural in character. These distinctions are explained and explored in greater detail in chapter 4.

This book thus expands the study of bureaucratic control by including at least two variables that are typically excluded: agent structure and principal preference. Of course, one cannot criticize scholars for not studying everything. What is problematic, however, is the manner in which the answers to the richer questions have been implicitly assumed. By treating the preference and agent structure variables as constants, previous studies may have attributed empirical variation in findings to variation in the term being studied: the principal. The reality may be quite different.

A study of hybrid organizations in action

The findings presented in the following pages are based upon a study of American, federal hybrid organizations. The research was designed to assess issues of bureaucratic control as described in the previous section and facilitate comparison of hybrids and traditional agencies, thus avoiding the primary shortcoming of existing work on quasi-government (as described in chapter 1).

Research design

Hybrids and government agencies were compared as they responded to preferences of Congress and the President in three policy areas. The policy spheres selected were housing, export promotion and international market development. Each area allows for comparison of organizations with different structural features as they undertake similar tasks, respond to similar sets of preferences and interact with similar sets of interest groups. Although there is variation in type of hybrid examined, this sample did not facilitate the study of every type of hybrid even at the American federal level. As has been discussed, almost every hybrid is unique. Thus, to conduct a truly comprehensive study, one would have to include every hybrid. For reasons already enumerated, that was simply impractical.

There is no way to assure the reader that the selected entities are representative of the entire population in terms of bureaucratic control. Would that this *were* possible; there would be no need for the research, as this is the dependent variable! Multiple types of hybrids (described in detail below) were sought for inclusion. In interpreting findings, careful attention was paid to the significance of features unique to each hybrid as they affected bureaucratic control. Reasons for skepticism are noted regarding the extrapolation of findings to the entire population of hybrids based on one or more of the hybrids studied.

The three policy domains selected were chosen because each offers multiple hybrids and traditional agencies. In each area specific principal preferences were identifiable and agent satisfaction of these preferences could be evaluated. In the course of presenting findings, reference is made to organizations within the policy area that were not principal subjects of this study.

Hybrids operating in other policy areas are occasionally discussed to illustrate points made with respect to subjects of direct study. Such examples provide additional illustration for findings or cautionary notes regarding the generalizability of the findings.

The research underlying this book was structured to limit the influence of excluded variables that logic, experience, and previous research suggest influence the bureaucratic control dynamic.

For example, the system of government almost certainly influences the relationship between principal and agent (Moe 1990, Moe and Caldwell 1994). A cross-national comparison of control over hybrid organizations would be interesting but this book is focused squarely on the United States federal government. Thus several variables (e.g., country, type of government, level of government, etc.) are effectively held constant. Although thousands of hybrid organizations are excluded from the study, interpretation of the findings is more straightforward as a result. Similarly, economic, social and political conditions likely affect the bureaucratic control dynamic, and thus comparisons must be made as institutions operate at the same time, under the same conditions.

The policy area in which the hybrid and traditional government agencies operate could also affect the control dynamic. For example, housing is an issue of great salience in domestic politics whereas foreign assistance is of little concern to most Americans. In this study, hybrids in the three different policy areas were considered not to test hypotheses regarding the importance of such differences but to ensure that the findings were not biased by focus on a single policy domain.

Another potentially complicating variable is the source of principal preferences. In a democratic political system, the normative significance of political control over bureaucracy is derived from the belief that the elected official is the conduit for expression of popular preferences. That is, it is assumed that the electoral connection between legislator and constituency is an efficient conduit of public preferences. If, however, the preferences of principals (say, Members of Congress) are *not* derived from popular preferences, the importance of their political influence is normatively diminished. Indeed, under such conditions bureaucracies more responsive to popular preferences than principal preferences might be characterized as more democratically legitimate. Alternatively, agents may influence the principal's choice of preference. This would turn the control idea on its head. Yet studies do not generally distinguish the origins of principal preferences, and with good reason; such differences are rarely transparent. Chapter 5 considers this problem in detail.

A truly comprehensive study would require analysis of variation on these and other potentially complicating independent variables. Perhaps an alternative research design calling for quantitative analysis of many organizations across jurisdictions could accommodate such variation but that is not the approach utilized herein. Each organization examined required extensive review of documentary materials as well as in-depth interviewing. Collection and interpretation of data required substantive knowledge of the policy area and the activities performed by the organizations under study. This book provides a solid foundation for future quantitative analysis by identifying salient characteristics to be considered.

Cases

In the chapters that follow, reference is made to the hybrid organizations and government agencies that were the subject of this research. These entities all operate in one of three policy areas: housing, export promotion and international market development. Their history and operations are described in detail in the appendix. The following descriptions are intended to provide some background sufficient to understand the analysis of this book.

Housing There is a complex network of organizations involved in federal housing policy that run the gamut from government agency to private company (see table 2.1). Of course, the federal Department of Housing and Urban Development is the centerpiece. The department is made up of several agencies that carry out numerous programs designed to accomplish a range of objective from building public housing to funding asbestos abatement. As the department will be compared with two hybrids in the business of housing finance, the part of HUD that is of primary interest is the Federal Housing Administration (FHA).

Table 2.1 *Federal housing entities*

Organization	Type	Ownership	Funds
HUD	Government agency	Public	Appropriations (and revenue)
Fannie Mae	Government-sponsored enterprise	Private	Revenue
Freddie Mac	Government-sponsored enterprise	Private	Revenue
Ginnie Mae	Government corporation	Public	Appropriations (and revenue)
Federal Home Loan Bank system	Government-sponsored enterprise	Private	Revenue

The FHA is the oldest part of HUD. It stimulates and stabilizes housing markets in the United States with multiple programs. Its core activity is providing insurance on mortgages to first-time homebuyers. This allows people who have never before had a loan to secure credit from banks and other lending institutions. The activities of the FHA are complemented by the work of the two prominent hybrid organizations that are the primary object of interest in the housing area.

The Federal National Mortgage Association (Fannie Mae) and the Federal Home Loan Mortgage Corporation (Freddie Mac) are government-sponsored enterprises. These profit-seeking companies are the best known of the hybrids examined in this book and arguably the most important. The two companies are now privately owned and their shares are traded on the New York Stock Exchange but they were created as government agencies during the Depression-era expansion of the federal government. They have grown into huge corporations, ranked second and sixth, respectively, among "Fortune 500" companies in terms of asset size. Their combined income in 2001 exceeded $10 billion (OFHEO 2001). The two companies are also linchpins of the financial infrastructure that allows millions of Americans to purchase their own home.

As explained in greater detail in the appendix, Fannie Mae and Freddie Mac help provide capital to American homebuyers by purchasing mortgages from lending institutions. That is, they provide a secondary market for mortgages, thus insuring that lenders do not "run out" of money to make new loans to homebuyers. In turn, the two companies either retain the mortgages as investments or pool them to create the basis for mortgage-backed securities that they sell to investors.

Fannie Mae and Freddie Mac are called GSEs because they are privately owned and profit-seeking yet endowed with certain privileges, including exemption from certain taxes, exemption from registration requirement on their securities and access to a line of credit with the Treasury. Because of these connections to the federal government, the market regards them as implicitly backed by the federal government (that is, investors believe that, if Fannie Mae or Freddie Mac were in danger of defaulting on their obligations, the federal government would make good on their commitments). As a result, the two GSEs pay interest on the money they borrow at only slightly higher rates than those paid by the federal government itself. Indeed, they pay lower rates – in the form of returns that investors realize on their debt securities – than even the most highly rated private companies.

As a consequence, the GSEs are subject to government regulation that has two broad purposes. One purpose is to ensure that the companies are operated in a fiscally prudent manner so that the federal government never does have to "bail out" these two entities. The second purpose is to guarantee that the companies fulfill the public purposes that they were created to address. The regulation of Fannie Mae and Freddie Mac is discussed in detail in chapter 5.

In addition to these three entities, reference is made to other organizations that are also key parts of the housing landscape. The Government National Mortgage Association ("Ginnie Mae") is a government corporation that operates as a part of HUD. It performs activities substantively similar to the GSEs but with a significant subsidy that enables focus on the most challenging borrowers. The Federal Home Loan Bank system is a network of lending institutions that is often characterized as a GSE because its securities have the same agency status. It does not, however, operate as a centralized single institution in the manner of Fannie Mae and Freddie Mac. Rather it is a network of institutions that borrow collectively and operate under a shared set of rules, regulations and programmatic objectives.

Export promotion   Three organizations are the focus of examination in the area of export promotion (see table 2.2). The Department of Commerce is the government agency compared with two government corporations, the Export-Import Bank of the United States and the Overseas Private Investment Corporation (OPIC).

The Department of Commerce includes a puzzling collection of agencies charged with tasks as varied as monitoring the weather and tracking American imports and exports. Of interest in this study is one of the department's core responsibilities: promotion of American products abroad.

Two government corporations are major elements of the United States government's efforts to increase sales of American products abroad. ExIm

Table 2.2 *Federal export promotion entities*

Organization	Type	Ownership	Funding
Department of Commerce	Government agency	Public	Appropriations
ExIm	Government corporation	Public	Revenue (and appropriations)
OPIC	Government corporation	Public	Revenue (and appropriations)
Other TPCC agencies: TDA, USTR, USDA, USAID, SBA, EPA	Government agencies	Public	Appropriations

provides loan guarantees to foreign purchasers of very expensive American goods. The most common product supported by this activity is commercial aircraft. Indeed, ExIm has sometimes been called "Boeing's Bank."

OPIC performs a related function. It provides loan guarantees to help finance major infrastructure projects in developing countries. For example, OPIC will help a nation finance a dam and hydroelectric plant. In addition to encouraging purchases of capital-intensive American goods (say, a General Electric turbine), this activity is intended to spur development and thus is not a purely export-related activity.

As government corporations, ExIm and OPIC operate as entities independent of any other federal agency. While they are exempt from many administrative laws and regulations that apply to federal agencies, they are subject to the requirements of the Government Corporation Control Act (GCCA). Additionally, the two corporations are integrated into the rest of the administration by virtue of presidential appointments to leadership positions and the incorporation of the two entities into the President's budget submission. More specification of the government corporation structure is provided in subsequent chapters as well as the appendix.

There are numerous other governmental entities that play a role in export promotion. Most notably, the Department of Agriculture (USDA) runs multiple programs devoted to increasing sales of American agricultural products abroad. The discussion of export promotion in the following pages explicitly precludes agriculture for reasons explained in the appendix (see page 199). Still, there are many agencies that are components of non-agricultural export policy. These entities are all part of the Trade Promotion Coordinating Committee (TPCC), a body located within the Department of Commerce that has as its objectives the harmonization and coordination of federal export programs.

International development Although they do not consume a large portion of the budget, programs aimed at spurring development outside the United States are spread over several federal entities (see table 2.3). Principal among them is the United States Agency for International Development (USAID). This agency runs projects around the world, relying in large part on contractors to employ personnel who work on the ground to enhance public health, education and economic development.

Research in this area focused on two sets of government-backed venture capital funds. One set was created by and overseen by OPIC, the government corporation described in the previous section. The second set, called Enterprise Funds, was created as a response to the collapse of the Warsaw Pact and the emergence of Eastern European countries trying to emulate

Table 2.3 *Federal market development entities*

Organization	Type	Ownership	Funding
USAID	Government agency	Public	Appropriations
OPIC	Government corporation	Public	Revenue (and appropriations)
Enterprise Funds	Government-backed venture capital fund	Private	Appropriations
OPIC investment funds	Government-backed venture capital fund	Private	Private investment and government-guaranteed loans

Western market systems. Both sets of funds are intended to spur economic development by seeding business with capital in countries that have precious little in the way of resources available to entrepreneurs.

The two sets of funds are structured somewhat differently. Enterprise Funds are privately incorporated but funded entirely by government appropriations. OPIC's investment funds are privately owned and managed but utilize government loan guarantees to solicit private capital and subsidize the rate of return to these investors. Funds in both programs emulate traditional venture capital funds as they seek out promising enterprises and invest in the hope of eventual profit.

As the descriptions may suggest, the activities of government-backed venture capital funds are quite different from those of USAID's programs. Thus the comparison is difficult. With respect to these hybrids, there is greater attention devoted to comparison across hybrid type rather than comparison of hybrid and government agency.

Reference is also made to similar organizations and entities sponsored by other governments or international organizations, such as the Inter-American Development Bank and the European Bank for Reconstruction and Development. Such entities provide additional insight into the consequences of hybrid structure in this field.

Measurement and interpretation

The basic form of the research followed the lead of other bureaucratic control studies. Essentially, this involves examination of an interrupted time series to evaluate organizational performance following a change in principal preferences. There are atleast three "shortcomings" in the bureaucratic control literature that were considered in framing the measurement strategies and interpreting the findings. First, findings regarding bureaucratic control tend to be expressed in dichotomous terms (e.g., control or no control). Second, the causal relationship between a principal's preferences and an organization's satisfaction of said preferences is generally assumed. Third, the results achieved by bureaucratic organizations tend to be conflated with the behavior of the same organizations. Different strategies were employed to avoid these pitfalls.

Non-dichotomous findings. The focus on control has, not surprisingly, led to interpretations that find control or lack thereof. This simplification has been moderated to some extent by the ascendance of "political influence" over bureaucracy in place of the control idea (e.g., Scholz, Twombly and Headrick 1991). Nevertheless, students of principal-agent dynamics have not consistently taken advantage of the rich diversity of conceptualizations regarding the ideal relationship between bureaucracy and other elements of government. As a consequence, there may be hidden variation in existing studies. Agencies that appear "beyond control" may be responsive to popular opinion or heed formal legal requirements. This would not be consistent with the control idea but also would not indicate the bureaucracy run amok suggested by the dichotomous "no control" finding.

The underlying premise is that there are gradations of control, to which the investigator must be sensitive. Combining extensive qualitative research with the collection of quantitative data, a balanced and comprehensive analysis was attempted in an effort to reach an accurate conclusion. Thus, for example, quantitative evidence that federal housing agencies appear to respond more quickly than hybrid organizations to the preference for more low-income loans was bolstered by information drawn from interviews and secondary sources. The data presented is not offered in the guise of econometric analysis; statistics summarizing organizational performance are illustrative.

The qualitative research agenda included over 115 interviews of hybrid and agency personnel, representatives of interest groups, trade associations, congressional committees and other informed sources. Secondary literature and official documents such as testimony, publications and court records were also collected and reviewed.

Causation problem. The reliance on poorly defined expressions of preference has already been noted as a common feature of bureaucratic control research that may lead to incorrect interpretation of data: false negatives. Recall that one study assumed that a change in administration represented a change in policy preferences, prompting a finding of "no control" when the organization did not alter its behavior.

The reverse problem also plagues control research. In studying bureaucratic behavior, researchers may identify changes in the performance of agencies that match the change in the principals' preferences. But organizational performance correlated with principal preferences is only circumstantial evidence of control. Without digging deeper, we might have a "false positive."

This problem is serious because there are ample reasons to believe that bureaucratic organizations could be responding to other "stimuli." For example, a principal's preference may change in response to some exogenous condition (e.g., an economic downturn) that independently prompts the agent to react. Similarly, an intermediary force might exert pressure (e.g., an interest group) on both the principal *and* the agent to alter both the principal's preference and the agent's behavior. Neither of these causal stories matches our expectation of "control." Thus evidence that the agent actually responded to its principals was always sought.

Again the qualitative research was a key response to this challenge. Interviews of people who work (or worked) for the organizations being studied made it possible to gain insight into the causal chain of activity. Did an organization really respond to a principal? Which principal? Why? Of course, the reports of such individuals may be biased, often in ways that are unknown to the researcher, but interviewing multiple subjects on a single case helps overcome this flaw. And, more importantly, potentially biased information provides greater insight than no information.

Defining performance. The third problem concerns the definition of organizational performance. This might be called the "input"/"output" problem. Each organization's "performance" really has two dimensions: the attempt; and the result.

One can evaluate the effectiveness of bureaucratic control by examining the effort of bureaucratic agents. Has the agent *tried* to satisfy the principal? This is a conception of performance focused on "inputs." Alternatively, one can measure the product of the agent's work; call these "outputs." What was the actual consequence of the organization's actions?

It is tempting to make two significant assumptions. First, if an organization increases its inputs, it will increase its outputs. Second, if an organization yields the same outputs from year to year, the inputs must be constant over that period as well. Unfortunately, neither of these assumptions is valid. Increasing inputs (expending more resources) does not guarantee any increase in outputs. An agency may spend more money or allocate more personnel to satisfy the preferences of some principal and still fail to achieve the desired outcome. Thus the failure to achieve any improvement as measured in outputs does not necessarily show lack of reaction to the principals' preferences.

When one speaks of control, great care must be taken to specify what is of interest: the principal's ability to compel an agent to *try* and satisfy preferences (inputs) *or* the principal's ability to secure the desired outcome (outputs).

Analysis of inputs and outputs may yield contradictory findings with respect to bureaucratic control. For example, suppose a congressional committee expresses a preference for cheaper military aircraft. Defense Department employees then dutifully work with contractors seeking opportunities for savings. If one measures the effort of these bureaucrats (inputs), evidence of control would be found. Still, they may fail to find any means of reducing cost. Thus, if one were to measure satisfaction of the principal's preferences (outputs), lack of control would be found.

The input/output problem is not addressed in most studies of bureaucratic control. Studies generally focus on outputs. This book presents similar data on performance of housing organizations, trade organizations and development organizations. But the potential pitfalls are recognized in the course of analysis. First, in some cases, the outputs are aggregated for multiple agencies. Disaggregating outputs in these cases can be difficult. Changes in outputs may reflect the work of one agent and not another. Second, outputs may be unrelated to the actions of any agent. Outputs may vary over time as a consequence of, say, changing economic conditions that improve or harm organizational performance.

Considerable effort has been devoted to the evaluation of inputs to complement the study of outputs and thus avoid misinterpretation of initial impressions. That is, in each case a determination was sought, in essence, as to whether the agent *tried* to satisfy the principal's preference. Inputs are also difficult to disaggregate. Organizations generally do not provide information on the assignment of resources divided by policy objective and, even when they do, organizational reports must be taken with a grain of salt since it is in the interest of an agent to report attempts to satisfy relevant principals. Thus subjective reports from interview subjects were relied upon to get a sense of agents' behavior with respect to principals' preferences.

This aspect of the principal-agent dynamic receives scant independent attention even though measuring control based on inputs seems most consonant with the "spirit" of bureaucratic control. That is, we may be disappointed that a principal's preferences cannot be satisfied but this does not seem to offend our understanding of accountability as long as the agent is *trying* to comply. Outputs are typically measured under the implicit assumption that they measure inputs as well. This makes no sense. Organizations frequently fail in their attempts to reach objectives. That does not indicate that they are beyond control.

In each policy area, an assessment is offered as to whether the principal's preference was satisfied by the bureaucratic agents. A comparative assessment of hybrids and traditional government agencies is emphasized because it is most germane to the research question: whether hybrid organizations are more or less difficult to control than government agencies. The emphasis on the likelihood of preference satisfaction also permits expression of findings in an understandable manner akin to a logit or probit analysis.

There is, of course, a crudeness to this characterization. In almost all cases, preferences are satisfied to a greater or lesser extent. Thus a cardinal approach might be more appealing. Still, assessments of degree are avoided because they only amplify the subjective nature of evaluating control.

Finally, the findings are not presented by policy area, as one might expect. Each chapter is devoted to a key finding of the research and draws upon the policy areas that best illustrate the point. In every chapter, reference is made to the three policy areas studied. Some observations were more pronounced in one field or another. Still, at no point is contradictory or confounding evidence excluded.

3

Administration by regulation

Principals rely upon a variety of tools to control their bureaucratic agents. Many hybrid organizations are differentiable from traditional government agencies by the set of tools available to principals seeking control. For example, Congress cannot use the annual appropriations process to compel government-sponsored enterprises to satisfy their preferences because GSEs are not included in the federal budget. Still, GSEs *are* subject to governmental regulation. This provides Congress opportunities for indirect influence through oversight of the GSEs' regulators.

Examining the consequences of such structural "substitution" is a logical starting point for a study of quasi-government. It is the elimination of traditional control mechanisms that arouses concerns of lost control when public policy responsibilities are delegated to hybrid organizations (Musolf and Seidman 1980).

In this chapter, two sets of control tools are differentiated, one associated with traditional government agencies and one associated with hybrid organizations. Principals attempt to control traditional agencies with what are here characterized as "administrative control tools." This includes the entire range of laws, structures, practices and conventions associated with the principal-agent relationships of US government agencies. This definition is elaborated below.

Principals seeking control of hybrid organizations, in contrast, must rely upon a reduced set of administrative control tools or an entirely different set of tools that are here referred to as "regulatory control tools." This phrase is intended to capture a heterogeneous set of institutional relationships between hybrids and their principals. It includes regulations, rules, contracts and procedural requirements. This too is specified below.

In essence, this chapter presents the claim that regulatory control tools are relatively unwieldy. Principals relying on regulatory tools to compel hybrid organizations to satisfy their preferences have a lower likelihood of success than they do using administrative tools to control traditional government agencies. Additionally, the soundness of regulatory infrastructure for hybrid organizations is more critical to effective control than the presence of some administrative ties. That is, hybrids with inferior regulatory infrastructure – even those subject to some traditional administrative control tools – are less likely to satisfy principals than a hybrid *without* the administrative ties but with a strong regulatory arrangement. In short, the principal-hybrid relationship is essentially regulatory in character and should be evaluated as such.

This chapter has three parts: (1) definition and differentiation of administrative and regulatory tools of control used by principals to control public bureaucracies; (2) presentation of empirical findings regarding satisfaction of principal preferences from a comparative study of hybrids and government agencies in the housing and international market development policy areas; (3) evaluation of the limits of regulatory control for hybrid organizations.

The tools of bureaucratic control

Principals in the American federal government have a wide range of control tools at their disposal. Although the focus of this book is on the implications of hybrid structure for congressional and presidential control, reference is made to the ramifications of hybrid structure for other actors in the American political system to provide a more complete picture.

The familiar catalog of control mechanisms available to political principals is here divided into two categories: administrative control tools and regulatory control tools. The sets are not mutually exclusive. That is, a relationship that is primarily regulatory in character may include one or more tools that are part of the administrative set and vice versa.

Administrative control tools

Principals may rely upon many tools to compel preference satisfaction from traditional government agencies. These are referred to as "administrative control tools" because they are associated with the classical model of public administration in the United States.

Legislation The most dramatic tool available to Congress is its authority to alter the structure, powers and status of any federal entity. Indeed,

Congress can create and eliminate federal agencies. Of course, this is rather uncommon. Restructuring or creating new organizations by legislation is a lengthy, resource-consuming process. Any Member of Congress, or group of Members, has limited ability to control the legislative process. The Member undertaking such a venture could expect opposition and long odds of success.

Thus, as a tool, legislation is difficult to wield and reserved for unusual situations (Dodd and Schott 1979). This chapter is focused on tools utilized in the course of ordinary policy-making rather than the extraordinary instances when Congress reshapes entire organizations. The implications of hybrid structure for extraordinary policy-making are considered in chapter 5.

The budget process Outside the power to rewrite federal law, the appropriations and authorization processes are Congress' principal control mechanisms. Congress specifies levels of spending, numbers of employees, and policy objectives in the annual budget. Although this activity is obviously legislative, it is not extraordinary. That is, no Member has to expend resources to initiate the process. It is part of the regular activities of Congress and thus it is distinguished from the previous category.

As part of the budget process, Congress holds regular hearings, requires annual and periodic reports, and commissions audits and investigations. Congress receives comment from affected interest groups on the performance and priorities of government agencies and adjusts its preferences accordingly. Thus the budget process allows Congress both to redefine and transmit preferences to bureaucratic organizations. Congress' use of the budget process as a control tool is discussed at greater length in chapter 6.

Control of the budget is also a critical tool of Presidential authority over the executive branch. The Office of Management and Budget is the clearing house and coordinating arm of the President. Agencies submit their budget proposals to the OMB, which sorts and prioritizes programs to come up with the administration's budget request. It is a bulwark against "freelance" agencies that might make independent deals with Congress and/or interest groups to further their interests regardless of presidential preferences (Heclo 1977, Wilson 1989). Notably, the power wielded by the OMB is better suited to trimming back agency ambitions than forcing agencies to undertake new presidential initiatives (Wildavsky 1992).

Appointment and confirmation The President's constitutional power to appoint personnel to executive positions in the agencies is another core control tool. Presidential appointees, loyal to the President and his agenda (in theory) steer the bureaucracy in the President's desired direction (Heclo 1977, Rourke 1984, Wilson 1989, Waterman 1989, Wood and Waterman

1994). Rourke chronicles the limits of appointment as an instrument for controlling the bureaucracy by examining President Reagan's influence on executive branch policy (1990). Despite rigorous ideological screening, Reagan's appointees either deviated from White House policy or ran into thoroughly entrenched policy networks that proved immoveable.

The Senate's confirmation authority also provides an instrument for congressional control. This is directed not only at specific nominees but, more generally, at the executive branch, which must clear personnel decisions. For example, President Clinton was essentially forced to appoint an individual for whom he did not care to the Federal Election Commission (FEC) in order to get several judicial nominees confirmed (Connolly and Allen 2000). Thus the ability to hold up nominations can compel compliance with a Senator's will.

Executive orders The most direct tool of control at the President's disposal is the executive order. Executive orders are legally binding declarations that can be utilized to move the bureaucracy in a desired direction notwithstanding objections from competing principals (Mayer 1999).

It has been argued that the President's ability to utilize executive orders is circumscribed despite the appearance of almost complete autonomy. Krause and Cohen (1997) found that Presidents' use of executive orders is constrained by their legislative performance, public prestige, the composition of Congress and national conditions.

Oversight Both Congress and the President rely upon a host of mechanisms to oversee the massive and complex federal bureaucracy. Government bureaucracies can be subject to high levels of scrutiny from other governmental entities (including legislative and executive organizations), the press, interest groups and the general public. This direct and indirect oversight is vital to all principals seeking control. It keeps the principal informed regarding the activities and performance of their agents. It lets them know if and when the agent is satisfying preferences. Without such knowledge, it is difficult for principals to maintain control.

As mentioned above, the budget process is the most regular form of congressional oversight. Yearly reports and hearings provide Congress with a regular stream of information on the activities of federal agencies. Additionally, the General Accounting Office and Congressional Budget Office (CBO) are congressional agencies that perform audits and research reports at the direction of Congress. Some of these reports are prepared regularly in line with requirements enshrined in legislation. Reports are also requested on an ad hoc basis by Members of Congress and committees. Not only do the reports provide vital information to principals, the information gathering required for thousands of reports keeps agents aware of the principals' attention and concern (Weiss and Gruber 1984).

Constituent service provides another form of oversight to Congress. One of the major functions of congressional staff is to help constituents negotiate interactions with the federal government. This activity, usually referred to as casework, involves assisting constituents with difficulties (e.g., "I didn't get my social security check!"). Not only does constituent casework fulfill an important ombudsman function, this mundane activity provides an important connection between the legislative and executive branches (Fenno 1978). It provides Congress a window into the actual operations of the bureaucracy. Thus Members, through their staffs, have first-hand knowledge of what it is happening "in the trenches" and their ability to communicate preferences to bureaucrats (Balla 2000).

Like Congress, the President relies upon the budget process as a regularized instrument of control and oversight. The Executive Office of the President includes a huge staff charged with transmitting the preferences of the President to the various federal agencies and monitoring them to ensure that his will is followed. And, of course, the political appointees that staff the top levels of executive branch agencies perform an oversight function in addition to the role as transmitters of presidential preference.

Inspectors General can prove both a help and a hindrance to presidential control of the bureaucracy by monitoring the activities of federal agencies and employees. An Office of the Inspector General exists within executive departments but it enjoys substantial independence to conduct audits and investigate allegations and suspicions of wrongdoing. Inspectors General are intended, according to law, to be free from the political influence of both the executive and the legislative branches (Light 1993, Newcomer 1998). While an Inspector General may alert the President – and Congress – to wrongdoing in a federal agency, he or she may also frustrate agency staff trying to carry out the will of the President.

Federal management laws Federal bureaucracies are subject to a wide range of legal requirements intended to ensure general "accountability" if not direct control. These are generally procedural in character but have serious implications. For example, the Freedom of Information Act (FOIA) and similar regulations guarantee public access to government documents. This provides opportunities for review by the press and general public, forcing bureaucracies to be prepared for informational requests. FOIA not only empowers outside groups, it can serve the interests of Congress and the President by allowing them to direct attention to oversight at decisive moments when critical interests (personal or political) are in jeopardy. It has been likened to a system of fire alarms, as opposed to the police patrols of regular hearings and reports (McCubbins and Schwartz 1984).

Other procedural laws provide opportunities for non-governmental groups to become involved in the policy-making process. For example, the Administrative Procedures Act allows interest groups to file opinions on new rules and regulations and bring legal challenges on procedural and, in some cases, substantive grounds. Other laws cover personnel practices, require public hearings, set contracting and procurement requirements, and set other common governmental activities with similar consequences.

Some scholars argue that such provisions are rarely neutral; rather, that they are tools of congressional control. Processes can be designed, in this view, to preordain specific outcomes (e.g., McCubbins, Noll and Weingast 1987, 1989, Epstein and O'Halloran 1996). For example, providing opportunities for legal challenges to agency decisions may be a means of limiting bureaucratic discretion. Although this type of control may be achieved through specialized requirements that pertain to a single organization, generalized management laws that apply to all or most federal organizations are less likely to fulfill this purpose.

Regulatory control tools

When confronting hybrid organizations, Congress and the President do not enjoy the use of all the tools described in the previous section. The justifications for their absence are varied. In some cases, organizations are exempted from laws that create administrative control tools in the interest of increasing their efficiency. For example, the designers of Enterprise Funds argued that the organizations would function more like private organizations if they were freed of governmental oversight (interviews 4, 5, 10). In other cases, organizations were transformed into hybrids by removing control tools. For example, when Fannie Mae was chartered as a private corporation, the imposition of federal management laws was impractical (Leazes 1987).

Principals often retain administrative control tools in indirect forms. That is, Congress and the President often delegate responsibility for oversight of hybrid organizations to regulatory agencies. These regulatory agencies are generally subject to the administrative control tools described above. In chapter 7, variation in the structure of the regulatory agencies is considered as a variable that affects principals' ability to control hybrids.

In tone, structure and operation the substitutes for administrative tools that apply to hybrid organizations resemble regulatory frameworks. That is, the relationships between the principal (or its intermediary) and the agent are defined by legal (or legalistic) documents laying out the rights and responsibilities of each party. Thus the tools often employed to control hybrids are here defined as "regulatory control tools." The regulatory control tools described below are utilized by Congress and the President (often through an intermediary, the regulatory agency) to compel hybrid organizations to satisfy their public policy preferences.

Laws and rules Federal hybrid organizations are subject to various laws, most of which are crafted with specific reference to each hybrid. The Government Corporation Control Act, however, applies to a large number of hybrid organizations, though certainly not all of them. This law, originally passed in 1945, provides standards for the accounting practices and legal activities of government corporations (see Leazes 1987 and Seidman 1954 for a fuller discussion of the GCCA). The law does not provide a clear definition of "government corporations," however, and Congress has changed the status of entities to be subject to or exempt from the law's requirements. The GCCA does not elaborate on the substantive purposes of individual government corporations.

Laws, rules and regulations specific to each hybrid can be employed as tools to steer organizations in desired directions. This can be thought of as a two-stage process, for Congress passes laws but generally relies upon executive agencies to write the regulations that fill in the details. Crafting laws and writing detailed rules that define desired outcomes (e.g., more affordable housing, investment in environment-friendly businesses, maintenance of safe business practices) is never easy. The performance of regulated organizations under new rules is often unpredictable.

The specificity of the laws upon which regulations are based varies tremendously. In some instances, Congress spells out with great precision its preferences regarding regulations for hybrid organizations. In other instances, often within the same law that includes specific direction, Congress essentially grants decision-making authority to its intermediary, the regulatory organization.

As a result, the nature of law- and rule-making for hybrid organizations varies by case. One aspect of the process that is uniform is its time-consuming nature. Even when Congress is relatively exact in its requirements, it takes time to translate the law into an intelligible, enforceable regulation. A proposed regulation must be published in the *Federal Register* for comment. After receiving criticisms and suggestions, the regulatory agency may publish a revised proposal, receive more comments and, only then, publish its final regulation. This process can take several years. In some cases, the regulator must perform significant research before even drafting the initial proposed regulation. This is more often the case when Congress assigns the regulator significant decision-making responsibility.

Monitoring   There are two elements comprising this type of control: measurement and standard setting. Successful regulation requires measuring the regulated entities' activity to evaluate compliance with stated expectations. This can be fairly straightforward (e.g., measuring vehicular speed to determine compliance with speed limits) or quite ambiguous (e.g., measuring consideration of minority job candidates to determine compliance with equal opportunity requirements).

The choice of measure can often determine whether a regulated entity will satisfy a proposed regulation. For example, emissions from a manufacturing plant might be considered acceptable if measured by net hazardous particulate matter released but unacceptable if hazardous particulate matter was measured as a percentage of total waste output. Measurement of hybrid organizations' performance with respect to principals' preferences generally requires assessment of their fulfillment of public policy needs. These are frequently the most difficult measurement challenges because assessment and quantification of need is invariably subjective.

Even if there is a clear measure of organizational performance available, setting a satisfactory level of performance may be difficult. This critical part of the regulatory function requires the establishment of a benchmark against which the organization's performance can be judged.

Sanctions and remedies   Any meaningful regulatory framework must include sanctions for non-compliance or, using a more expansive definition, incentives for successful performance. Penalties can take many forms ranging from verbal reprimands to fines to judicially imposed administrative takeovers. Determining sanctions for hybrid organizations can be particularly challenging because the ultimate consequence of any penalty could be a reduction in the penalized organization's capacity to achieve its public policy objectives. This is a truly perverse outcome with respect to hybrids. Sanctioning the hybrid for failure to fulfill its public policy purpose would then make fulfillment of its public policy purpose that much more difficult!

Some regulatory designs include remedial mechanisms. Remedies may involve mandated action or the placement of an organization into receivership, but generally remedies are less extreme. They require an organization to submit for approval a plan to reach compliance in the near future. This is, for example, the first sanction to which Fannie Mae and Freddie Mac are subject if they fail to meet target levels of financing for affordable housing.

Litigation and mediation   A prominent feature of the regulatory relationship is the potential for dispute between the regulator and regulated entity being carried to the courts. For example, the regulated organization feels that the regulator has not considered all data in crafting a new rule. Litigation may be initiated by the regulated organization to challenge the judgment of the regulatory body or its sanctions. The investment funds overseen by OPIC, for example, have signed detailed loan agreements providing both the funds and OPIC with opportunities for legal challenges.

Alternative means of dispute resolution are sometimes available to avoid time-consuming and costly court proceedings. Mediation or binding arbitration can settle appeals and establish protocols of compensation for unjust impositions of regulatory burdens. Often disputes between regulator and regulated organizations are concluded with binding agreements that stipulate the terms of the decision or settlement.

Administration by regulation

There is reason for skepticism regarding the efficacy of regulatory tools as substitutes for administrative tools. This application represents a departure from classic uses of regulation. The general form of justification for government regulation is that some feature or deformation of the market requires governmental intervention in the name of the public interest. Specific justifications fall into one of the following six broad categories (Breyer 1982). Any given policy may contain elements of several justifications.

1. *Control of monopoly power.* When a market can support only one firm, governments frequently step in to control price, ensure fair treatment of all customers and limit the power of producers.
2. *Control of rents.* When a limited mismatch in production costs and market prices (as opposed to wise investment strategy or investment of equity) allows for individuals to make extraordinary profits, governments may regulate price.
3. *Compensation for spillovers.* Market prices may not reflect true social costs. Regulation can prevent the social wastefulness caused by individual firms adopting inexpensive behavior that is collectively costly.
4. *Inadequate information.* Regulation is often justified by the need for access to information.
5. *Excessive competition.* Governments prohibit predatory pricing and other practices that quash competition, lead to business failures and produce unwanted monopoly conditions.
6. *Other justifications.* Governments invoke less frequently the need for rationalization (coordination in planning and operation to maximize efficiency), paternalism and protection from scarcity (when rising prices might result in serious hardship).

Intra-governmental regulation is often justified by the first rationale – regulation of a monopoly. The Postal Service and electric utilities are prominent examples. Additionally, some self-regulation results from government undertaking a regulated private sector activity. For example, public housing authorities are subject to safety requirements imposed on all landlords, and federal agencies are subject to Equal Employment Opportunity Commission (EEOC) review.

Regulation intended to guarantee that a quasi-public entity *fulfills its public policy purpose*, however, does not fit easily into Breyer's scheme. The intra-governmental regulation to which hybrids are often subject is intended to ensure that these governmental entities perform their public policy responsibilities.

Barry Mitnick has noted that governments sometimes resort to "regulation by directive" (1980). That is, governments pull private-sector institutions into the governmental orbit by bringing them under the authority of administrative command. A dramatic contemporary example of this phenomenon is the federal government's assumption of responsibility for airport security. The proliferation of hybrid organizations essentially does the opposite. Quasi-government transfers administration of public programs to semi-private entities. This necessitates *directive by regulation,* adapting regulation for the transmission of public policy objectives. The consequences of this substitution are discussed below.

Having the right tools: explaining the control challenge for hybrid organizations

The purpose of this book is to explain differences in principals' abilities to compel hybrid organizations to satisfy their preferences compared with traditional government agencies. Building upon the distinction laid out in the previous section, this chapter focuses on the different sets of control tools available to principals as the causal factor explaining observed differences. The empirical findings indicate that hybrid organizations are somewhat less likely to satisfy the principal's preferences. The relative ineffectiveness of the regulatory control tools as a substitute for administrative tools provides a partial explanation of this observation.

It is not suggested that principals can *never* compel hybrids to satisfy their preferences. Nor is it assumed that principals can *always* compel government agencies to satisfy their preferences. Rather, it is argued, based on the comparative study of hybrids and agencies underlying this volume, that hybrid organizations are less likely to satisfy a principal relying upon regulatory control tools than a government agency responding to a principal using administrative tools.

The following section reports observations from the study of hybrids and agencies in two policy areas: housing and international market development.

The control mechanisms available to principals with respect to the hybrid organizations are specified and a detailed account of the responses of hybrid and agency to changes in principals' preference is presented. The final section of this chapter (starting on page 66) summarizes these findings and offers implications for students of bureaucratic control and policy-makers interested in employing hybrid organizations.

Financing home loans with regulations

Since its creation in 1938, the public policy priorities of Fannie Mae (and its younger sibling, Freddie Mac) have evolved. Fannie Mae was originally created to expand the availability of mortgage credit as a means of boosting the United States out of the Depression. Fannie Mae and Freddie Mac are now charged by Congress and the President with extending credit opportunities to underserved communities while continuing to facilitate home purchases by middle-class Americans.

In 1992, Congress passed the Federal Housing Enterprises Financial Safety and Soundness Act (FHEFSSA). This law overhauled the regulatory infrastructure for both Fannie Mae and Freddie Mac. The legislative history of this Act is detailed extensively in chapter 5. Essentially, Congress divided regulatory authority between two entities: the Department of Housing and Urban Development and the Office of Federal Housing Enterprise Oversight. HUD is responsible for programmatic regulation – regulation that deals with the substantive policy objectives assigned to Fannie Mae and Freddie Mac. OFHEO is responsible for safety and soundness regulation – regulation to ensure that the two GSEs are well managed and maintain a healthy capital reserve as a cushion against potential losses.

These two regulatory organizations are the intermediary agents through which Congress and the President must compel Fannie Mae and Freddie Mac to satisfy their preferences. Each has a set of regulatory mandates established by Congress that define (in varying degrees of specificity) the objectives to be pursued by Fannie Mae and Freddie Mac and the regulatory tools available to compel compliance.

Programmatic regulation by HUD   The 1992 law called for HUD to create a multi-part regulation that set clear goals for the GSEs. In addition to formalizing the regulatory authority of HUD, the law also expressed a clear congressional preference for Fannie Mae and Freddie Mac to focus on making more credit available to low- and moderate-income borrowers and to borrowers in underserved communities. Implementation of the law fell to appointees of President Clinton, including his first Secretary of Housing and Urban Development, Henry Cisneros. Both Clinton and Cisneros expressed strong support for the programmatic goals included by Congress in the legislation (*Mortgage Marketplace* 1993, Senate Banking Committee 1994).

The law establishes goals for Fannie Mae and Freddie Mac in three areas: low- and moderate-income borrowers; special affordable housing; and central cities, rural areas and other underserved areas. The low- and moderate-income goal is described in modest detail to give a flavor of the regulation. The law directed the Secretary of HUD to establish a goal for Fannie Mae and Freddie Mac taking into account "national housing needs," the "performance and effort of the enterprises toward achieving the . . . goals in previous years," the "ability of the enterprises to lead the industry in making mortgage credit available," and the "need to maintain the sound financial condition of the enterprises" (12 United States Code 4,561 §1,332(b)). The law established an interim goal of 30 percent (of total units financed by each company) for the two years immediately following passage of the law.

The enforcement powers of the Secretary of HUD were also spelled out. If the GSEs fail to meet the regulatory goals, the companies' managers are notified and have an opportunity to respond in writing. The Secretary, if still finding the company out of compliance, can then order creation of a "housing plan" that would remedy the situation (12 USC 4,561 §1,336(c)(1)). The plan must be approved by the Secretary. If an acceptable plan is not submitted or the GSE in question does not make a "good faith effort" to achieve the goals, the Secretary can seek a court order requiring the company to do so (§1,341 (b)(2)). After fulfilling various procedural requirements, the Secretary of HUD can request that the Attorney General move for civil monetary penalties against the company (§1,345(a)).

The striking feature of the legislation is the nature of HUD's enforcement authority. The Secretary has weak authority to require remediation plans and Draconian authority to request that the Attorney General pursue civil action. Given the dramatic nature of the latter option, critics – and HUD staff – have argued that the real enforcement authority is quite limited (interview 82).

Safety and soundness regulation by OFHEO The impetus for the 1992 law was not programmatic concern but safety. Following the savings and loan crisis of the late 1980s and the resulting bailout, Congress was alerted to the potential liability posed by Fannie Mae and Freddie Mac. The safety and soundness regulation of these two large corporations was found to be woefully inadequate – essentially a handful of HUD employees with little in the way of resources or authority (GAO 1991, US Department of the Treasury 1991, CBO 1991). After a long and contentious process (see chapter 5), Congress created an entirely new regulatory entity to ensure the financial safety and soundness of the two GSEs.

OFHEO, which was founded in June 1993, is an "arm's length" agency of HUD. OFHEO's status is akin to bank regulatory agencies that are affiliated with but technically not part of the Treasury Department. An arm's length agency is organizationally part of a cabinet department but its head retains decision-making independence. OFHEO has two central responsibilities: the creation and development of capital regulations; and the regular examination of the business practices of the two companies.

The purpose of capital regulations is to create a cushion in the event of financial difficulties. There are two capital regulations to which Fannie Mae and Freddie Mac are subject. The minimum capital requirement was largely specified by Congress in the 1992 law. It sets a minimum level of capital that the GSEs must have on hand based on a relatively simple formula taking into account the companies' liabilities. There is also a risk-based capital standard that required OFHEO to design a complex model of the GSEs' business. A computerization of this model is then used to simulate the effects of massive downturns in the economy on Fannie Mae and Freddie Mac. The risk-based capital requirement is thus a moving amount that is required by each company to withstand this "stress test" given their financial obligations in any given quarter.

The minimum capital requirement was implemented shortly after OFHEO's creation (OFHEO 1994). The risk-based capital regulation, on the other hand, was approved after eight years of research, development and drafting (Collins 2001). It went into effect in September 2002 (*American Banker* 2002).

Remaining administrative tools In addition to the regulatory control tools, some administrative tools remain that may provide opportunities for influence. Most obviously, the President appoints five of each company's thirteen board members, with the Senate's approval. The board members appointed by the President are not distinguished from the other members by an obligation to represent the President, the administration, or the public in board proceedings (Musolf 1983).

Although Fannie Mae and Freddie Mac are not included in the annual budget process, representatives of the two companies appear frequently at congressional hearings. Both companies fund research into housing and housing finance and, as a result, they are considered invaluable sources of information. In addition to hearings related to general housing policy, Congress sometimes addresses Fannie Mae and Freddie Mac, their role in the American housing system, and the regulations being drafted by OFHEO and HUD. The companies are always given an opportunity to be represented at such hearings. In recent years, the two GSEs have received more attention on matters ranging from securities regulation to the limits of their mission (Bailey 2000, Fernandez 2002b).

Fannie Mae and Freddie Mac are occasionally the subject of reports by the GAO and CBO. The companies cooperate with these inquiries as required by their charters. Also, as publicly traded companies on the New York Stock Exchange, both GSEs publish annual reports and various supplements that provide information regarding their performance and financial status. Wall Street analysts evaluate the companies for potential investors and the financial and housing industry press follow their activities closely as well.

Likelihood of preference satisfaction is lower for Fannie Mae and Freddie Mac

The revamped regulatory infrastructure increased the ability of principals to transmit their preferences to Fannie Mae and Freddie Mac. It also increased the likelihood of preference satisfaction. Still, based on the organizations' performance and the nature of their relations with Congress, the administration and their regulators, Fannie Mae and Freddie Mac remain less likely to satisfy their principals than HUD. This finding is illustrated with a comparison of the organizations' provision of housing assistance to low-income borrowers since Congress and the President made clear their preference for this outcome.

The Department of Housing and Urban Development is a large agency carrying out a variety of programs. The Federal Housing Administration, located within HUD, is the entity most readily comparable with the GSEs in judging organizational activity in reaction to Congress and the President. As described in chapter 2, the FHA is not a hybrid by the definition utilized for this study. It relies upon appropriations to cover a significant portion of its costs and, perhaps more importantly, functions effectively as an office of HUD.

As part of HUD, the FHA's commissioner is a presidential appointee who reports to the Secretary of Housing and Urban Development. The FHA's budget is included with the department's in the OMB's annual budget submission. For appropriations and authorization purposes, the FHA is considered along with the rest of HUD's programs.

The FHA performs a function related to, if not equivalent to, the GSEs'. It essentially insures lenders against default by certain borrowers, generally first-time buyers purchasing a home with value below a prescribed level. While Fannie Mae and Freddie Mac were being pushed to increase their performance among minority borrowers and residents of low-income and underserved areas, the FHA was under the same pressure. Although both GSEs have increased their performance in these areas, they have not kept pace with HUD, as reflected in the performance of the FHA.

As indicated in figures 3.1–3.3, the FHA has done a better job ramping up its performance in serving borrowers in high-minority areas, underserved

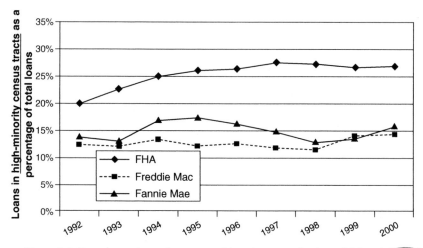

Figure 3.1 Programmatic performance of housing organizations (high-minority census tracts), 1992–2000

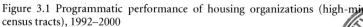

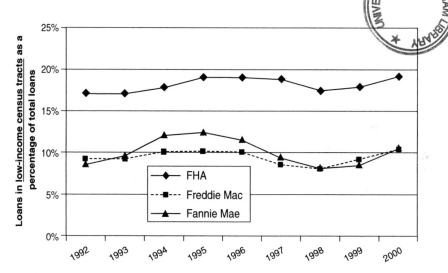

Figure 3.2 Programmatic performance of housing organizations (low-income census tracts), 1992–2000

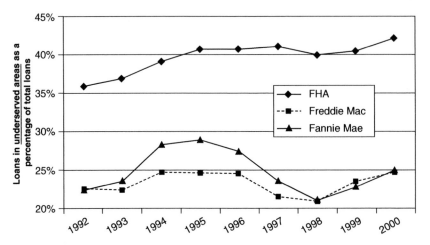

Figure 3.3 Programmatic performance of housing organizations (underserved areas), 1992–2000

areas and low-income census tracts. Fannie Mae and Freddie Mac have improved, but at a slower rate. As figure 3.1 shows, the percentage of FHA loans that went to individuals purchasing homes located in high-minority census tracts areas climbed from 20 percent to 27 percent between 1992 and 2000. In comparison, Freddie Mac increased from 12 percent to 14 percent over the same period. Fannie Mae roughly matched Freddie Mac, increasing from 14 percent to 16 percent from 1992 to 2000.

The performance among low-income borrowers is similar (figure 3.2). The FHA increased its share of loans to low-income borrowers from 17 percent to 19 percent between 1992 and 2000. Fannie Mae had a similar increase, from 8.7 percent to 10.5 percent (although it did get as high as 12.5 percent in 1995). Freddie Mac trailed both, climbing from 9.2 percent in 1992 to 10.4 percent in 2000.

The pattern was the same with respect to underserved areas (figure 3.3). The FHA managed to increase the percentage of loans going to these areas from 36 percent to 42 percent between 1992 and 2000. Fannie Mae raised its performance from 22.5 percent to 25.0 percent as Freddie Mac went from 22.6 percent of its loans going to underserved areas to 24.7 percent at the end of the nine-year period.

Two points of qualification are in order. First, the FHA's relative performance is made more significant by its higher baseline. It is somewhat more difficult to register improvement when the starting point is higher. Moreover, the behavior of the organizations is as important as their performance. This relates to the input/output distinction discussed in chapter 2. While the

FHA embraced the goals, Fannie Mae and Freddie Mac have both resisted the efforts of Members of Congress and the administration to raise the levels of expected performance (e.g., Nitschke 1998). Indeed, it must be noted that the disparity described above has been the subject of heated debate between HUD and the GSEs. Fannie Mae and Freddie Mac reject HUD's interpretation of the data, which is similar to the preceding paragraph, arguing that Fannie Mae does not have the same ability to adjust performance as the FHA (Raines 2000). The GSEs, Raines argues, cannot purchase uninsured loans and nor can they compel lenders to sell them loans if they prefer to hold them in portfolio. Neither claim is especially persuasive as virtually all loans in the targeted communities carry the FHA insurance (the FHA's improvement suggests an *increased* pool of insured loans), and lenders serving such markets are highly unlikely to prefer retaining the credit risk on low-value loans when they could be sold to Fannie Mae or Freddie Mac.

Second, the GSEs' contention that they have done as much to satisfy Congress and the President as HUD is underscored by their performance in terms of the regulatory goals. The data presented in these three figures is useful because it places Fannie Mae, Freddie Mac and FHA on the same scale. However, the GSEs' performance can also be judged – perhaps *should* be judged – by their performance vis-à-vis the goals mandated by the 1992 legislation overhauling the regulation of the two companies. HUD issued regulations establishing targets in 2000 following on the interim goals that it had established earlier. The GSEs have met the gradually rising targets.

The goals are divided into three categories: low- and moderate-income borrowers, geographically targeted areas and special affordable. For each goal, HUD established a goal for 1996 and for 1997–2000. Fannie Mae and Freddie Mac both met the goals in each category in all the years since 1996.

Fannie Mae and Freddie Mac have arguably been somewhat more responsive to OFHEO's capital regulation than the calls for increased allocation of resources to low-income communities. Recall that there are two aspects to the capital requirements put in place as part of the revision of safety and soundness regulation: minimum capital requirements and risk-based capital requirements.

As seen in figure 3.4, both companies have met the minimum capital requirement. In fact, Fannie Mae and Freddie Mac began increasing their capital levels in anticipation of the law's passage and since 1993 have maintained levels at or slightly above the requirement stipulated in the regulation (OFHEO 2001).

The risk-based capital requirement proved far more contentious. As OFHEO developed the stress test and proposed the regulation, Fannie Mae and Freddie Mac have criticized the agency and its approach (e.g., Brockman 1999b). In this manner, they have attempted to influence the final regulation.

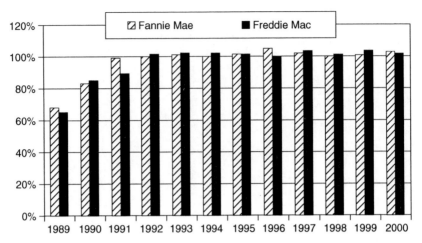

Figure 3.4 GSEs' retained capital (as a percentage of minimum capital requirement), 1989–2000

Even as the regulation neared finalization, the companies sought delay and modifications (Rehm 2001). Still, the companies have complied with the requirements set forth in the final regulation and have allocated the capital specified (OFHEO 2001).

There is no easy comparison available for the capital regulation. The FHA is not subject to this type of oversight. The capital regulations applied to private financial institutions by financial regulators are similar to those being implemented by OFHEO but the differences in institutions and the nature of the relationships make the comparison uneasy.

The relative effectiveness of the two types of regulation – financial safety and programmatic – is considered at length in chapter 4. It appears that the programmatic regulation that embodied principals' preference for greater activity in low-income areas proved somewhat less effective than the safety and soundness regulation. It certainly took longer for this declaration of preference to be translated into action and results by the GSEs than it did by the FHA. The capital regulation – judging primarily by the experience with the minimum capital requirements, which were put in place very shortly after passage of the 1992 law – almost immediately altered the behavior of the hybrids.

This suggests that the quality of regulation – its clarity, specificity and enforceability – is the key to "controlling" hybrid organizations. Preferences that require regulating agencies to carry out research, set controversial benchmarks and objectives, and translate these measures into rules and regulations are less likely to be satisfied by the GSEs in a timely fashion than agencies. Still, the effectiveness of the regulation of Fannie Mae and Freddie Mac, in absolute terms, also demonstrates that regulation is a more reliable means of control than the remaining administrative connections (e.g., directors appointed by the President). It was, in the final analysis, regulation that moved the GSEs to increase their activities in underserved areas and add to their capital reserves.

Regulating the wild world of venture capital

The two government-backed venture capital fund programs discussed in this volume are designed somewhat differently (see appendix for detail). Here the extent of control over Enterprise Funds and OPIC investment funds is the primary consideration while some reference is also made to the US Agency for International Development, the government agency with activities most similar to the funds. The control tools available to principals with respect to Enterprise Funds and OPIC investment funds are described before the evaluation of their satisfaction of a range of principal preferences is presented.

Although the comparison of hybrid organizations with government agencies is the primary objective of the research behind this book, the two venture capital fund programs present an opportunity to study the consequences of variation in structure *among* hybrids. Specifically, the tools available to overseers of the two sets of funds are different. The OPIC-sponsored investment funds are structured in such a way that satisfaction of principals is more likely than in the case of Enterprise Funds. This difference is explained below.

Enterprise Funds   Confronted by Eastern European countries hungry for American assistance, Bush (the elder) Administration officials and Republicans in Congress did not have faith in the ability of USAID to develop the private-sector institutions seen as the key to economic and political development (interviews 5, 4, 2, 24). This attitude, reminiscent of the feelings that led to OPIC's separation from USAID years earlier, led to the creation of the Enterprise Funds. Thus it is not shocking that the administrative ties between the Enterprise Funds and the federal government are weak. In the years since the creation of the Funds, Congress, the administration and the Funds have struggled with the extent to which the principals ought to influence the agents.

This project considered all European Enterprise Funds operating as of 1999. However, research efforts were concentrated on a few funds to get a more nuanced picture of the relationship between the Enterprise Funds and their overseers at USAID and the State Department.

The Enterprise Funds have a common skeletal structure that differentiates them from traditional government agencies and the largest class of hybrid organizations, government corporations. The Support for Eastern European Democracy (SEED) Act establishing the first Funds allows them to carry out their activities "notwithstanding any other provision of the law" (22 USCA §5,421(c)). This clause has been interpreted, after some agitation, to exempt the Funds from all federal management laws, including the Government Corporation Control Act (Cox 1990).

There is tremendous variation across Funds. The government's financial commitment, the level of disbursement and the strategic approach all vary quite significantly from Fund to Fund. Congress emphasized some strategic objectives to all Enterprise Funds, including investments that encourage stock ownership plans for employees, the establishment of credit unions and the modernization of telecommunications. The legislation provides tremendous latitude to the Enterprise Funds; they can make grants, loans or capital investments or deliver technical assistance. One clause explicitly permits the Polish Fund to channel money to the Solidarity Party (22 USCA §5,421(f)).

Congress placed some "limitations" on Fund activities in the limply worded "Matters to be Considered by Enterprise Funds" but provided no enforcement mechanism:

> Each Enterprise Fund shall take into account such considerations as internationally recognized worker rights and other internationally recognized human rights, environmental factors, United States economic and employment effects, and the likelihood of commercial viability of the activity receiving assistance from the Enterprise Fund, (22 USCA §5,421(g))

A vague instruction that compensation for Fund personnel be "reasonable" was subsequently translated in to a more concrete $150,000 cap, to which the Enterprise Funds agreed (Atwood 1993). This specification came following a minor "scandal" concerning the compensation of a politically connected individual hired to manage an enterprise owned by the Hungarian American Enterprise Fund (HAEF) (interviews 19, 2).

In addition to the SEED Act, there are essentially three tools of control available to influence Enterprise Funds: (1) presidential designation of directors; (2) negotiated grant agreements, corporate by-laws and Fund policies and procedures; (3) ongoing oversight by USAID and the State Department.

Designation of directors   The Enterprise Funds are chartered as non-profit corporations in the state of Delaware and governed by boards of directors. Enterprise Fund directors are reimbursed for expenses but are not compensated. As officers of private corporations, Enterprise Fund directors are not appointed by the President per se. Rather they are "designated" by the President and elected by the existing board. The founding boards incorporated their Funds following their presidential designation.

Enterprise Fund directors must be citizens of the United States or the host country and can be designated only after "consult[ing] with the leadership of each House of Congress" (22 USCA §5,421(d)(1)). Consultation is informal without hearings or votes. The choice of directors, in practice, is largely a matter of presidential prerogative. Directors, the majority of whom must be American, must have "relevant expertise" and commitment to the establishment of "democracy and a free market economy" (22 USCA §5,421(d)(3)(b)).

The first Enterprise Fund directors, John Whitehead of the Hungarian Fund and John Birkelund of the Polish Fund, are highly respected senior members of the investment banking community, to whom the President was deferential on the selection of additional directors (interviews 4, 5, 74, 77). The early boards were bipartisan (or non-partisan) in composition and included persons with distinguished records either in financial pursuits or in matters pertaining to the host country. Critics have noted that recent appointments have been more political in nature and handled through the White House personnel office, unlike the selection of the Polish and Hungarian Enterprise Fund directors, and less concerned with substantive qualification (interviews 4, 5, 8).

There are no formal reporting requirements or liaisons within the White House or the administration for the directors of Enterprise Funds. Many of these individuals do have frequent informal contact with administration officials but board members, even chairmen, are not involved in regular foreign policy discussions, even those concerning the region in which their Fund operates (interviews 20, 21, 77).

Most board members are not involved in the day-to-day operations of the Funds (interviews 15, 20, 21, 62, 64). Enterprise Fund directors select a president, who manages in-country operations. Some Enterprise Funds have US offices; this allows greater involvement of the chairman, who is generally well apprised of Fund activities. The board itself typically meets four times per year (at least once a year in the host country). Some Funds have investment committees that meet more frequently (usually by teleconference) than the entire board to review major proposed investments. By and large, the boards defer to Fund management (interviews 15, 19, 60, 62, 65).

Negotiated terms of incorporation, by-laws and policies Before the chairman of the first Fund had been designated by President George H. W. Bush, USAID personnel took the first steps towards establishment of the Funds. They engaged lawyers, who began drafting incorporation papers, and put

out a request for proposals (RFP) from contractors who would run the
Funds for the boards (interviews 17, 10, 5). When the first two boards were
named, the chairmen quickly abandoned the USAID efforts and informed
the agency that they would be setting up new, independent organizations.

Many within USAID favored this approach and encouraged the Enterprise
Funds, essentially, to go their own way (interviews 4, 5, 10, 80). The State
Department's SEED coordinator, the individual designated to oversee the
Enterprise Funds, also favored the independence of the Funds (interview 17).
Thus, even though some career USAID staff were wary of the Funds, their
directors and managers were granted substantive latitude (interviews 5, 17).

Negotiations regarding the terms of grant agreements, corporate by-
laws and policies and procedures were necessary (interviews 4, 10, 17).
Hammered out by USAID officials and counsel hired by the Enterprise
Funds, these documents added flesh to the skeleton provided by the
SEED Act and defined the relationship between the Enterprise Funds
and the government overseers. A brief explication of their terms is
helpful.

Corporate by-laws and the certificate of incorporation formalize the requirements of the legislation. This includes selection procedures for directors and
other matters including non-profit status, distribution of assets, and other
procedural issues. Almost no attention is given to the Fund's mission other
than a general statement that its purpose is development of the private sector.

Grant agreements focus on the distribution of Funds from USAID to
the Enterprise Funds and the requirements placed upon both the agency
and each Fund to facilitate payment. These requirements are largely driven
by budget rules and do not include any imposition of policy direction as
condition for obligation of funds.

Policies and Procedures lay out guidelines on managerial matters, including procurement, expenses, salaries, hiring and other administrative matters.
These requirements generally call for "reasonable" behavior and documen-
tation rather than establishing strict rules.

The structure and practice of control over the Enterprise Funds has
evolved since the creation of the first two Funds. Driven in part by "problems" with two Funds, both the administration and Congress have gradually
asserted more authority in the form of beefier reporting requirements. This
type of "oversight creep" is neither unusual nor unexpected (interview 24).
In a system that emphasizes "fire alarm" oversight, the discovery of a fire
frequently results in the creation of additional alarms and lessened resistance
to their installation (McCubbins and Schwartz 1984).

Oversight and coordination   USAID and the State Department play the
role of regulator for the Enterprise Funds. Within the Eastern Europe bureau
of USAID a group of three or four Fund overseers track the Funds' activities

(i.e., office operations, potential investments, status of programs) and communicate regularly with Fund staff. There are two so-called "SEED coordinators" in the State Department responsible for monitoring the Enterprise Funds and considering them in discussions of regional policy.

USAID's formal power as overseer of the Enterprise Funds is quite limited. Recall that the creators of the Fund program – even those within USAID – were suspicious of the agency's ability to let these new organizations operate in a non-bureaucratic fashion. Thus Enterprise Fund overseers at USAID and the State Department SEED coordinators are informed of pending deals but have no authority to veto a deal or force a Fund to proceed on a particular proposal. They may raise questions regarding proposed projects and suggest their doubts, reservations or enthusiasm (interviews 9, 11, 12, 13).

The most significant contact between Enterprise Funds and USAID concerns money. The first Enterprise Funds expected to receive a lump payment of their entire allotted sum from USAID and then to operate free and clear of any supervision (interviews 4, 5, 8). This is not how the program ended up functioning. Money is disbursed in chunks as needed until the total commitment is met. The Funds make annual requests based on their anticipated slate of investments. These yearly disbursements come out of the USAID budget for that year (and region). Thus there can be tension between the Enterprise Funds and other USAID operatives in a given region (interviews 13, 72). They are competing for the same finite resources.

The SEED Act and grant agreements require Enterprise Funds to produce public annual reports. The reports outline the yearly activities of the Funds, including new investments, the size and performance of the existing portfolio and future projects. The reports do not provide detailed financial information on each investment as that might reveal proprietary business information. Although project-specific information is available to USAID, public evaluation of an Enterprise Fund's portfolio is difficult (*Annual Reports* of Enterprise Funds).

Enterprise Funds are required to report results of independent private audits. The General Accounting Office may also conduct periodic reviews. Finally, the Inspector General of USAID has authority to review the Funds' compliance with their own policies and procedures (described below).

The current reporting requirements are significantly broader than those applied to the Funds early in the program's development. First, they expanded in response to "incidents" that made oversight of the Enterprise Funds an issue. Held responsible for the alleged misdeeds, USAID negotiated with the Enterprise Funds for more comprehensive reporting requirements (interviews 19, 13). USAID overseers also conduct semi-annual reviews, including a required report on the status of new and existing investments as well as meetings with Enterprise Fund boards and management (interviews 3, 11, USAID 1998).

Second, the Government Performance and Results Act (GPRA), enacted in 1996, created a requirement that USAID formalize its strategic objectives. As the Enterprise Funds are within USAID's portfolio, the agency now requires the Enterprise Funds to fill out a "performance matrix" that includes aspirations for the short- and long-term futures. There is no indication that the performance matrix plays an important role in the decision-making of any Fund manager or board but it does compel them to provide USAID with additional information.

Assessment Issues of control were hardly considered in two early studies of the Enterprise Funds. A GAO report pointed out the shortcomings in USAID's oversight authority but noted that this was a consequence of legislative design (GAO 1994). As a result, the GAO concluded, the Enterprise Funds have a great deal of latitude and it is difficult even to evaluate their performance. Development Alternatives, Inc. (DAI), a Washington-based development contractor commissioned to write a report on Enterprise Fund performance, found the Enterprise Funds limited as developmental tools – as did an internal USAID report (DAI 1995, Fox 1996). Evaluators concluded that the monitoring performed by USAID was not sufficient to generate good information. The reviews examined only the first four Enterprise Funds and took place before significant formalization of USAID's oversight.

This study found limited effective authority to compel any behavior from the Enterprise Funds. This is evident in considering Enterprise Fund performance with respect to the goals stated in the SEED Act. For example, the legislation explicitly directs the Enterprise Funds to invest in the telecommunications sector (103 Stat. 1,306 §201(f)(4)). This is the clearest indication of congressional interest in a particular goal as one can find.

As table 3.1 illustrates, the Funds have not demonstrated any emphasis on telecommunications. As of 1999, only three of the ten Funds reported any investment in telecommunications. Note that this is not a criticism of the Funds. There are sound reasons why telecommunications investment was not pursued. Moreover, the administration did not press the Funds to carry out this mandate, demonstrating the perils of relying upon an intermediary (interview 80). Another legislatively articulated objective produced a similar outcome. Despite a legislative directive to pursue joint ventures with American businesses, there have been only four successful joint ventures with American firms in the history of the Enterprise Fund *program*.

An overriding preference applying to Enterprise Funds (and OPIC investment funds) is the avoidance of financial malfeasance (i.e., improper use of government or government-guaranteed funds). Enterprise Funds, by the admission of overseers of the program, had many problems with this in the early years of the program (interviews 1, 8), culminating in

Table 3.1 *Enterprise Fund investment in telecommunications*

Fund	Telecommunications [sector activity]	
	Loans	Equity
Albanian American Enterprise Fund (1998 AR)	0	0
Baltic American Enterprise Fund (1997 AR)	0	N/A
Bulgarian American Enterprise Fund (1997 AR)	0	0
Central Asian American Enterprise Fund (1997 AR)	0	0
Czech and Slovak American Enterprise Fund (1997 AR)	0	0
Hungarian American Enterprise Fund (1998 AR)	N/A	N/A[a]
Polish American Enterprise Fund (1998 AR)	0	0
Romanian American Enterprise Fund (1997 AR)	0	$0.8 million[b]
US Russia Investment Fund (1997 AR)	0	$5 million
Western NIS[c] American Enterprise Fund (1997 AR)	0	0

AR = *annual report* N/A = loans/investment not reported by sector.
[a] AR does highlight at least one $0.7 million investment in telecommunications firm.
[b] Based on percentage figure for telecommunications and total investment.
[c] Newly Independent States.

Rep. David Obey's 1993 investigation of the Hungarian American Enterprise Fund following revelation of two questionable decisions by HAEF management (Maass 1993a, Maass 1993b). The firestorm of attention brought the Fund program to a temporary halt and led the Hungarian Fund's president to resign (interviews 19, 80, Denton 1993). In the most dramatic failure of oversight, the Czech and Slovak Fund suffered an effective meltdown amidst lurid tales of intra-office romance (and promotions), faked bidding on contracts and misled board members (Ottaway 1996). USAID eventually pressured the board of directors to resign and a new board started essentially from scratch (Wald 1996a).

As a consequence USAID overseers beefed up the reporting and oversight requirements (interviews 19, 13). Still, there is no explicit authority in the hands of USAID's Fund overseers to punish "wayward" Funds and problems remain. Fund records on file with USAID indicate persistent problems with waste of Fund resources, small-scale theft and possibly fraud (Brauer 2001).

OPIC investment funds The OPIC investment funds were structured to facilitate equity investment utilizing OPIC's statutory authority to provide loan guarantees. The first few funds – experiments created on an ad hoc basis – proved popular and were replicated. The creators of the funds acknowledge that the development of oversight capacity trailed the creation of the funds. Only after personnel with both government and venture capital experience were brought in did the process for creating and overseeing the investment funds take on structure (interviews 23, 27).

Subsequent to the creation of the first investment funds, Congress has included language in foreign assistance legislation instructing OPIC to create additional investment funds to serve particular regions, but the OPIC statute has not been altered to include explicit provision for the investment fund program (22 USCA §2,194, §2,194(b)).

As discussed in the previous chapter, the OPIC funds have received very little attention. This is not only a function of lack of interest, but of the secretive nature of the program. OPIC fund managers argue that the legal requirement for business confidentiality precludes releasing most information regarding the funds (interviews 87, 88, 89). Thus evaluation is quite difficult – a challenge encountered in carrying out research for this book.

OPIC's control tools: fund selection The earliest investment funds were created in a haphazard manner. OPIC approached private fund managers with ideas for new investment funds or entertained unsolicited proposals. In response to criticism that the program was influenced by political considerations, the process for soliciting and evaluating new bids for investment funds has gradually been formalized. OPIC advertises its intention to start a fund for a particular country or sector to interest potential fund managers.

The organization has developed criteria on which applications are evaluated. All proposals are judged on the fund manager's ability to attract private investment, identify and manage equity investments, and apply substantive knowledge of the proposed target country, region or sector (interviews 23, 31). OPIC also utilizes policy-related criteria in evaluating competing bids for a proposed fund. For example, competing prospective fund managers have highlighted investment strategies targeting woman-owned businesses or labor-intensive businesses (interview 31). Thus the selection process provides an opportunity for OPIC to give substantive direction to the investment fund.

OPIC's control tools: negotiated terms of loan guarantees Once a fund manager is selected, the terms of the loan guarantee are hammered out in a process resembling the negotiation of the charter and by-laws of Enterprise Funds. OPIC is guaranteed a pre-set return on its loan regardless of the profit (or lack thereof) generated by the investment fund. The loan is the primary financial obligation of the fund. That is, in the event of a fund's failure, all recovered assets must be dedicated to repayment of the loan before equity investors are made whole (Stillman 1996). OPIC thus refers to the private investments as an "equity shield" on the guaranteed loans.

There are numerous details to be determined and incorporated into the loan agreements, such as the length of payment grace periods, profit stages, interest rates, etc. OPIC also gets a portion of the "management carry" – the fund manager's profit – related to the risk of each arrangement.

Restrictions on the funds are drawn from the restrictions placed on all OPIC programs by Congress. OPIC cannot undertake programs that have harmful effects in the United States (i.e., that "export jobs" by financing enterprises that compete with American employers) or that fund companies that violate worker rights or that contribute to the degradation of the environment (22 USCA §2,191(3)). Additionally, the programmatic purpose of a particular fund imposes restrictions (e.g., a small business fund is limited to investment in companies of a certain size).

OPIC's control tools: scrutiny OPIC fund overseers review proposed investments for compliance with the loan agreements. Each proposed investment must be approved by the OPIC fund manager and a review committee before the money is released from the lender to the investment fund. This includes the three major restrictions applicable to all OPIC programs as well as any specific constraints incorporated into a particular fund's agreement. For example, a fund operating in multiple countries may have a distribution scheme stipulated. OPIC overseers will review investments to ensure that the fund is, in fact, allocating its investment according to the negotiated distribution.

Deals are rarely rejected formally because the fund managers are unlikely to propose an investment to the review committee at risk of rejection (interview 109). Fund managers and OPIC staff emphasize that the review does not pertain to the financial aspects of the deal. That is, OPIC does not review the fund's evaluation of the business in terms of the market for the company's product or its likelihood of good economic return (interviews 109, 120, 87, 89). OPIC also periodically conducts site visits to ensure continued compliance with standards on environmental pollution, child labor, etc. Some critics argue that high-quality investment professionals are unwilling to manage OPIC investment funds under these restrictions (interview 79).

Control tools: OPIC as part of the administration As OPIC is the overseer of the investment funds, it is important to outline the extent to which it is subject to the executive and legislative controls applicable to OPIC itself. OPIC is subject to many federal management laws, including the Government Corporation Control Act. Its employees are compensated on the same scale as federal employees and must comply with ethics requirements and abide by the Freedom of Information Act, among other rules. One important caveat involves the shielding of private business information. OPIC personnel cite their legal obligation not to divulge any proprietary information of entities with which it does business when describing the activities of investment funds (interviews 31, 87, 88, 89). This means that the private fund managers do not divulge the names of their investors, the companies in which they are investing or the returns on these investments.

OPIC is governed by a board of directors, chaired by the administrator of USAID, that includes ex officio six representatives of the administration as well as seven other presidential appointees (22 USCA §2,193(b)). OPIC's president/CEO and senior officials are appointed by the President of the United States with advice and consent from the Senate (§2,193(c)). OPIC is represented in administration working groups and discussions related to its mission. It is part of the Trade Promotion Coordinating Committee, a "toothless" entity created to coordinate American trade activities across agencies.

OPIC is included in the federal budget. Its appropriations request is submitted through the Office of Management and Budget, where inter-agency negotiation of demands takes place. Although OPIC is typically a net positive on the budget – bringing in more revenues than outlays – an appropriations request is required for OPIC's yearly credit reserve. That is, the administration must include in the budget a reserve calculated as a percentage of all OPIC financial commitments to be made during the budget year. This creates a limit on OPIC activity that can constrain programmatic activity.

OPIC historically enjoyed a low profile on Capitol Hill until targeted by Rep. John Kasich in his 1996 crusade against "corporate welfare." Kasich argued that OPIC subsidized American companies that profited at taxpayer expense (Blustein 1996). After a bruising re-authorization battle, OPIC narrowly survived by the unusual step of re-authorization through the appropriations bill. OPIC has experienced heightened levels of attention ever since and is often targeted, at least rhetorically, as an example of corporate welfare (Schaeffer 1996, Doherty 1996, Savage 1997).

The periodic re-authorization and yearly appropriations processes include congressional hearings. OPIC also submits annual reports and communicates regularly with congressional staff. Relatively little information is transmitted regarding the investment funds. Each annual report includes new investment funds with the amount of loan guarantee committed to that fund, along with other projects financed in a given year. That does not reveal the *actual* amount of loans drawn upon by those investment funds or the total investment in the funds program. Committee staff members do not display a strong interest in the activities of the investment funds or a particular thirst for additional information. By their own admission the committee staff assigned to the program have little time to engage (interviews 16, 3, 6, 2). As one staffer put it, "We'll wait for something to blow up and then take a look" (interview 16).

Assessment of OPIC's control tools OPIC's control tools with respect to its investment funds are more regulatory in character than those to which the Enterprise Funds are subject. This appears to explain the finding that OPIC appears to have more reliable control of its investment funds than USAID enjoys with respect to the Enterprise Funds. This is not to suggest Enterprise Funds run amok. But, based on this comparison, OPIC fund managers seem better able to acquire relevant information in a timely manner, scrutinize investment funds' activities and ensure compliance with loan agreements. This can be seen in several comparisons.

The OPIC funds have not appeared to have problems similar to those experienced by the USAID funds in terms of financial malfeasance. This is due in large part to two differences. First, the more formal loan agreements between OPIC and investment funds specify appropriate uses of funds, thus reducing ambiguity for OPIC fund managers. Second, the participation of private investors in the OPIC investment funds introduces a third party with a strong interest in monitoring the management and use of resources.

There is also a disparity between the two types of funds when comparing the satisfaction of preferences related to the substantive activities of funds. For example, the SEED Act articulated investment in telecommunications as a priority for Enterprise Funds. Barely any investment in this area has been registered by the Funds. Similarly, efforts to coordinate standards of environmental review for the Enterprise Funds fell upon deaf ears (interview 11).

OPIC's fund managers have an advantage in this regard. Substantive targets can be stipulated in loan agreements. For example, the Modern Africa Fund is required to distribute its investments to various countries according to a formula included in the loan agreement (Modern Africa Fund undated). This gives OPIC leverage to require compliance with the agreement during the review process.

Still, several funds have been unable to fulfill the objectives specified in the loan agreements (interviews 29, 31, 109). This is a point that is difficult to substantiate due to OPIC's unwillingness to divulge data on fund performance. But examples illustrate the observation. The West Bank and Gaza Fund was created at the behest of Congress. Although this fund had an OPIC commitment for $125 million, it had invested only $2.6 million as of March 1999 (US State Department 2000). It has had a difficult time raising capital and finding suitable investments. Neither OPIC nor any investment fund can mandate investment by private investors to satisfy principals' preferences.

The limits of regulatory control

One can draw two key inferences about the consequences of substituting regulation for administration with respect to hybrid organizations. First, reliance on regulatory tools makes the satisfaction of principal preferences more difficult and less likely. Second, in situations where principals rely upon a mix of administrative and regulatory tools, the soundness of the regulatory infrastructure influences the likelihood of effective control more than the presence of administrative ties.

Regulatory control tools are more difficult to wield effectively

Effective regulatory control requires meticulous crafting of detailed laws and regulations that define preferences in specific measurable terms, set sanctions for non-compliance, provide opportunities for mediation or appeal, and establish protocols of compensation for unjust impositions of regulatory burdens. This can create barriers to the satisfaction of preferences.

Although the concepts underlying public policy programs are often straightforward, definitions can prove elusive. For example, the definition of "low-income" for the purposes of HUD's regulation of Fannie Mae and Freddie Mac has proven contentious and time-consuming. Low relative to what? The city? The state? The region? And even when a goal can be defined, establishing the appropriate standard of achievement can be difficult. HUD argues that Fannie Mae and Freddie Mac should exceed the performance of the market generally while the two companies argue they can be expected only to match private market participants.

Even if these obstacles can be overcome, the regulatory process is clearly time-consuming. The law mandating new regulations for Fannie Mae and Freddie Mac was passed at the end of 1992. OFHEO's risk-based capital standard took effect in the fall of 2002. Thus, even to the extent preferences are satisfied, it takes a long time. As many public policy needs require immediate or rapid redress (particularly from the viewpoint of elected political principals), delayed satisfaction of preferences may be tantamount to no satisfaction.

Effective regulation is key

The finding that the OPIC fund program seems better suited to satisfy principals' preferences than the Enterprise Fund program may be surprising. Conventional understanding of control would lead one to the opposite hypothesis. That is, one might expect *greater* control of Enterprise Funds than OPIC investment funds for three reasons. One, Enterprise Funds rely upon government appropriations as opposed to OPIC investment funds, which mix guaranteed loans and private capital. Thus Enterprise Funds are subject, as part of USAID, to the yearly appropriations review. Two, OPIC investment funds are not subject to nearly the same level of public scrutiny as Enterprise Funds. They do not produce publicly available annual reports or submit audited financial statements for congressional review. Even Members of Congress have complained that the funds resist even modest requests for information. Three, Enterprise Fund directors are designated by the President. OPIC fund managers are selected by OPIC under a formal review process and must subsequently solicit private investors for capital. Thus the Enterprise Fund directors more closely resemble the political appointees relied upon as loyal agents of the President.

But, in the context of hybrid government, these three traditional administrative tools – appropriations, public scrutiny, and presidential appointment – are not reliable instruments of control. That is because the relationship between government and hybrid is essentially regulatory. The rights and responsibilities of the venture capital funds directors, managers and overseers are defined in legal agreements.

In such relationships, the dominant considerations are the structure, character and quality of the "regulation." The administrative linkages are essentially vestigial. The OPIC fund program has a stronger regulatory framework in two respects: OPIC has formal regulatory powers of enforcement with legal sanction; and OPIC investment funds have more clearly articulated missions to which the fund managers can be held accountable.

As lender to the investment funds, OPIC has legal rights and remedies should the terms of the loan agreement be violated. Indeed, OPIC investment funds can be legally compelled to divest a particular investment if it is found to violate any of the strictures of the loan agreement (interviews 15, 27). OPIC managers visit the investments and express discontent when failings are noted. It has not been necessary for OPIC to invoke these rights and privileges formally, but the action has been threatened and the requirements of the agreement are frequently debated between OPIC, the investment funds and their lawyers (interviews 109, 110). USAID has no equivalent "stick" to wield over the Enterprise Funds.

OPIC's advantages have origins in the negotiation of terms for the venture capital funds. Investment funds are generally created at the discretion of OPIC and in all cases fund managers are selected from a group of prospective managers. Unhappy with the terms proposed by prospective fund managers, OPIC can simply walk away. Enterprise Funds, in contrast, begin with a board of directors designated by the President and cannot be terminated by the supervising agency.

Unlike OPIC officials setting the terms of loan agreements with the investment funds, USAID and State Department negotiators have no choice but to work out a deal with the Enterprise Fund directors. This gives USAID considerably less leverage in negotiating the terms of the agreement. That is not to say OPIC simply dictates its terms. Private fund managers must be able to solicit investment from private investors. If the terms imposed by OPIC seem to make profitability less likely, this will be difficult if not impossible. Indeed, the loan agreements create a legal impediment to OPIC influence on the funds. If OPIC pressures the fund into taking actions that prove financially damaging, OPIC may be legally liable (interview 87).

An important caveat is required regarding OPIC's oversight of its investment funds. Although the investment funds face more stringent controls than the Enterprise Funds, it should be noted that their sole "examiner" is OPIC. Any control to be exerted by other agencies, the President or Congress must be routed through OPIC. Most administration officials and congressional staff admitted that they know little about the investment funds and their operations or made this fact abundantly clear in the course of interviews. Limited public access to materials related to the investment funds makes dependence on OPIC review and regulation more profound. Any breakdown in OPIC oversight leaves the investment funds essentially unsupervised. This introduces the embedded principal-agent problem, which is discussed at length in chapter 7.

Conclusion

The basic lesson of this chapter is that the relationship between the hybrid organization and the government should be conceived in regulatory rather than administrative terms. Despite its intra-governmental appearance, the relationship between principal and hybrid organization most closely resembles the relationship between a regulatory agency and regulated organization. The terms of that relationship are defined in legal documents. The extent of principal influence is determined by the content of those documents.

The relative strength of OPIC is a function of the superior regulatory infrastructure created by the legally binding loan agreements. The absence of traditional tools of administrative control with respect to the OPIC investment funds was insignificant. The Enterprise Funds, in contrast, have many traditional administrative linkages in place including presidential appointment of each Fund's board of directors. These ties give only the illusion of control. USAID simply does not have sufficient regulatory powers to compel the Enterprise Funds to satisfy principal preferences.

The lesson is amplified by the study of housing hybrids. Fannie Mae and Freddie Mac performed better with respect to the safety and soundness regulation than programmatic regulation. This is due, at least in part, to the more concrete nature of the safety and soundness regulation and the relative ease in translating the preference for reduced financial risk into regulations. Moreover, the presence of administrative linkages in the case of Fannie Mae and Freddie Mac appears to provide nothing more than window dressing. The directors appointed by the President did nothing to compel the companies to satisfy the elected principals.

This lesson should be extended to future hybrid organizations. Greater attention should be paid to the development of well-conceived regulatory frameworks, including clear goals and limits, well-articulated performance standards and suitably equipped regulators. Insistence upon token appointment of directors does little, if anything, to enhance the principal's ability to satisfy preferences.

It is important not to overstate the consequences of differences in control tools. Although regulatory tools are relatively unwieldy in comparison with administrative tools, the differences in preference satisfaction observed in the course of this research indicate that hybrids are more difficult to control regardless of the tools at the disposal of the principal. The subsequent chapter focuses on the nature and structure of hybrid organizations as impediments to reliable control for Congress and the President.

4

Principal's preference, organizational structure and the likelihood of control

It may seem obvious that *what* you want affects the probability that you will get it. Yet studies of bureaucratic control typically do not differentiate among types of preferences. That is, the following two assumptions are implicit in most academic discussions of bureaucratic control:

1. If Principal A can secure Preference P from Agent X, then Principal A can secure Preference Q from Agent X; *and*
2. If Principal A cannot secure Preference P from Agent X, then Principal A cannot secure Preference Q from Agent X.

But these are tenuous assumptions. Differences in the character of the desired outcome may affect the ability of the principal to compel some behavior from the agent. For example, the President may be able to induce *more* rigorous enforcement from the Environmental Protection Agency but be unable to prompt *less* rigorous enforcement from the same agency. Such differences would consistently affect the likelihood of preference satisfaction. Thus they are an important part of the bureaucratic control story.

This chapter introduces a refinement of the bureaucratic control literature. The comparative study of hybrids and agencies underlying this book revealed an interaction effect with this previously overlooked variable: preference type. Hybrid organizations are, on average, less likely to satisfy principal's preferences than government agencies. But it is also clear that the preferences that *are* satisfied by hybrids share characteristics, as do those that are not satisfied. Accounting for differences in the performance of hybrid organizations and government agencies thus requires identification of influential variations in preference type. This chapter proposes two dimensions on which preferences vary.

70

First, "positive" and "negative" preferences are differentiated. Inducing a bureaucratic agent to undertake some substantive action is materially different from restricting or constraining the same agent. Hybrid organizations are more likely to satisfy negative preferences than positive preferences.

Second, preferences related to the definition of a hybrid organization's mission are less likely to be satisfied than non-mission-related preferences. For example, the imposition of procedural requirements that do not fundamentally alter the focus of an organization is more likely to succeed than an effort to reshape organizational goals.

Three comparisons provide evidence for these two claims: hybrids versus traditional agencies; positive versus negative control preferences; and mission-related versus non-mission-related preferences. Before illustration and explanation of the claims regarding the importance of preference type, the distinctions among types of preferences are elaborated. An explanation of the connection between hybrid structure and the difficulty in satisfying certain types of preferences precedes presentation of lessons for students of bureaucratic control and for policy-makers considering the use of hybrid organizations.

Differentiating types of preferences

Existing research has emphasized the relative strengths of various competing principals (see chapter 2). By comparing hybrids and traditional government agencies, the importance of agent structure is illuminated. In the course of carrying out this comparison, however, it became clear that part of the explanation for differences in the extent of control lies beyond consideration of principals and agents. Differentiating types of preferences provides a fuller explanation of why some attempts at bureaucratic control are successful and others are not.

As in the previous chapter, no prediction of "control/no control" is offered based on preference types. Rather, probabilistic assessments of a principal's chances of satisfying types of preferences are offered. That is, different preference types (based on the two dimensions identified briefly above) are associated with high, medium or low likelihood of effective control over an agent.

Positive versus negative control

Preferences vary in the type of response required by a compliant agent. In some cases, principals want bureaucratic agents to take some particular action. For example, Congress directs the Immigration and Naturalization Service to devote more resources to the interdiction of illegal immigrants.

These can be called "positive" control preferences. In other cases, the principal's preference requires an agent to cease some behavior. For example, the President issues an executive order forbidding purchase of vehicles manufactured outside the United States. This can be called a "negative" control preference.

Essentially, positive and negative control preferences differentiate a desired outcome "Z" versus a desired outcome "Not Z." The following examples help clarify:

Positive preferences	Negative preferences
• Fannie Mae should devote more resources to low-income homebuyers	• HUD should not reject borrowers on the basis of race
• Export-Import Bank should emphasize exports to Africa	• OPIC should not provide risk insurance to companies that produce alcoholic beverages
• Enterprise Funds should make investments in agricultural businesses	• Investment funds should not support companies that harm the environment

There is an intuitive appeal to the idea that initiating and terminating an agency's activity require different levels of control. Every parent knows that it is easier to stop a child from doing some forbidden activity (e.g., confiscating the ball being bounced off the living room wall) than it is to prompt some desired action (e.g., studying for tomorrow's exam). It is reasonable to hypothesize that the same is true for bureaucracies. One interviewee pointed this out, noting that moving a government agency to do something new is like "pushing on a string" (interview 78).

There is more than intuition behind this distinction. Positive preferences require an agent to allocate resources differently in order to satisfy the principal. This will require reductions in some other area or an increase in total available resources. At the very least, satisfaction of positive preferences is likely to require more additional resources than satisfying negative preferences because ceasing some activity generally does not consume an organization's time or money.

Mission- versus non-mission-related preferences

Mission-related preferences strike at the center of an organization's function. Satisfaction of such a preference requires an agent to change organizational objectives. For example, a congressional committee wants the Department of Transportation to redirect resources to mass transit from highway expansion, or the President attempts to make environmental protection the highest priority of the Bureau of Land Management. Although mission-related preferences are frequently related to the prioritization of an organization's objectives, they may also concern the manner in which the organizations pursues goals. For example, some Members of Congress have pressed for regulatory agencies to utilize "cost-benefit analysis" of all proposed new regulations – an approach that regulatory proponents allege is intended to stifle new regulations (Nakashima 2002).

Mission-related preferences can also be thought of in the terms suggested by James Thompson (1967). That is, mission-related preferences relate to the utilization of an organization's core technology or competence. For the National Aeronautics and Space Administration, for example, a mission-related preference would be for the agency to emphasize unmanned missions. Setting such preferences apart from those that do not relate to an agency's core, substantive concerns makes sense. Mission-related preferences are likely to be of concern to key organizational personnel and constituencies that have an investment in such matters, and are therefore likely to encounter resistance from some quarters.

Non-mission preferences relate to the manner in which an agency pursues its policy objectives and are often procedural in character. Requiring competitive bidding before contracts are awarded is an example. Other non-mission preferences relate to the individual behavior of organizational employees. For example, Congress decrees that the government will not pay for business-class airfares. Non-mission preferences are distinguished by their broadness. They frequently apply to governmental organizations across a wide range of policy areas and are prompted by considerations that are not unique to any particular policy area.

Note that both mission-related and non-mission-related preferences can be positive or negative in character, and vice versa. For example, a congressional mandate that the Department of Agriculture develop alternative uses of tobacco would be a positive, mission-related preference. A law prohibiting subsidization of tobacco farmers who sell to cigarette manufacturers targeting children would express a negative, mission-related preference. In contrast, an executive order prohibiting government purchase of pencils made from rainforest timber would constitute a negative, non-mission-related preference. Requirements that government agencies advertise all positions in widely read newspapers before hiring establish positive, non-mission preferences. Thus the two distinctions can be combined to create a two-dimensional typology of preference types (see table 4.1).

Findings regarding the likelihood of effective control for preferences that fall in each of the four categories are presented in this chapter.

From a theoretical point of view, recognizing distinctions of preference type is important. Equating all types of control across preference type may mislead researchers regarding the consequences of structural or environmental variation. Results may be misinterpreted if a non-preference variable is correlated with variation in preference type. While it may appear that the ability of a principal to control an agent is a function of, say, alterations of formal powers or the ascendancy of a new governing coalition, the reality may be different. Differences may, in fact, be driven by variation in preference type.

As a practical matter, policy-makers choosing institutions ought to know the limitations of each proposed structure under consideration. The suitability of a particular design may be related to the ability of principals to assert negative control over the organization without much concern for positive control. Policy-makers may be perfectly comfortable ceding non-mission-related control in the name of efficiency if they retain mission control.

Note that neither distinction implies greater normative value for one type of preference. To one individual, the ability of a principal to exert positive, mission-related control may be of paramount importance. To another, satisfaction of non-mission preferences (e.g., procedural requirements) may be the most important issue. The objective in drawing these lines is to produce a more refined reading of findings and understanding of quasi-government.

Finally, a word is required regarding the permeability of categories (suggested by the dashed lines in table 4.1). There is, to be sure, a large gray area that can rightly be described as positive and/or negative control. In some instances, a bundle of negative controls may be employed to approximate positive control (e.g., imposing a set of limits that makes only a single course feasible). Similarly, some seemingly non-mission preferences may be mission-related in disguise. Procedural requirements intended to steer an organization towards a certain end, for example, could be characterized as such. But difficult-to-classify cases do not undermine the distinction between the two categories, just as uncertainty regarding the location of the French/German border would not negate the differences between France

Table 4.1 *Two-dimensional typology of preference types*

		Positive v. negative	
Mission v. Non-mission	Positive, mission		Negative, mission
	Positive, non-mission		Negative, non-mission

and Germany. As the findings demonstrate, both distinctions are robust enough to observe patterns when evaluating the data. That is the ultimate test of the usefulness of any typology.

Negative, non-mission preferences are most likely to be satisfied

The central observation of this chapter is that negative, non-mission-related preferences are more likely to be satisfied by hybrid organizations than positive, mission-related preferences. Moreover, differences in the likelihood of control for hybrids and traditional agencies are likely to be greatest with respect to positive, mission-related preferences. That is, one would not expect stark differences in the control exercised over hybrids and agencies with respect to negative, non-mission preferences.

In the three following subsections, accounts of the findings from the export promotion, housing and venture capital fund studies are presented to illustrate this conclusion. This is followed by more general explication of the findings as they relate to all hybrid organizations (see page 89).

Export promotion: implementing administration policy

The United States government supports the export-related activities of American business with several government programs. Entities involved in export promotion include the Department of Commerce and two hybrids, the Export-Import Bank and the Overseas Private Investment Corporation, both government corporations. Although these organizations perform different functions, they share a common premise: that increasing the international activity of American business creates (or protects) jobs domestically. These organizations are described in detail in the appendix.

Foreign policy concerns inevitably influence the administration of export promotion programs. For example, the United States prohibits exports to Cuba as a means of pressuring the Castro regime. Both Congress and the President attempt to influence the activities of some or all of the export promotion organizations to serve various foreign policy objectives as well as domestic considerations.

Responses to four policy objectives were recorded for all the organizations. A negative objective (sanctions against China) and three positive preferences (emphasis on environmental technology, small business and Africa in export promotion) are examined. All fall in the mission-related preference category. Ideally, variation on this dimension of preference type would have presented itself. Unfortunately, non-mission preferences applicable to all three organizations were not available. This is due, in large measure, to the significant differences in the manner in which each organization pursues its objectives.

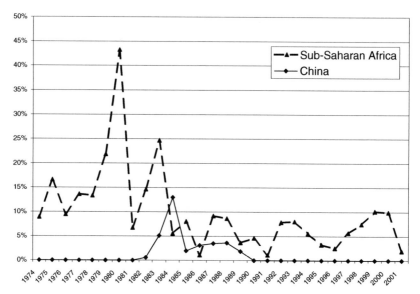

Figure 4.1 OPIC commitments by region (as a percentage of total OPIC commitments), 1974–2001

Following the 1989 massacre of pro-democracy demonstrators in Tiananmen Square, the prevailing sentiment in Congress was that the United States had to register its disapproval. This was expressed in a law restricting foreign aid – including OPIC programs – to the People's Republic of China (Holmes 1990). This is clearly a negative, mission-related preference. The agents were required to cease operations in a substantive area that constituted a significant segment of the organizations' activities.

The record shows that Congress' preference for a cessation of trade assistance to China was satisfied by all three agents. The Commerce Department curtailed activities in China and overall exports to the country declined following implementation of the sanctions. Agency staff recall a "180° turnaround" from emphasis on Chinese trade to avoidance of the country.

OPIC activity in China was also curtailed quite dramatically. As figure 4.1 demonstrates, activity dropped from about four percent of OPIC's total yearly commitment in 1988 to zero percent in 1990. ExIm's response was less stark. This is explained by the latitude Congress gave President Bush to waive the law with respect to ExIm if doing so was deemed in the interest of the United States (Lawrence 1989). Several large deals were allowed shortly after the sanctions were passed. Still, by 1991 ExIm's authorization for exports to China was nearly zero percent of its total authorization (figure 4.2).

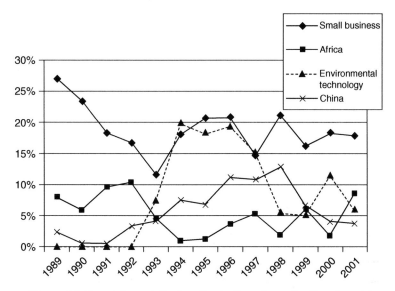

Figure 4.2 Export-Import Bank authorizations by region/investment type (as a percentage of total ExIm authorizations), 1989–2001

In contrast, the response of the organizations to three positive, mission-related preferences was less consistent. When President Clinton took office, he and his appointees quickly declared their interest in international trade. In particular, they stated a desire to increase exports to African markets, by small businesses, and of environmental technology. All three objectives had been neglected previously by the export promotion organizations (Bradsher 1993, Beamish and Lane 1993, TPCC 1997).

The complications described in chapter 2 regarding inputs and outputs come into play when evaluating satisfaction of these three positive, mission-related preferences. For example, the Commerce Department reports total exports to Africa. This statistic includes the outputs of *all* export promotion agencies (including OPIC and ExIm). It is impossible to identify the department's output per se. Similarly, inputs are difficult to disaggregate by, say, sector. For example, OPIC advertises its programs broadly; any statement regarding how much of its advertising budget is directed at small business, for example, is likely to be speculative.

Still, the Clinton Administration's stated interest in environmental technology, small business and African markets seems to have compelled activity (inputs) from federal agencies to a greater degree than OPIC or ExIm. Additional staff were assigned responsibility for these areas, a new office was established within the Commerce Department devoted to environmental technology, and attempts to bolster environmental technology exports were featured prominently in agency literature. The Trade Policy Coordinating Committee, an inter-agency group created to align trade-related activities, established multi-agency working groups devoted to environmental technology and small business. Publications and websites emphasize these areas of activity (TPCC 1997).

Several high-profile trips and announcements to spur African trade reflect the Commerce Department's heightened interest in the subject and an increase in inputs. Department staff members attribute this to Secretary Ron Brown's agreement with the President's policy preference and the loyalty of other political appointees at the department. Interview subjects in all organizations report an emphasis on the President's areas of interest by presidential appointees (interviews 22, 35, 41, 46, 47).

Notably, increases in staff activity and allocation of resources (inputs) have not as yet yielded dramatic changes in exports (outputs). Unfortunately, the data on small business exports are collected only every five years. Since 1992 the share of exports generated by small business as a share of total American exports has climbed slightly from 29.5 percent of total US merchandise exports to 30.6 percent (ITA 1999). Although the figures indicate a 3.1 percentage point increase from 1987 (26.4 percent) to 1992, the TPCC report notes that improved measurement of small business exports accounted for some or all of that apparent increase (TPCC 1997, 63). Total exports to Africa have increased by about $2 billion since 1991 but exports to Africa as a percentage of total American exports dropped from a high of 2.2 percent in 1992 to 1.4 percent in 2000 (see figure 4.3).

Although changes in environmental technology exports are difficult to judge – it has only been tracked as a sector for about five years – the recent emphasis on this area appears to have yielded results. The Department of Commerce established an office dedicated to "green exports" and tasked numerous personnel to this bureau. In the subsequent years (1993 to 2000), American environmental exports have increased from $9.4 billion to $22.4 billion (see figure 4.4, *Environmental Business Journal* 2002). Moreover, the market for environmental technology has expanded – an increase to which American efforts contributed – and the American share of the non-US market has increased from 3.6 percent to 6.9 percent (figure 4.4).

The hybrid organizations have been slower to take up the administration's causes than the Commerce Department (and other traditional agencies that participate in the Trade Policy Coordinating Committee). Indeed, frustrated by ExIm's inattention to small business, Congress designated one of the organization's five directors as the "point man" for small business. But, according to a long-time senior ExIm official, even this change had little impact until a new ExIm president sympathetic to the small business cause

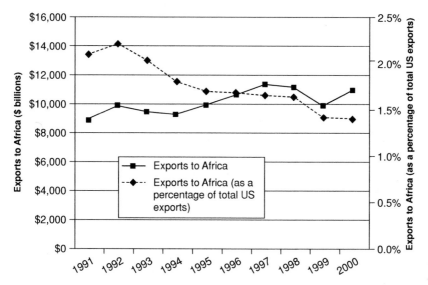

Figure 4.3 United States exports to Africa, 1991–2000

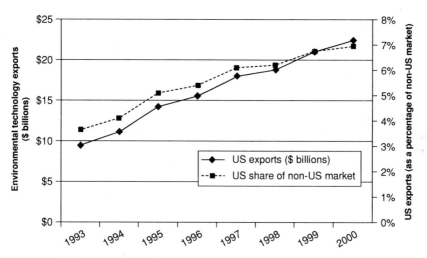

Figure 4.4 United States environmental technology exports, 1993–2000

took office (interview 78). Even now, ExIm has complied with the preference of Congress and the President only by ceding much of its insurance
functions to the Small Business Administration when small businesses are
involved (interview 41). Thus there was no marked organizational reori-
entation to emphasize small business activity by ExIm after Clinton took

office (interview 78). This is reflected in the data. ExIm authorization of loan guarantees for small business exports saw an increase only between 1993 and 1996 (from 12 to 21 percent of total authorization). As of 2001, small business authorizations have dropped back to 18 percent, roughly the same as 1991 (figure 4.2).

Although OPIC has printed materials directed at small businesses, it does not appear to have reallocated resources to develop small business projects. This is, in part, a structural constraint. Businesses must seek out OPIC. Thus the most significant adjustment the government corporation can make to alter its clientele is targeted advertising. The organization does not report any increased allocation of funds for advertising or other outreach activities. In its 2001 *Annual Report*, OPIC reported a steady increase in the number of "Small Business Projects" supported by the organization. In 1997, five years after the small business preference was articulated, OPIC published data involving small businesses; that year twelve such projects were reported, with the number reaching eighty-two in 2001 (2001 *Annual Report*, 4). This was accomplished, in part, through a "structured arrangement" with the SBA, making it difficult to assess just how much changes in OPIC practices contributed to the reported improvement (2001 *Annual Report*, 4).

The hybrids also appear to have adjusted more slowly to the emphasis on environmental technology. Despite the overall growth in environmental technology exports noted above, neither ExIm nor OPIC has registered significant improvement in this area. Even the apparent increase in ExIm activity can be accounted for (according to ExIm officials) by the refinement of measurement (interviews 37, 78).

Congress created an environmental director for ExIm to prompt additional attention to environmental issues, similar to the small business director. However, the "environmental director" relies largely on a single individual to reorient the bank (interviews 37, 39). Thus it is not terribly surprising that the effects have not yet registered strongly in outputs. ExIm authorizations for environmental technology show a significant increase between 1992 and 1996 as the organization started measuring this category separately. The entry for 1992 – zero percent of ExIm authorizations – reflects lack of measurement. Nevertheless, this category constituted 19.6 percent of ExIm authorizations in 1996. Since then "environmentally beneficial exports" (a new label that suggested an increasingly inclusive measure) dropped to single digits in 1998 and 1999 before hitting 11.6 percent in the final year of the Clinton Administration (see figure 4.2).

OPIC has similarly developed promotional and educational materials regarding its efforts to promote environmental technology, but it does not report any increase in the financing of projects that result in American exports of environmental technology. Given the expansion of the market reported above, this is somewhat surprising. It would have been reasonable to expect that OPIC-supported exports might have paralleled the expansion of this market.

Finally, OPIC's and ExIm's responses to emphasis on Africa resemble their responses to the environmental technology and small business initiatives. Staff report increases in inputs. There is some evidence to support this; both agencies, for example, participate in inter-agency discussions regarding African trade. All the same, there is no evidence of increased outputs. ExIm authorizations for exports to Africa (expressed as a percentage of total ExIm authorizations), an output measure that reflects the dollar value of loans guaranteed in a particular area, fell from 10 percent in 1992 to about 1 percent in 1994. They fluctuated between 1 and 6 percent through 2000. OPIC commitments, also an output measure, follow a similar pattern. Commitments to sub-Saharan Africa reached 10 percent of total OPIC commitments in 1999 and 2000, two percentage points higher than the 1993 level.[1] Note that the similarity in the pattern of ExIm authorizations and OPIC commitments suggests the influence of factors beyond the control of either organization. This is discussed in the analysis of findings.

In this area, then, all agencies satisfied the negative preference – cessation of China-oriented activity – but the hybrids were less effective than the Commerce Department in satisfying the positive preferences for increased exports to Africa and increased exports in environmental technology and small business products.

Housing: the challenges of GSE regulation

The Federal National Mortgage Association (Fannie Mae) and the Federal Home Loan Mortgage Corporation (Freddie Mac), both privately owned, highly profitable GSEs, are here compared with the Department of Housing and Urban Development. The history, structure and functions of these organizations are described in detail in the appendix. Of interest is the responsiveness of these organizations to Congress' and the administration's positive, mission-related preference for increased allocation of credit to low-income homebuyers. And, in the case of Fannie Mae and Freddie Mac, the effectiveness of financial regulation that required increased allocation

---

[1] It is worth noting that in 2001, the first year of the George W. Bush Presidency, OPIC commitments to sub-Saharan Africa dropped to only 2 percent of total OPIC commitments. This could be interpreted as an indication of the new administration's relative lack of interest in Africa and an affirmation of the commitment of OPIC's previous leadership to the Clinton Administration's objectives.

of capital to reserves – a preference classified as positive, non-mission related – is considered as well. This preference has no analog for the government agencies.

The positive, mission-related preference for increased credit opportunities in low-income communities was articulated in legislation and policy pronouncements. In legislation overhauling the regulatory infrastructure for Fannie Mae and Freddie Mac, Congress included programmatic provisions that directed HUD to establish and enforce targets for performance in low-income areas. This legislation is described in detail in chapter 5. Shortly after the law was passed, Bill Clinton was elected President. He appointed Henry Cisneros as Secretary of Housing and Urban Development, and both Clinton and Cisneros expressed a strong preference to increase the provision of mortgage credit to low- and middle-income borrowers in underserved communities (e.g., Cornwell 1993). Thus there was relatively little conflict among principals on this point, and there is a clear shift from the status quo. Under the Bush and Reagan Administrations, the expansion of borrowing opportunities in underserved communities had not been emphasized.

HUD has the regulatory authority to create portfolio targets for Fannie Mae and Freddie Mac. These targets concern the quantity of loans to low- or moderate-income homebuyers purchased by Fannie Mae and Freddie Mac, expressed as a percentage of all loans purchased by the two GSEs (Day 1999). This is a positive control objective, setting the levels of programmatic achievement.

The effort to subject the two companies to programmatic regulation was slowed by battles over definitions and data sets. HUD released its final regulation in accordance with the 1992 law calling for affordable housing goals in 2000. This regulation established that 50 percent of the loans purchased by the two companies should be for low- and moderate-income families (Feigenbaum 2000). According to HUD, both companies have thus far met the targets established under the new regulation (Manchester 2002).

There is also some prior track record to evaluate. First, interim regulations have been in place since 1993. Second, the consideration and passage of legislation clearly established a congressional interest in boosting affordable housing performance, an objective endorsed by the Clinton Administration. Thus one can look at the performance of the companies prior to the finalization of the law and regulations.

Both Fannie Mae and Freddie Mac met most of the interim housing goals established by Congress, although they have failed (with no resulting penalty) in the "Central Cities" category on several occasions (Bunce and Scheessele 1998). These goals were not particularly demanding; the GSEs did not need to alter their inputs significantly (i.e., pursue business in previously neglected areas) or outputs to comply. So, while we might take Fannie Mae and Freddie Mac performance as evidence of control, the data may reflect what the GSEs would have done anyway.

Fannie Mae and Freddie Mac made subsequent improvements – as noted above, they are in compliance with the affordable housing regulations – but their performance has not matched the response of the Department of Housing and Urban Development to the same imperatives. Note that, in order to compare the organizations, the data referred to below are not in the same categories as those in the regulations.

Recall the explication of these figures from the previous chapter. As figure 3.1 shows, the percentage of Federal Housing Administration loans that went to borrowers in census tracts with a concentration of minority residents climbed from 20 percent to 26.8 percent between 1992 and 2000 – an absolute increase of almost seven percentage points and a relative increase of 33 percent. In comparison, Freddie Mac increased from 12.4 percent to 14.3 percent over the same period. Fannie Mae roughly matched Freddie Mac, increasing from 13.9 percent to 15.8 percent from 1992 to 2000. The results for performance among low-income borrowers is similar (figure 3.2). The FHA increased its share of loans to low-income borrowers from 17.1 percent to 19.2 percent between 1992 and 2000. Fannie Mae had a similar increase, from 8.7 percent to 10.5 percent. Freddie Mac trailed both, climbing from 9.2 percent in 1992 to 10.4 percent in 2000.

A bit of qualification is in order. The FHA's performance vis-à-vis the goal is made more significant by its higher baseline. It is somewhat more difficult to register improvement when the starting point is higher. And, as noted in the previous chapter, the FHA embraced the goals while the GSEs resisted the ratcheting up of expectations.

The disparity in performance has been emphasized by HUD officials. Criticizing the two GSEs for their failure to increase their lending in minority communities substantially, the head of the FHA pointed to the superior performance of private-sector market participants (Day 2000a). Not surprisingly, the leaders of Fannie Mae and Freddie Mac took exception to this comparison, noting the differences in the structure and function of the organizations (Day 2000b, Bergquist 2000).

The positive, *non*-mission preference that applies only to Fannie Mae and Freddie Mac concerns the maintenance of capital buffers. This is a component of financial safety and soundness regulation carried out by the quasi-independent Office of Federal Housing Enterprise Oversight. OFHEO evaluates the GSEs' capital reserves to determine whether the two companies can withstand severe economic circumstances and reviews business practices to ensure that the GSEs are not exposing the federal government to unnecessary risk. If OFHEO finds either company "undercapitalized," it can order them to retain more capital as a buffer against potential losses. Thus safety and soundness preferences can be positive but they are not directly related to the companies' mission.

Safety and soundness regulation has thus far proven a moderate success. The regulatory agency, OFHEO, founded in 1993, has applied the minimum capital standards as defined, for the most part, by Congress. Both Fannie Mae and Freddie Mac have increased their capital levels to meet these minimum requirements. As figure 3.4 shows, the two companies began increasing their capital allocation in anticipation of implementation of the minimum capital rule.

OFHEO was also charged with creating a risk-based capital regulation. This involved creating a computer-based simulation of the GSEs' business as a means of testing the capital required by each company to withstand an economic shock (see chapter 5). After eight years of development, a final rule was published that required the two companies to increase capital holdings substantially (*Mortgage Servicing News* 2001). OFHEO has been criticized for taking a long time to develop the regulation (e.g., Julavits 2002). And, although some consider the regulation weaker than it could be, it has produced the desired outcome. The GSEs have devoted greater resources (inputs) to the evaluation and measurement of risk and increased capital levels (outputs) in response to the articulation of preferences. The risk-based capital requirements were not enforced until 2002 but there is little doubt that the GSEs complied with the regulation. Thus evidence of control is available.

OFHEO has also conducted regular examinations of the two companies, finding them operating in a safe and sound manner (although not without fault), and offering numerous suggestions for improvement (OFHEO 1997).

These findings reveal that Fannie Mae and Freddie Mac have more consistently satisfied the non-mission capital preferences than the programmatic affordable housing preferences, although the companies have, for the most part, met programmatic requirements. Focusing on the comparison of hybrid and agency, however, reveals that HUD appears to have better satisfied its principals' preference for greater activity in the low-income segment of the homebuying population than the hybrids.

Not only did the FHA's performance appear superior to the GSEs; the data do not reflect the difficulty in exerting control over Fannie Mae and Freddie Mac due to the significant political clout possessed by these GSEs (Matlack 1990, Nitschke 1998, Kulish and Schlesinger 2001). This political influence allows Fannie Mae and Freddie Mac to shape the preferences of Members of Congress and the administration alike, as is discussed in detail in chapter 5. Many critics, including Members of Congress, note this influence and argue that the programmatic regulations are not demanding enough as a consequence (US House 1991). Thus, these critics imply, satisfaction of the goals creates a false impression of control. This hypothesis is considered in detail in the next chapter.

International market development

In this area, two sets of government-backed venture capital funds are considered with only limited reference to a government agency. Enterprise Funds focus on the post-Communist countries of Eastern Europe and the former Soviet republics. OPIC's investment funds target developing countries all over the world. In some sense, their activities are comparable to those of the United States Agency for International Development. These organizations are described in detail in the appendix.

Both sets of venture capital funds present similar control challenges. Funds in each program must pursue, evaluate, select and oversee investments in ventures large and small. The opportunities to squander resources (by intention or incompetence) are many. The most significant preference expressed by all principals falls into the negative, non-mission category. Principals have a low tolerance for financial malfeasance. A second set of negative control preferences are restrictions placed on fund investments by Congress and/or the administration. For example, both sets of funds are prohibited from investing in companies that produce armaments. Such preferences are mission-related in the sense that they affect the pool of potential investments.

There are also positive, mission-related preferences. Such preferences relate to the substantive targets of fund investments, such as the emphasis on investment in the telecommunications sector directed at Enterprise Funds. OPIC is often encouraged by Congress and/or the administration to focus investment in one region or another.

In 1993, US Rep. David Obey led a group of members in expressing a strong negative preference: stop perceived inappropriate behavior by the Enterprise Funds. Obey initiated an investigation of the Hungarian American Enterprise Fund after he got word of a HAEF project that involved 100 percent financing of a Hungarian merchant bank to be run by two Americans earning $350,000 salaries (Maass 1993b). Controversy was fueled by the disclosure that the Fund was paying a portion of the salary of a Hungarian-American running the Hungarian government's privatization program (Maass 1993a). Neither problem was mission-related.

In neither instance was it clear that the HAEF violated any rule; there are almost no rules specified in the legislation to violate. Still, Obey's investigation and criticism of the Fund's leadership provoked negative attention and ultimately led the Hungarian Fund's president to resign (Denton 1993).

There were other failures. The most dramatic involved the collapse of the Czech and Slovak Fund. In that case, USAID successfully pressured the board of directors to resign and a new board started essentially from scratch (Wald 1996a).

The management of the Enterprise Fund program changed as a result of Obey's investigation. USAID overseers, caught off guard by the controversy, were held partially responsible for the alleged misdeeds and pressured the Funds to submit to more meaningful supervision (interviews 19, 13). Although there is no explicit authority in the hands of USAID's Fund overseers to punish "wayward" Funds, there are now more frequent required reports, formal reporting requirements and the possibility of investigation by the USAID Inspector General. Thus the negative preference for unimpeachable conduct on the part of the Enterprise Funds has been better satisfied through the Funds' acceptance of more attentive oversight and reporting requirements.

The OPIC investment fund program was quite ad hoc at the outset. By admission of the staff who created the program, proper oversight of the various funds was developed well after the funds had already begun operating (interviews 23, 27). What evolved was a system based on contractual agreements between OPIC and the managers selected to run each fund. These agreements give OPIC rights of review and are the basis of their monitoring. As OPIC became more experienced with the programs, the typical agreement to provide effective oversight was revised.

Most of the constraints placed on the investment funds serve preferences of the negative, non-mission variety. There are clauses inserted to prevent financial malfeasance and a few mission-related prohibitions that reflect requirements that Congress has placed on OPIC itself. Specifically, the OPIC investment funds cannot invest in projects that degrade the environment, harm US workers (i.e., export jobs) or violate human rights.

Political principals have also expressed positive preferences regarding both venture capital fund programs. These include creation of new funds to serve particular geographic areas or directives that one type of investment or sector of the economy be emphasized. For example, Enterprise Funds are directed in the SEED Act to seek investment opportunities in the telecommunications sector. Regional investment funds often have country-by-country distribution goals (e.g., percentages of total portfolio investment expected per country). Such emphases may be sought for political, strategic, philosophical or economic reasons; the motives are not of concern.

Most fund managers and their overseers note that funds are not directed to approve specific projects (notwithstanding the occasional congressional reference on behalf of a constituent or an unsolicited call to a fund director), but administration officials have been known to offer Enterprise Fund managers advice (interviews 12, 13, 74). For example, the Polish Fund undertook a successful micro-lending program, by most accounts, at the suggestion of USAID and State Department overseers. Although such instances of positive influence can be identified, most attempts to satisfy positive preferences result in little or no activity. An illustrative example concerned an effort to have Enterprise Funds utilize common environmental impact review procedures by holding a conference with experts in the field. The Funds simply refused to attend and the conference was scuttled (interview 11).

The response to the most formal suggestions made to the Enterprise Funds underscores their resistance to positive control. The only specific industry targeted in the SEED Act creating the first two Enterprise Funds was telecommunications. Even this legal mandate has not prompted a particular emphasis on telecommunications by the Funds. Only three of the ten Funds reported any investment in telecommunications as of 2000. As noted in the previous chapter, this is not a criticism of the Funds. Telecommunications investment was not pursued, based on the Funds' calculation that investment in this area was either not needed or not promising. Recall the similar experience with another preference articulated by Congress. Despite the stated desire for investment in joint ventures with American businesses, only four such enterprises have succeeded. These examples demonstrate the limited ability of Congress to satisfy positive, mission-related preferences with respect to Enterprise Funds.

The OPIC funds are even less suited to the satisfaction of positive preferences. Loan agreements do not include provisions for the transmission of positive preferences; private investors would be deterred from investing funds that could have goals imposed by government other than maximizing return. If potential investors in an OPIC-backed fund could not be guaranteed that the government would not impose policy-driven burdens on the funds that might impede profitability, they would be less likely to invest. Thus attempts at "positive" control might undermine the program (interview 31). Indeed, OPIC efforts to steer the investment funds toward a specific investment or even a type of investment could create a legal liability in the event of a fund's failure (interview 81). Enterprise Funds do not face this constraint because they are funded entirely by government appropriations.

OPIC can and does utilize policy-related criteria in evaluating competing bids for a proposed fund, thus acquiring a modicum of positive control (interviews 31, 89, 109). A senior OPIC official offered the following example. Two prospective managers competing for a fund in Africa pitched their proposals. One highlighted an investment strategy targeting woman-owned businesses. The other proposed an investment focus on labor-intensive businesses that would maximize employment effects (interview 31). Thus the selection process does provide an opportunity for OPIC to give direction to the investment fund.

Still, the *creation* of an OPIC investment fund is the *only* positive preference likely to be met. Both the administration and Congress have recognized this and called for the creation of new funds to serve particular areas (the West Bank and the Caucasus region). But even this type of control is limited in effect. In both cases, the funds were created to satisfy principals. But both funds have had difficulty finding investors interested in risking their capital and viable businesses in which the fund can invest (US State Department 1999). Although the investment levels of OPIC funds are not published, interview respondents acknowledge that funds created to serve severely underserved markets have encountered significant impediments to success.

Several Enterprise Funds have experienced similar difficulties (though they do not need to raise capital). Poland and Hungary, recipients of the first two Enterprise Funds, had market foundations in place when the SEED Act was passed, but several of the subsequent target countries have not. As a result, the Bulgarian American Enterprise Fund, the Western NIS Enterprise Fund and the Central Asian American Enterprise Fund (1998 *Annual Reports*) have experienced difficulty finding suitable investments (outputs) despite their best efforts. In each case, the political and economic conditions made responsible disbursement of fund resources challenging.

Thus the comparison of the two different venture capital fund programs demonstrated findings consistent with observation of other hybrids. The organizations satisfied principals' negative, non-mission preferences with a relatively high degree of reliability. Both sets of funds were less likely to satisfy positive, mission-related preferences.

Summary

Across the policy areas, a pattern emerges. Overall, hybrid organizations are less likely than traditional government agencies to satisfy principal preferences. This chapter indicates that this general finding is driven by significant differences related to preference type. Specifically, hybrid organizations are less likely to satisfy positive preferences and mission-related preferences. This was true in the three policy areas studied. Housing hybrids resisted attempts to increase low-income loan volume, export promotion hybrids were slow to increase activity related to small business, Africa and environmental technology, and government-backed venture capital funds failed to reorient in response to regional and sector preferences expressed by Congress.

The cases examined also suggest additive effects between the two dimensions of preference type. That is, the low likelihood of a hybrid organization satisfying a positive preference is slightly increased if it is a non-mission, positive preference rather than a mission-related, positive preference. Conversely, the likelihood of a hybrid organization satisfying a principal's non-mission preference is decreased if that preference is

Table 4.2 *Hybrid organizations' likelihood of preference satisfaction (by preference type)*

		Positive *v.* negative	
Mission *v.* Non-mission		Low	Medium plus
		Medium minus	High

positive non-mission rather than negative non-mission. These relationships are summed up in table 4.2.

Note that the findings represented here appear to apply to a lesser extent to traditional government organizations as well. That is, there is an interaction between preference type and organizational structure. The differences in control related to organizational structure are driven by hybrid organizations' greater sensitivity to preference type.

The discussion below offers an explanation for the finding that hybrids are less likely to satisfy principal preferences than traditional government agencies. Hybrids' sensitivity to preference type is a function of their design.

Preference type and the dynamics of bureaucratic control

This section explicates the connection between structure, preference type and the relative likelihood of preference satisfaction. The explanation is complex for not only are there multiple structural features at work, there are both additive and interaction effects among the variables. Thus each case is, in some respect, unique. The following explanations are general lessons that do not necessarily apply with equal weight to all hybrids. There are essentially three aspects of hybrid government that render them sensitive to preference type: the different set of control tools outlined in chapter 3; the reliance on market-oriented partners to achieve objectives; and the competing objectives pursued by hybrids.

Different control tools

Control tools available for hybrid organizations are typically regulatory rather than administrative (chapter 3). That is, principals, both legislative and executive, must rely upon laws, regulations, contracts and enforcement mechanisms to induce desired behavior. The adaptability of these regulatory tools as substitutes for administrative tools appears to be linked to preference type. Specifically, the satisfaction of positive control preferences is difficult. Effective regulatory control requires meticulous crafting of detailed laws and regulations that define the nature of preferences, sanctions for non-compliance, opportunities for mediation or appeal and protocols of compensation for unjust impositions of regulatory burdens. Regulation inevitably draws both the regulator and regulated into a legal paradigm, where finely articulated standards, controlling precedents and binding obligations are key.

This helps account for the relatively high likelihood of satisfying negative preferences. Simply put, negative preferences are more easily translated into regulation than positive preferences. Listing impermissible activities, forbidden countries or products and inappropriate practices is easier than specifying affirmative objectives and goals. Two facets of regulation make the satisfaction of positive preferences relatively difficult:

Definition. Although the concepts underlying public policy programs are often straightforward, definitions can prove elusive. This is true with programmatic regulation of the housing GSEs. The desire to increase the availability of affordable credit to low- and moderate-income homebuyers seems straightforward. Yet specifying the meaning of "low-income" can be contentious. "Low" relative to what? The city? The state? The nation? Answering such questions is critical to the construction of an effective regulatory regime and the satisfaction of preferences. It is the marker against which the hybrid shall be measured and the target at which hybrids must aim.

While the GSEs' critics argue that Fannie Mae and Freddie Mac try to minimize the burden of programmatic regulation by lobbying for definitions that will effectively allow them to focus on more profitable loans, there are legitimate substantive questions that can create conflict. Thus the definition problem is not only a manifestation of a hybrid's interest in some competing objective.

Measurement. Even when a goal can be defined, establishing the appropriate standard of achievement can be difficult. For example, improved performance in terms of credit provision to low-income homebuyers could be measured by the median income of *new* borrowers or the median income of *all* borrowers with loans outstanding. In the case of export loan guarantee programs, one could measure the percentage of loans guaranteed to a particular market or the percentage of total guaranteed funds allocated to a particular market. These measurement decisions may determine whether a preference is satisfied.

Additionally, establishment of a benchmark is difficult. When judging the performance of a hybrid, the only basis for comparison is the non-existent alternative state in which the organization does not exist. Thus any benchmark is inherently contestable. Setting targets *before* creating the hybrid does not alleviate this problem. In the absence of performance data, there is no credible evidence regarding the hybrid's potential. It is the inverse problem. Assumptions regarding the nature of the market and the appeal of proposed services are also contestable.

Under such circumstances, standards of measurement and definition of targets are a product of persuasion as much as reason. This is not an issue for negative preferences. The ban on venture capital fund investment in pornography and the sanctions against China do not hinge on the establishment of benchmarks.

These problems are also less pronounced with respect to preferences that are not mission-related. Such preferences are often translated into procedural requirements that are less ambiguous and do not require complicated definitions, measures or benchmarks. Moreover, because non-mission preferences do not strike at the core of an organization's function, there are generally fewer interested parties willing to register opposition and expend resources in the event of conflict.

Ceding control to the market

The most oft-mentioned advantage of hybrid and private organizations is market-based efficiency. It is an accepted (if questionable) truism that profit-seeking entities are disciplined by the need to survive in a competitive market place and thus root out inefficiencies. This study demonstrates that the use of private-sector mechanisms can also result in an unforeseen alienation of public policy control.

Many hybrid organizations attempt to modify the economics of business calculations. That is, by altering the costs, risks or expected returns on a prospective deal, the hybrid induces the participation of a private-sector entity that otherwise would not be feasible or optimally profitable. As a consequence, a hybrid relying on this approach cannot satisfy a desired policy preference if that preference cannot be made economically attractive to the market participant. This limits the ability of a hybrid to satisfy the positive preferences of principals.

The consequence of this constraint is best seen with the export promotion organizations, ExIm and OPIC. In these cases, not only did overall performance relate to prevailing market conditions, but the ability to pursue specific policy priorities was limited by the availability of businesses sharing that interest. This is an important observation. The absence of market interest is presumably the reason the hybrid was directed to pursue the objective in question. Thus the incompatibility of policy goal and market inclination is not anomalous but to be expected. When market resistance exceeds the hybrid's capacity to alter the economics of a potential deal, the hybrid will be unable to yield outputs to the satisfaction of the principal.

Note that, once again, the satisfaction of negative preferences does not face such a contingency. Neither the existence of business interests with a desire to do deals in China nor Chinese interest in welcoming American investment limited OPIC's ability to satisfy the strong congressional preference for sanctions. Similarly, venture capital funds can decline to participate in deals that threaten US jobs regardless of market conditions.

Competing considerations

In each policy area, hybrid organizations are differentiated not only by their structure but by competing objectives that government agencies do not share. These considerations limit the likelihood of control because they orient hybrid organizations towards non-programmatic objectives that often compete with policy goals. Moreover, the non-programmatic objectives can create interest groups with a stake in the outcome of deliberations regarding hybrid organizations. Thus, under quasi-government, difficult administrative decisions take on the character of political mud wrestling. The net result is the principals' reduced likelihood of satisfying mission-related preferences with respect to hybrid organizations.

The most obvious competing concern for many hybrid organizations is profitability. Of course, traditional government agencies are limited by monetary concerns. Unlike government-sponsored enterprises, no government agency, however, has shareholders who expect a reliable profit stream and sustained stock performance from year to year. OPIC's investment funds must also seek profitable investments to satisfy their private investors. The implications of the "profit" difference can hardly be overstated.

Private participation in the publicly sponsored program is often induced with the assurance that public policy goals will not cut into profits. Once in operation, efforts to steer the hybrid organization towards one type of activity or another for public policy purposes would be seen as wholly inappropriate and offensive to private investors. Shareholders expect their companies to generate profits, which obviously presumes at least enough revenue to cover costs. Any imposition of policy-derived requirements that threaten this feature is fundamentally inconsistent with the model of a profitable hybrid. Indeed, the profitability of Fannie Mae and Freddie Mac is enshrined in their charters (12 USC §1,716). This is also the case with OPIC investment funds, which obviously eschew unprofitable investments.

Mission-related preferences generally require adjustment of the public policy responsibilities of a hybrid. Such demands threaten parties with an interest in the non-policy goals of the organization. Too much weight on the public aspect of the hybrid's mission and the profit-making side may not be viable or as lucrative.

Although non-mission preferences can and do raise similar disputes, they do not strike as frequently at the core compromise of the hybrid model. For example, the safety and soundness regulation of the GSEs, while highly relevant to the profitability of the two companies, does not by definition call into question the fulfillment of the entities' mission. Moreover, safety and soundness regulation is more consonant with the profit side of the equation; shareholders have an interest in corporate stability and sound management (though, to be sure, no interest in overly conservative financial practices). Private investors in OPIC funds are as concerned with the safe and sound management of their investment as the government. Thus insistence on measures intended to reduce financial malfeasance does not face resistance equal to that generated by mission-related preferences.

Competing objectives are not only an issue in for-profit hybrids; they affect the workings of government corporations as well. For typical federal agencies, expenditure levels are negotiated and set during the congressional appropriations process. This follows the prior steps of the budget process wherein spending levels are set and each committee is allotted an amount to appropriate. There is no expectation of "balance" in any given agency's budget. That is, a typical government agency is not expected to generate revenues to cover costs. Even agencies that *do* generate revenue are neither limited to nor promised that revenue.[2] Thus they are not constrained by the bottom line.

Hybrid organizations, in contrast, operate on the premise that they can generate revenue that (at least) covers their own costs. This is explicit in the case of OPIC (22 USC §2,191(a)). Of course, there is no legal requirement that *all* hybrid organizations break even, and many (including ExIm, at times) do not. However, the *expectation* that a hybrid will not draw on the federal budget diminishes the ability of policy-makers to place demands that do not enhance revenue. This creates a dynamic similar to that described with respect to profitability. Resistance to preferences that increase costs without increasing revenue is great.

A senior official at Ginnie Mae, a government corporation similar in function to Fannie Mae and Freddie Mac, noted that his organization limits the size of its trailer home loan program because of the high default rate associated with such loans (interview 81). Allowing that program to grow could threaten the solvency (on paper) of Ginnie Mae. The success of the Polish

---

[2] There are some exceptions to this generalization. For example, the National Park Service effectively secured the right to keep all the revenues generated by user fees and concession contracts.

American Enterprise Fund (PAEF) had the unexpected effect of extending the same imperative to the other Enterprise Funds. Despite the fact that the program's originators never envisioned return of the US government's initial investment – let alone profitability – the boards and managers of the Enterprise Funds feel pressure to break even at least (interview 80).

This limitation on control applies to both positive and negative preferences. Empirically, however, it almost always affects positive preferences, because positive preferences generally require the hybrid to pursue some less profitable, policy-oriented objective. In the cases where negative preferences reshape the mission (e.g., restricting business in certain countries), they rarely result in the elimination of alternatives that serve the hybrid's non-public objectives. For example, forbidding both sets of government-backed venture capital funds from investing in producers of armaments left a healthy range of investment opportunities available.

Implications

The most practical implication of this study is that hybrid organizations should be employed in situations where the satisfaction of positive preferences and mission-related preferences is not critical. Such situations are distinguished by clear, non-controversial public policy goals that can be easily articulated. The very existence of the hybrid should, in effect, accomplish the goal that prompted its creation. A few examples help clarify this point.

Proposals for the partial privatization of the air traffic control function of the Federal Aviation Administration have been circulating for several years. This seems to meet the "test" laid out above. An air traffic control hybrid would have a clear purpose (to manage American airspace) with easily defined objectives (the efficient and safe movement of aircraft), relatively unambiguous measurements (recorded performance data on delays and accidents) and a reliable source of revenue (fees charged to carriers). Of course, there are subjective policy decisions involved (the balance between volume and safety), but many of these decisions can and have been handled at the legislative level. Negative controls could be maintained, perhaps in a modified form, by law or regulations.

Some cases, seemingly straightforward, can prove ambiguous. It has been suggested that the Patent and Trademark Office (PTO) be transformed into some sort of hybrid (Dean and Seidman 1988). Until recently, this organization would also seem to meet the "test" laid out above. A PTO hybrid would have a clear purpose (to process patent and trademark claims) with easily defined objectives (timely and reliable processing), relatively unambiguous measurements (recorded processing times and service reports) and a reliable source of revenue (patent filers).

But growing concern over patent decisions in the fields of information and biotechnology has demonstrated the policy sensitivities in even the most apparently mundane functions. The PTO has been granting patents to many Internet companies for business practices that competitors consider common sense (Salkowski 2000). Critics argue this practice will frustrate the growth of Web-based business. Similarly, the PTO has granted patents to biotechnology companies for DNA sequences even though applicants cannot specify the role of the sequence (Clark 2000). Thus the PTO is sure to be at the center of heated policy debates. If the PTO *was* transformed into a hybrid organization, would Congress and/or the President have less power to reshape the organization's decisions?

Finally, the Environmental Protection Agency is an example of an organization that is ill-suited to hybridization. The EPA is frequently required to make subjective mission-related decisions regarding enforcement priorities, new regulations, inter-agency cooperation and a host of other policy matters. The loss of control in this case would represent a serious cost in terms of indirect popular sovereignty even if non-mission, negative preferences were satisfied.

In a more theoretical vein, the differentiation of types of control, however preliminary, adds subtlety to the study of bureaucratic control – an area of research now dominated by broad brush strokes. Treating all attempts at control as equivalent is the obfuscation of interesting variance. Hybrid organizations are clearly "different" from traditional agencies in terms of control but that difference is not captured by a characterization of "more" or "less."

In fact, hybrid organizations *and* traditional government agencies are somewhat less likely to satisfy positive, mission-related preferences than negative, non-mission preferences. It turns out that the difference in likelihood of preference satisfaction for hybrids and agencies is largely explained by the *greater* sensitivity of hybrids to differences in preference type. Hybrids are much less likely to satisfy positive, mission-related preferences whereas government agencies are only somewhat less likely. This is a function of the structural features that define hybrids. Thus it demonstrates the benefit of examining agent structure *and* preference type – two neglected variables in the bureaucratic control equation.

The two dimensions of variation in preference type identified in this book are surely not the only distinctions that have relevance for bureaucratic control. For example, the nature of the policy area in which the organization operates is likely an important factor. Policy domains with large, active interest group communities are probably particularly treacherous for principals interested in reshaping an agent's behavior. There are also difficult-to-measure differences among preferences that seem intuitively important. For example, the intensity of principals' preferences surely affects the likelihood of satisfaction. These are areas for further exploration.

There is a danger in social science of creating ever more complex typologies until understanding is diminished, not enhanced. This study demonstrates that inclusion of the preference term is not such a gratuitous project. It is an important next step in the development of the bureaucratic control field.

5

Hybrid organizations and the alignment of interests: the case of Fannie Mae and Freddie Mac

Principals' control of bureaucratic agents is only a piece of the political puzzle. How does hybrid structure alter the political dynamics of the governmental process? Based on a detailed analysis of a legislative case study involving Fannie Mae and Freddie Mac, two answers to this question are presented in this chapter: (1) the characteristics that distinguish government-sponsored enterprises from traditional government agencies and private companies endow Fannie Mae and Freddie Mac with unique political resources; and (2) the alignment of interest groups around Fannie Mae and Freddie Mac creates opportunities for strategic manipulation. A triangular model of this alignment is proposed and employed to analyze the drafting and passage of the Federal Housing Enterprises Financial Safety and Soundness Act (FHEFSSA) of 1992.

This chapter is an important complement to the other sections of this book. It considers the consequences of hybrid structure during periods of extraordinary policy-making. Most research on bureaucratic control, including this book, focuses on the day-to-day interaction between principals and agents, referred to in these pages as ordinary policy-making. Extraordinary policy-making, large-scale legislative activity that reshapes institutions and occupies multiple players in the governmental process for extended periods of time, receives minimal attention. Although infrequent, such seminal moments of change in policy and/or organizational structure are, of course, crucial. They shape all subsequent ordinary policy-making interactions.

At the heart of this chapter is the FHEFSSA, a law that reshaped the regulatory infrastructure for two government-sponsored enterprises, Fannie Mae and Freddie Mac. The three-year process of study, drafting and negotiation was precipitated by the costly bailout of the savings and loan industry.

The legislative history presented in this chapter was constructed from official records, trade magazines and newspapers, and extensive background interviews with participants from all sides, including representatives of all the organizations that participated in the development of the legislation: Fannie Mae, Freddie Mac, the Treasury Department, the Department of Housing and Urban Development, the Office of Management and Budget, non-profit and industry interest groups, and committee staff from the relevant committees and subcommittees on both the House and Senate sides of Congress.

Although this chapter deals with Fannie Mae and Freddie Mac, two organizations that are distinguished by their reputed political influence, the lessons are applicable to other hybrids. That is because the essential point of the following pages applies well to all hybrids. These organizations introduce a unique alignment of interests that is subject to strategic manipulation by interested parties.

Hybrid characteristics and GSE influence

On matters pertaining to housing and housing finance, Fannie Mae and Freddie Mac are influential political players in Washington (Matlack 1990, Labaton 1991, Bradsher 1992, Nitschke 1998). This surprises those who presume that the two GSEs are "part of the government," not organized interests. In fact, that confusion helps explain the two companies' political power. Fannie Mae and Freddie Mac are powerful because they possess resources generally associated with both private- and public-sector institutions.[3]

No pejorative connotation should be inferred from this description of Fannie Mae and Freddie Mac. Although contemporary discourse frequently paints "political influence" in negative terms, it is not here intended to convey nefarious intentions or deeds. Fannie Mae and Freddie Mac have been successful in pursuing their legislative agendas; this chapter simply offers an explanation. That success is explained below as a function of the GSEs' unique combination of "private-ness" and "public-ness" in a single package.

The private Fannie Mae and Freddie Mac: GSEs as interest groups

The political activities of Fannie Mae and Freddie Mac are only restricted, as are those of any private company. Both companies lobby Congress, build

---

[3] While the term is used repeatedly, the vexing issues of "power" described by March (1966), Dahl (1957) and others are skirted in this chapter. A simplistic definition – the ability to get what one wants – is utilized for the analysis of this case.

relationships with individual politicians and cultivate a network of other interest groups. This is a brief summary of the "private-sector" characteristics that provide Fannie Mae and Freddie Mac with potential influence.

Resources and incentives Like many large profitable corporations, Fannie Mae and Freddie Mac devote resources to political activities. Political expenditures can take many forms: personnel devoted to legislative or political liaison, development of educational materials and advertising. Federal Election Commission records reveal that executives of both companies contributed heavily to the political campaigns of relevant committee members during the years in which the FHEFSSA was under consideration, and Fannie Mae and Freddie Mac appear on congressional honoraria reports for speaking engagements. Fannie Mae, for a time, ran a political action committee ("Fannie PAC") that was disbanded after publicity brought criticism (Abramowitz 1988, Garsson, McTague and Zboril 1988). Both companies frequently advertise in popular media and publications aimed at Members of Congress and their staff, such as *Roll Call, The Hill,* and *The Washington Post* (Kosterlitz 2000a).

Fannie Mae and Freddie Mac enjoy financial resources not by chance but as a function of their structure. They enjoy legally protected partial franchises and are profitable, at least in part, due to the implicit support of the federal government. And, since every aspect of their operations can be affected by congressional action, Fannie Mae and Freddie Mac have powerful incentives to devote significant attention to Congress and politics in general. Thus one can conclude that GSEs *will* possess resources and motive to expend these resources for political advantage.

Electoral connection As purchasers of mortgages in every congressional district in the United States, Fannie Mae and Freddie Mac are of potential interest to every Member of Congress. Their centrality in the American system of home finance makes issues related to Fannie Mae and Freddie Mac salient for representatives interested in the financial well-being of their constituents; an effective hook on which to hang lobbying efforts.

Understanding this, Fannie Mae and Freddie Mac employ strategies to reinforce their connection to members' districts. Fannie Mae, for instance, produces computer-generated maps that graphically display how much business the company is doing in each congressional district. The two companies also steer corporate attention to members. At announcements of new affordable housing initiatives and other lending programs, elected officials are given the opportunity to bask in the positive attention generated by Fannie Mae or Freddie Mac. *The Wall Street Journal* reported that Fannie Mae held 200 events with Members of Congress in 2000 (Kulish and Schlesinger 2001).

Loyal allies Lenders, realtors, and other housing-related trade organizations dependent upon Fannie Mae and Freddie Mac for their business can be mobilized to bolster the GSEs' political strength. Once again, the dominance of Fannie Mae and Freddie Mac in the mortgage industry ensures the availability of this resource. The GSEs' status secures their hold on a large share of the residential mortgage market. Thus relationships with partners are asymmetric and Fannie Mae and Freddie Mac have historically enjoyed consistent support from organizations with national memberships.

Critics have accused Fannie Mae of being heavy-handed in its efforts to maintain solidarity. In 1986, Salomon Brothers opposed Fannie Mae's bid to amend its charter and expand its business. Not only did Salomon fail to stop Fannie Mae, it was subsequently cut off from the lucrative underwriting business Fannie Mae had steered towards the Wall Street firm (Taub and Gold 1989, Matlack 1990). Fannie Mae withdrew advertising from *The Economist* after several articles – and editorial cartoons – portrayed Fannie Mae and Freddie Mac unfavorably (Matlack 1990). Fannie Mae has also been accused of using donations from its charitable foundations to coerce political support from dependent non-profit organizations such as the Association of Community Organizations for Reform Now and the Low-Income Housing Information Service (Zuckman 1991b, Jacoby 2000). More recently, representatives of financial services companies reported that Fannie Mae and Freddie Mac threatened to withhold business as a means of forcing their executives to resign from a group that opposed the two GSEs (Wilke and Barta 2001).

As the previous sentence suggests, the landscape is changing. In recent years, the support enjoyed by Fannie Mae and Freddie Mac *has* eroded. The 1999 formation of "FM Watch," an interest group created by mortgage industry businesses and trade associations, signified the shifting terrain. FM Watch is a response to the feared expansion of Fannie Mae and Freddie Mac into new areas of the mortgage business (Schroeder 1999). Although both companies are dominant in the market, they have committed to sustained growth. Thus companies in fields related to the GSEs' core business (e.g., mortgage insurance, underwriting) feel threatened (Stevenson 2000, Barta 2001).

Recent events have also contributed to the emergence of GSE critics. The Enron scandal has focused attention – some of it unfavorable – on disclosure and corporate governance practices at Fannie Mae and Freddie Mac (Gilpin 2002). Attention has also been directed at the GSEs' exemption from Securities and Exchange Commission (SEC) securities registration requirements (Fernandez 2002a). Both companies have been adamant in response to these criticisms but their regulator, OFHEO, has been moved to investigate and suggest new regulations (Garver 2002).

Network dominance Former, current and potential Fannie Mae and Freddie Mac employees constitute an extensive network in the housing finance community. The two GSEs offer the opportunity to work on housing-related issues with private-sector compensation and unparalleled levels of substantive engagement. As one former congressional aide now working for a GSE put it, "If you're interested in housing and finance in the United States, there is no better place to be working than at Fannie Mae or Freddie Mac" (interview 95).

As a result, Fannie Mae and Freddie Mac personnel rosters boast numerous alumni of the executive and legislative branches, with both the Democratic and Republican parties well represented. For example, current CEO Franklin Raines returned to Fannie Mae after heading the Office of Management and Budget. Former House Speaker Newt Gingrich signed on as a consultant to Freddie Mac. Through their personnel, the two companies gain expertise and connections to key players in the legislative process and the administration's policy formulation. Furthermore, there is an impressive history of GSE executives crossing back into government service, giving the company advantages in terms of access, and sympathy, at the highest levels. Raines, for example, was a top executive at Fannie Mae *before* joining the Clinton Administration. Robert Zoellick left his position as executive vice-president at Fannie Mae to join the administration of George W. Bush. Zoellick had previously served under the first President Bush in the State and Treasury Departments.

The public Fannie Mae and Freddie Mac: GSEs as powerful bureaucracies

Multiple models have been offered to capture the place of bureaucracy in the governmental process; all agree that public bureaucracies possess resources that can be utilized for political influence (Rourke 1984, Hill 1991). The public aspects of government-sponsored enterprises endow them with many of the resources attributed to public bureaucracies. This influence complements the private-side resources.

Unassailability Fannie Mae and Freddie Mac are in a unique position to claim that their successful performance is a matter of national importance. Chartered by Congress, the two GSEs represent a governmental effort to help Americans purchase their own homes. Housing is, in the words of one Fannie Mae executive, a "white hat issue" (interview 93). Fannie Mae and Freddie Mac can strategically "wrap themselves in the flag" and make attacks politically costly.

Both companies cultivate this advantage through advertising. Advertisements on television and in print remind Americans of the companies' role in home purchases. And, as pointed out above, the GSEs also remind members of Congress by advertising in newspapers aimed at them and their staff.

Expertise   Experience, information and technical expertise sometimes give bureaucracies the upper hand in negotiations with Congress, interest groups and executive branch agencies (Rourke 1984). In the case of Fannie Mae and Freddie Mac, non-profit organizations and congressional committees do not have the resources to conduct research and develop arguments with a breadth and depth equal to the GSEs. Even HUD can be overmatched because it cannot devote the personnel or resources to carry out the research provided by Fannie Mae and Freddie Mac.

This advantage was particularly evident during consideration of legislation pertaining to the capital stress tests – computer simulations that would determine capital requirements for each GSE. Individuals with sufficient technical proficiency to challenge the GSEs' claims were sprinkled throughout the administration and congressional staff. These individuals were, by their own accounts, outgunned (interviews 102, 103, 107, 108). As a result, the GSEs dominated the crafting of legislation regarding these tests (interviews 98, 99, 102, 103, 105).

Insiders   Fannie Mae and Freddie Mac are historically and structurally linked to the federal government. Loans insured by the federal government are purchased by Fannie Mae and Freddie Mac. Both companies have worked with HUD on program evaluation and innovation. Like many housing organizations, HUD relies upon the GSEs in such partnerships because they offer expertise and financial resources. Finally, the GSEs' long-term repeated interaction with members of Congress and their staff has given them the opportunity to build strong relationships.

Fannie Mae and Freddie Mac emphasize different strategies. One senior GSE officer noted that Freddie Mac has focused on maintaining strong relationships with the executive branch while Fannie Mae has traditionally maintained strong ties on the Hill (interview 93). Thus the companies collectively protect against hostility in either branch.

The best of both worlds: more powerful than agency or private company

The conclusion is that Fannie Mae and Freddie Mac possess more resources as hybrids than they would as fully private or fully public entities. This point is driven home with consideration of two *fictitious* mortgage-purchasing entities. Consider the Federal Mortgage Agency, part of the executive branch, and Acme Mortgage Corporation, a private company.

The Federal Mortgage Agency would be subject to political control, run by a political appointee and answerable to the President. It could not take retributive actions against businesses or interest groups that failed to endorse its legislative agenda. As a result, the Federal Mortgage Agency's behavior would be limited. It could not take positions independent of the administration. Without the latitude to punish clients and partners who do not act as allies in the political realm, it could not coerce surrogates. The Federal Mortgage Agency could not independently lobby Congress. It could not serve particular areas selectively and strategically. Moreover, the agency would be subject to a host of federal management laws and regulations that govern everything from compensation to procurement. In all these respects, our fictional Federal Mortgage Agency is identical to the real FHA.

Now consider another fictitious entity, the privately owned Acme Mortgage Corporation. Acme could spend large sums of money to cultivate political goodwill with impunity. It could enlist support from dependent institutions on key policy issues. However, as a private corporation, Acme Mortgage Corporation would be restricted by federal financial laws. It would not have the implicit backing of the federal government or exemption from federal regulations and state or local taxes. Finally, Acme would not enjoy the imprimatur of public purpose and the mandate of the federal charter.

In short neither the Federal Mortgage Agency nor the Acme Mortgage Corporation would likely wield the same economic and political influence that Fannie Mae and Freddie Mac display. As government-sponsored enterprises, Fannie Mae and Freddie Mac have *all* the advantages possessed by our fictitious entities and none of the disadvantages. It is not surprising that Fannie Mae and Freddie Mac have generally resisted calls for their complete "privatization," severing the remaining ties to the federal government. As one congressional staff member who has worked closely with the GSEs concluded, Fannie Mae and Freddie Mac are "more powerful than if they were private or if they were public" (interview 103).

The alignment of interests around GSEs

Terry Moe (1989) argues that interest groups can shape bureaucracies to their own advantage. Although this chapter confirms Moe's hypothesis, it offers an additional claim that is, in a sense, the converse of Moe's. The structure of institutions can shape the preferences of interest groups. In this case, the arrangement of interests around Fannie Mae and Freddie Mac reflects the organizational features of GSEs. Furthermore, this alignment of interests was pivotal in determining the outcome of the legislative process when Congress was considering the Federal Housing Enterprises Financial Safety and Soundness Act of 1992. The following sections describe the alignment of interests around Fannie Mae and Freddie Mac and illustrate the significance of this arrangement with examples from the drafting of the FHEFSSA.

The alignment of interests around Fannie Mae and Freddie Mac

Government-sponsored enterprises have three objectives:

1. To fulfill programmatic policy purposes. In the case of Fannie Mae and Freddie Mac, this means providing greater access to mortgage credit markets.
2. To maintain a financially safe and sound operation that minimizes risk to the federal government.
3. To operate as a profitable private company that maintains consistent return to shareholders.

Each objective is potentially in conflict with the other two. Reckless pursuit of profits could undermine the achievement of public purposes and expose the federal government to financial risk. Overly risk-averse regulation of financial safety and soundness could hinder the GSEs' abilities to meet programmatic goals or limit profitability. Overly ambitious programmatic goals could adversely affect the GSEs' profitability or even financial safety and soundness.

As a result, parties with an interest in Fannie Mae and Freddie Mac are organized in a triangular arrangement around the GSEs (see figure 5.1). Each node of the triangle is potentially at odds with the other two. A brief description of the interest groups at each node of this triangle introduces the source of conflict between interests in the case of Fannie Mae and Freddie Mac.

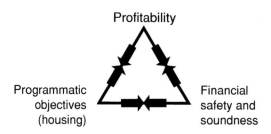

Profitability

Programmatic
objectives
(housing)

Financial
safety and
soundness

Figure 5.1 Triangular model of interests around Fannie Mae and Freddie Mac

Programmatic considerations   Fannie Mae and Freddie Mac are regarded by Congress, the executive branch and housing specialists as part of the federal response to the public's housing needs. Although created to stabilize mortgage markets, eliminate regional disparities in credit availability and facilitate home-buying by middle- and working-class Americans, Fannie Mae and Freddie Mac ought now – in the view of policy-makers who see a mature efficient market for middle-class home buyers – focus on providing credit opportunities for underserved markets and borrowers. Thus proponents of housing for low- and moderate-income communities – generally non-profit organizations and the elected officials that serve such communities – press Fannie Mae and Freddie Mac to devote additional resources to housing for less affluent Americans. The Department of Housing and Urban Development generally shares this interest in the GSEs' programmatic function.

Profitability Fannie Mae and Freddie Mac are both profit-seeking companies. This orientation is codified in the GSEs' charters. Even the clause pronouncing Fannie Mae's obligation to provide assistance to low- and moderate-income borrowers specifies that the company is entitled to a "reasonable economic return" on *all* programs (12 USC 1,716, emphasis added).

Of course, the parties most interested in the profitability of Fannie Mae and Freddie Mac are their owners and managers. Stockholders' desire for the companies to maintain their market status creates a powerful incentive for executives. Like many corporate managers, executives at both companies are judged and compensated, in large part, on the basis of stock performance. Thus the corporate leadership predictably resists legislation that makes maintenance of stock value more difficult.

The normative question of whether government-sponsored enterprises *ought* to be profit-oriented is not relevant. The fact that GSEs *are* profit-seeking entities is integral to explaining their behavior. The ownership of Fannie Mae and Freddie Mac constitutes an interest group concerned with the profitability of their companies and brings a distinct set of interests before Congress.

The profitability of other companies may also be at stake when Congress considers government-sponsored enterprises. Primary market lenders (banks, thrifts, mortgage bankers) depend on Fannie Mae and Freddie Mac. Without the stream of capital the GSEs guarantee, many lenders could not function. Home-builders, realtors, mortgage insurers, contractors, landscapers and other housing-related industries recognize the critical role of Fannie Mae and Freddie Mac; more loans mean more business. Similarly, Wall Street firms that handle the multimillion dollar issuances of Fannie Mae and Freddie Mac securities have a strong interest in the two companies. The more business the GSEs are doing, the more income such firms earn by underwriting the sale of debt and mortgage securities to investors.

Of course, there can be serious disagreements among these groups. For example, some financial institutions that depend upon Fannie Mae and Freddie Mac complain that they cannot compete with GSEs because of their preferential status. One should not assume that all mortgage-related businesses would naturally endorse proposals beneficial to Fannie Mae or Freddie Mac. As noted above, there is increasing fear that Fannie Mae and Freddie Mac could expand their businesses, thus threatening other mortgage industry companies (Barta 2001). This has reduced the GSEs' influence, if only because there is now a well-financed group, FM Watch, that is offering rebuttals to the arguments made by Fannie Mae and Freddie Mac.

Financial safety and soundness   The combined outstanding debt of Fannie Mae and Freddie Mac is over $1.3 trillion (OFHEO 2001). Fannie Mae and Freddie Mac guarantees cover over $1.5 trillion in outstanding mortgage securities (OFHEO 2001). To give some perspective, the housing GSEs' $2.8 trillion combined liability is greater than the actual or projected total outlays of the US government in any single year. Indeed, a few years ago the Treasury Department was reducing the federal government's outstanding debt, fueling speculation that the securities issued by Fannie Mae, Freddie Mac and smaller hybrids might establish the benchmark of creditworthiness for the bond market (Stevenson 2000). Dramatically increased federal borrowing has deferred that possibility.

Although such large numbers seem abstract, the risk presented is quite real. The financial conditions of Fannie Mae and Freddie Mac, for example, are very sensitive to interest rate movements. Unforeseen shifts in the market can have catastrophic consequences. Fannie Mae absorbed "substantial losses" in the early 1980s when interest rates rose and Fannie Mae's borrowing costs greatly exceed its revenues (BNA *Banking Report* 1990). Freddie Mac has written off millions of dollars in losses on poorly managed programs (*The Economist* 1989). If, for example, even one GSE were unable to meet its current outstanding obligations, the federal government could be stuck with a bill for hundreds of billions of dollars.

Interest groups concerned with the financial safety and soundness of Fannie Mae and Freddie Mac are not readily apparent. If Fannie Mae can produce a higher rate of return for the stockholder by maintaining a small cushion of reserve capital, the stockholder benefits. The increased risk is borne by the federal government and the stockholder can bail out if the company's fortunes deteriorate. Wall Street investment banks are equally unconcerned with financial safety and soundness. As long as investors are confident that the federal government guarantees Fannie Mae and Freddie Mac securities, their business is not affected.

At stake, then, is the creditworthiness of the federal government. Unfortunately, the public good of "creditworthiness" is diffuse and non-divisible – difficult to organize an interest group around. This is a logical extension of the observations that Stanley Surrey offers on the politics of tax breaks; the cost of tax loopholes is so diffuse as to be non-existent (Surrey 1976). The costs to taxpayers presented by GSEs is even more diffuse. In fact, there is only a *risk* of cost. By analogy, then, legislative resistance to GSE risk should be lower than it is for tax breaks.

The strongest institutional advocate for fiscal prudence has been the Treasury Department; its staff took the lead in drafting the safety and soundness legislation. A handful of "public interest" groups and Members of Congress have also raised the risk presented by government-sponsored enterprises. It is telling, however, that perhaps the single most effective advocate for safety and soundness regulation has been a private individual: Thomas Stanton, a Washington attorney, former Fannie Mae associate general counsel and self-appointed activist for financial safety and soundness. Stanton's 1991 book *State of Risk* and his personal lobbying were influential in the legislative process leading to the passage of the FHEFSSA (Rauch 1991, Matlack 1990).

Alignment in action: redesigning a regulatory framework

The most significant business advantage Fannie Mae and Freddie Mac enjoy by virtue of their GSE status is low borrowing costs. Because of the implicit federal guarantee behind their securities, the companies borrow at interest rates only slightly higher than those paid by the United States Treasury. Even companies evaluated as "AAA" by corporate rating firms pay higher interest rates than Fannie Mae or Freddie Mac (Moe 1983). Prior to the savings and loan crisis in the 1980s, Congress ignored the tremendous government liability created by this implicit guarantee.

The savings and loan debacle served a painful reminder that off-budget liability could become quite tangible. Congress included a provision in the 1989 savings and loan bailout law calling for a study of the government's GSE liability.[4] The subsequent budget reconciliation act called for additional reports and mandated congressional action on GSE regulatory reform, setting the stage for the legislative struggle to revamp regulation of Fannie Mae and Freddie Mac.[5]

Signed into law by President George Bush, the Federal Housing Enterprises Financial Safety and Soundness Act of 1992 had taken shape over three years. Fannie Mae and Freddie Mac worked with the administration on the development of the initial proposal and later negotiated with congressional

---

[4] Section 1004 of FIRREA, the 1989 law that overhauled regulation of the savings and loan industry, required the Comptroller General of the United States to prepare a study of government-sponsored enterprises, including Fannie Mae and Freddie Mac, to determine: (1) the financial soundness and stability of GSEs; (2) the need to minimize any potential financial exposure of the federal government; and (3) the need to minimize any potential impact on the borrowing of the federal government.

[5] The Omnibus Budget Reconciliation Act of 1990 required the Treasury Department and the Congressional Budget Office to prepare additional reports on GSE regulation and required Congressional consideration of GSE legislation by September 1991. Failure to consider legislation would result in a mandatory vote on a proposal to be presented by the Treasury Department.

staff. This gave the GSEs, as a former OMB official described it, "two bites at the apple;" once while working with the administration and again while negotiating with Congress (interview 99).

The alignment of interests, combined with the resources available to the GSEs, often allowed Fannie Mae and Freddie Mac to shift debate from disadvantageous issues to more favorable ground. Yet the history of the legislation shows that opponents could recognize this strategy and, to some extent, compensate successfully. This section considers three key elements of the FHEFSSA: regulatory structure, capital standards and affordable housing goals. Each is explained and the history of the legislation is recounted to provide insight into the character of GSE influence.

Regulatory structure   Prior to passage of the FHEFSSA, regulatory authority over Fannie Mae and Freddie Mac was vested entirely in the Department of Housing and Urban Development. HUD's limited regulatory authority over Fannie Mae and Freddie Mac had rarely been utilized due to chronic lack of resources, expertise and political leverage. In 1989, the Financial Institutions Reform Recovery and Enforcement Act legislation added oversight of Freddie Mac to HUD responsibilities and required the issuance of new regulations for the GSEs. By the time regulation of Fannie Mae and Freddie Mac was being restructured, no final regulations had been issued under the 1989 law.

The new law divided regulatory authority between a new, quasi-independent agency, the Office of Federal Housing Enterprise Oversight, and HUD itself. OFHEO was made responsible for safety and soundness regulation while HUD's responsibility was for programmatic regulation. This outcome resulted from a combination of congressional politics, fear of regulatory capture and the GSEs' desire to maintain Congress' role in the oversight process.

The fear of regulatory capture came from all nodes of the interest group triangle. Safety and soundness advocates worried that a small independent regulatory agency could be influenced by Fannie Mae and Freddie Mac and that HUD would subordinate safety and soundness to programmatic goals. Affordable housing advocates were wary of Treasury regulation because safety and soundness might dominate programmatic considerations. The GSEs were leery of any regulator that might hinder their ability to pursue profits and other objectives successfully.

A May 1991 GAO report to Congress recommended the creation of a Federal Enterprise Regulatory Board to oversee all government-sponsored enterprises (1991). Such a regulator would have "the visibility and capability to act promptly and effectively if a government-sponsored enterprise experiences severe difficulties" (GAO 1991, 46). The "super-regulator" idea, however, was doomed from the outset. The proposed super-regulator would have overseen agricultural, educational *and* housing GSEs. Thus the agriculture and education committees would likely have lost jurisdiction over *their* GSEs to the banking committee. Such changes are not generally welcomed enthusiastically (Fenno 1973). Furthermore, existing regulators resisted efforts to strip away their authority and, in some cases, their reason for existence.

Thus the critical issue was whether HUD should retain regulatory authority or whether a new regulatory agency should be created to oversee Fannie Mae and Freddie Mac. The GSEs took different positions regarding the optimal regulatory structure. Fannie Mae argued that HUD should continue in its role as regulator. A politically insulated independent regulator might diminish the value of relationships with HUD and Congress that Fannie Mae had long cultivated. Freddie Mac, on the other hand, favored the independent regulator proposal. One independent regulator with safety and soundness as well as programmatic authority over the two housing GSEs, Freddie Mac argued, would produce more coherent regulation.

The disagreement revealed differences between the two companies. At the time that the FHEFSSA was under consideration, Freddie Mac had been a private company for only two years. Prior to the introduction of stock ownership and the creation of a board of directors, Freddie Mac, in the words of an administration official, functioned "like an agency not a private corporation" (interview 102). The leadership at Freddie Mac did not have the political experience or perspicacity that Fannie Mae strategists displayed. The contrast between Leland Brendsel, Freddie Mac's CEO, and Jim Johnson, Fannie Mae's CEO, is telling. Brendsel is a Ph.D. economist. Johnson was a top aide to Vice-President Mondale and a successful Wall Street investment banker.

With the transformation from government agency to private corporation, Freddie Mac had moved to the profitability node of the triangle – but had not yet adapted. As a congressional aide put it, "Freddie Mac was operating under an organizational culture reflecting past interests" (interview 100). Fannie Mae, on the other hand, recognized the virtue of keeping authority within HUD, a government agency that, like many interest groups called upon to support the GSEs' positions, relied on partnerships with Fannie Mae.

The Treasury Department had favored the creation of a single, independent regulator while HUD was loath to surrender its regulatory authority. The Bush Administration's desire to maintain a united front in the face of intense GSE lobbying forced a compromise: the separation of safety and soundness from programmatic regulation *within* HUD. Treasury was satisfied that the director of OFHEO was sufficiently insulated from the secretary

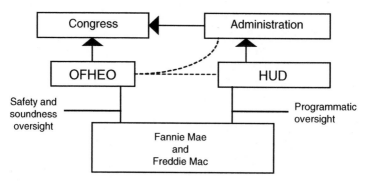

Figure 5.2 New regulatory structure created by FHEFSSA

of HUD. According to the statute, "The Director is authorized, without the review or approval of the Secretary, to make such determinations, take such actions, and perform such functions as the Director determines necessary . . ." to set capital standards, issue and enforce regulations, and examine Fannie Mae and Freddie Mac (12 USC 4,513).

Still, the secretary of HUD retains the right of approval over any OFHEO actions not directly required by the legislation. OFHEO submits its appropriations request and clears drafts of proposed regulations through the Office of Management and Budget. The director of OFHEO is appointed by the President, with Senate confirmation, to a five-year term. Fears that the safety and soundness regulators would dominate the programmatic interests were allayed because the secretary retained direct authority over programmatic oversight (see figure 5.2).

Several Senators and their staff disliked the compromise. Expressing their sentiments, Senator Carl Levin (D – MI) commented that "the better course of action would have been to place the regulator of housing enterprises outside of HUD" (Senate 1992, S8,652). But the Senate gave the House the structure it wanted in exchange for concessions in the areas of capital standards and the affordable housing goals. Congressional staff note that Fannie Mae lobbied heavily with more sympathetic House members to maintain HUD's authority. The compromise, it was concluded, was the best available deal. "They could have been stronger," said Levin, "but at least the regulator does not report to the Secretary when it comes to safety and soundness" (Senate 1992, S8,614).

As a final bit of protection, Fannie Mae fought to keep channels of congressional review in place as an insurance policy in the event the regulators proved overly aggressive. Significant examples of this strategy include the requirements that OFHEO clear all proposed regulations through oversight committees and go through the yearly appropriations review (a requirement to which bank regulators are not subject). Critics of the final law note that, because the independent safety and soundness regulator was subject to the congressional appropriations process, the GSEs would have "a chance to exercise influence over the regulator by lobbying the appropriations committees" (Taylor 1992). Administration and congressional staff explain that they understood why Fannie Mae wanted the appropriations clause inserted and that it could cause difficulties for OFHEO in the future (interviews 102, 103). Nevertheless, the clause was accepted to get the bill passed. In subsequent years, OFHEO itself has argued for removal of this provision because of the constraints it imposes (OFHEO 2002).

Although there is some substantive justification for the division of regulatory responsibility, this case study supports Terry Moe's glum conclusion that, given the objectives and influence of interest groups, the democratic process is unlikely "to promote effective organization (Moe 1989, 329).

Setting capital standards   Three congressionally-mandated reports on the regulation of government-sponsored enterprises recognized the need for meaningful capital requirements to ensure that the GSEs have enough money to cover losses. With each loan purchased, Fannie Mae and Freddie Mac assume credit risk (the borrower may not repay the loan) and interest rate risk (Fannie Mae or Freddie Mac may have to pay higher interest rates on debt than it receives from borrowers). Although maintaining reasonable capital is prudent, holding excess capital is inefficient; reserve capital does not maximize return. Thus there is tension between the need for capital reserves and the desire to utilize capital profitably.

The general approach suggested by the reports and agreed to by the administration and the GSEs was a two-part capital standard: a minimum capital standard (a baseline ratio of retained capital to liabilities) and a risk-based capital standard – a more complex requirement derived from projected losses under computer-simulated economic scenarios. The initial question was how much latitude Congress should grant OFHEO to translate the law into precise regulations

The GSEs disagreed on the desirability of regulatory discretion to specify the capital standards. Freddie Mac favored regulatory discretion but Fannie Mae sought to have Congress define as much of the risk-based capital standard as possible to constrain any future regulatory agency. The Treasury Department wanted OFHEO to have complete discretion in setting capital standards.

Fannie Mae invoked programmatic concerns when arguing against discretion. A company spokesman suggested that a regulator with discretion could impose "such a high capital standard that the corporation would be unable to fulfill its housing mission" (Zuckman 1991a), an argument endorsed by corporate supporters (*Housing and Development Reporter* 1992). The final legislation did spell out most of the minimum capital requirement and a great deal of the risk-based capital requirement. Keeping the determination of capital standards in the legislative domain was consistent with Fannie Mae's strategy throughout the legislative process: to capitalize on the good congressional relationships cultivated and maintained over several years.

Although Fannie Mae and Freddie Mac expressed different views on several specific questions, the two GSEs both argued against any legislation that would raise capital levels. Once the capital standards battle was kept in Congress, the GSEs focused on shaping the regulations. Leland Brendsel, the chairman and CEO of Freddie Mac, and Jim Johnson, the chairman and CEO of Fannie Mae, both testified before Congress that overly demanding capital standards would threaten the GSEs' ability to perform their programmatic functions (Senate Banking Committee 1991, 197; House Housing Subcommittee 1991, 36). By invoking the housing functions of their companies, as they did in arguing against regulatory discretion, the two executives portrayed the capital standards debate as a conflict between programmatic goals and fiscal safety. This deflected attention from the profitability node of the metaphorical triangle.

Other interest groups interested in profitability joined this chorus. Stephen Ashley, president of the Mortgage Bankers Association, warned that "excessive capital requirements are not necessary and, in fact, would limit credit availability and raise interest rates for homebuyers" (House Housing Subcommittee 1991, 72). Not coincidentally, that would mean a loss of business for the members of Mr Ashley's organization. The California Association of Realtors argued that "any increase in required capital for the FNMA and FHLMC will reduce the supply of lendable funds in the primary mortgage market and raise mortgage interest rates . . ." and dismissed the prospects of a taxpayer bailout as "extremely remote . . ." (Senate Banking Committee 1991, 380).

More tellingly, the interest groups clustered around the *programmatic* node rallied against stringent safety and soundness regulations. In their testimony before Congress, affordable housing advocates argued against higher capital standards. Paul Grogan, president of the Local Initiatives Support Corporation, a national non-profit development organization, raised the danger that safety and soundness regulation would adversely affect affordable housing programs, saying that ". . . a regulator focusing only on safety and soundness will not take into account the impact of its actions on low-income housing and communities" (House Housing Subcommittee 1991, 412). Such statements were not uncommon among affordable housing advocates (*Housing and Development Reporter* 1991).

The mobilization of both sets of interest groups suggests the consequences of the alignment of interests. In a conflict between profitability and safety and soundness, the programmatic node was a swing faction. Fannie Mae and Freddie Mac used their resources to recruit groups clustered around this node. The Treasury Department, the only institutional advocate of safety and soundness, had no such ability.

In advocating more stringent capital standards for the GSEs, Treasury's representatives sought to distinguish between the nodes of opposition. A central theme of Under-Secretary Robert Glauber's testimony before Congress was that higher capital requirements do not necessitate reductions in affordable housing support or increases in interest rates or fees charged to American homebuyers. "It should be possible for these institutions to raise significant amounts of capital and do so without raising their prices," explained Glauber. "What it would mean would be somewhat of a reduction in the rate of return that they make" (House Housing Subcommittee 1991, 24). Under questioning from Senator Jake Garn (R – UT) on the impact of increased capital requirements on mortgage interest rates, Glauber reiterated, "If anybody bore the burden, it would be the shareholders and not homebuyers" (House Housing Subcommittee 1991, 23).

The problem with Glauber's claim lay in the structural independence of Fannie Mae and Freddie Mac. Given the absence of direct governmental control over the two companies, there was no guarantee that increased capital standards *would not* adversely affect housing programs. While the companies *could* lower their rates of return, they could just as easily raise the fees charged on borrowers. Both the GAO and CBO recognized this possibility and even calculated the potential adjustments in rates paid by borrowers that would be required to help GSEs meet higher capital requirements. A 1996 CBO report on the GSEs made the point more starkly, noting that Fannie Mae and Freddie Mac effectively decide how much of the federal subsidy they receive is passed on to borrowers.

Negotiations between Senate staff and representatives of Fannie Mae and Freddie Mac resulted in the risk-based capital requirement (more stringent than the House version) that was included in the final bill. The conference committee adopted the Senate's capital standards and parameters for a risk-based capital stress test. When the GSEs faced an unpalatable component of the capital standard in Congress, they settled for regulatory discretion, hoping to fight the battle another, more advantageous, day.

Suffice it to say that the compromise solutions left ample room for dispute between the new regulator and the GSEs. For example, one version of the risk-based capital rules required that the regulator identify the worst historical interest rate shocks for use in the stress test. The GSEs resisted this clear requirement and insisted that the final bill require only that the interest rate portion of the stress test be "reasonably related" to the worst historical experience. This left the door open for future dispute (and negotiation) with OFHEO. The frequent appearance of the phrase "reasonably related" suggests the appeal of this solution. Fannie Mae was able to extract such concessions because the Bush Administration and several Senators were eager to pass the law and feared the ability of the GSEs to delay passage, at the very least. By creating mechanisms to exert pressure on their regulators through Congress, the GSEs maintained the value of their good relations on Capitol Hill.

The unanswered questions of the capital standards have consequence measured in millions of dollars for each GSE. Even seemingly simple issues can be vexing. For example, the risk-based capital standard required by Congress calls for a stress test. A computer simulation is utilized to determine how much capital the GSEs require to withstand a horrendous economic scenario as bad as the worst ten-year period experienced in any region of the United States. This simplified clause gives some sense of the difficulty of the task. What is a region? The legislation says only that a region is ten contiguous states. Which ten states? This question is critically important; it will define how bad the worst-case scenario is for the GSEs. Development of the capital standards required that the regulator resolve scores of such difficult questions – a partial explanation for the fact that OFHEO took eight years to produce the regulation.

The legislative history of the capital standards confirms the influence of Fannie Mae and Freddie Mac. Not only were the GSEs able to employ their considerable political power, but the organization of interests around government-sponsored enterprises allowed Fannie Mae and Freddie Mac to enlist groups with programmatic interests for their battle against stringent capital standards. Furthermore, the triangular arrangement of interests dictated the strategic behavior of the Treasury Department. In practice, this meant trying to drive a wedge between the programmatic and profitability nodes by arguing that the GSEs could cut profits to meet stricter capital requirements rather than paring affordable housing programs. Given the resources at the GSEs' disposal, this strategy proved unworkable.

Housing goals   There is tension between the programmatic mission of the GSEs and both profitability and safety and soundness. Although the programmatic goals are publicly unassailable, there *is* resistance on the part of the GSEs to the additional burden of programmatic regulation. While fighting higher capital standards, programmatic goals were invoked by Fannie Mae, Freddie Mac and allies to dull the impact of safety and soundness regulations. In the case of affordable housing goals, Fannie Mae and Freddie

Mac attempted to enlist groups clustered at the safety and soundness node and profitability node to thwart the efforts of housing proponents at the programmatic node.

With Congress overhauling the regulation of Fannie Mae and Freddie Mac, interest groups that had been pressing the GSEs to contribute more to the development of low-income and affordable housing saw an opportunity. The affordable housing aspect of the legislation was introduced when House Banking Committee chairman Henry Gonzalez inserted a provision requiring the GSEs to allot an amount equal to 20 percent of the previous year's dividend payments to the Federal Home Loan Banks' "Affordable Housing Program" that subsidizes rental units for low-income families. Fannie Mae and Freddie Mac were animated in their opposition to Gonzalez's subsidization provision (Senate Banking Committee 1991, House Housing Subcommittee 1991). Their testimony on the subject was vehement, they marshaled significant resistance from their allies, and the subsidization program was eventually removed from the bill (with the blessing of many Members of Congress, who argued the provision was a corruption of the GSEs' mission).

The battle was revealing as a parade of Fannie Mae and Freddie Mac allies rose to their defense. The comments submitted by a host of Wall Street investment firms indicated that the profitability node was as significant in the resistance to the affordable housing goals as was safety and soundness. For example, Jonathan Gray, a Sanford Bernstein analyst specializing in GSEs, asked members of the House subcommittee, "how would you feel, placing your money at risk, in a venture whose profits accrue to you only after a third party has extracted an interest, the amount of which interest is subject to change at any time?" (House Housing Subcommittee 1991, 406). Many financial sector participants that depend on Fannie Mae and Freddie Mac to provide a large, lucrative share of their business urged members to recognize the importance of the profitability node. It, they suggested, was crucial to the success of government-sponsored enterprises. Unlike Fannie Mae and Freddie Mac, which, as GSEs, risked offending the public with overt emphasis on profitability, these firms were politically safe to argue from the profitability node and understood that it was in their business interest to support Fannie Mae and Freddie Mac.

The backlash prompted Gonzalez to scrap his proposal and order the GSEs and housing groups to reach a compromise. This proved controversial. In an episode recalled by some participants as a conference and others as an intimidation session, representatives of the affordable housing groups met with representatives of the GSEs and negotiated language that was inserted into the first House bill. The two paragraphs created a weak requirement "that *a reasonable portion of the corporation's mortgage purchases* be related to the national goal of providing adequate housing for low- and moderate-income families, *but with reasonable economic return* to the corporation" (H. R. 2900, September 17, 1991, 20; emphasis added).

Some observers and participants, including Rep. James Leach (R – IA), cried foul and argued that Fannie Mae had bought off the affordable housing groups with financial support donated through its foundation, the Fannie Mae Foundation. Housing groups dependent on the money, it was alleged, were forced to choose between supporting Fannie Mae or sacrificing funds (Zuckman 1991b). In his dissenting views on H. R. 2900 reported out of the House Committee on Banking, Finance and Urban Affairs, Leach expressed his dismay over this phenomenon: "The committee's judgment on the housing provisions of the bill unfortunately was clouded by the endorsement of the approach favored by Fannie and Freddie by a variety of activist consumer groups which without notification to Congress became recipients of substantial contributions from the two GSEs" (House Banking Committee 1991). According to committee staffers, members of the committee chose not to fight for tougher regulations when the affordable housing groups signed off (interviews 95, 100).

The situation was different on the Senate side. A bipartisan group of Senators, of varying ideological backgrounds, called for greater dedication to programmatic goals. Chairman Donald Riegle (D – MI) and Ranking Minority Member Jake Garn both supported more ambitious affordable housing goals. Riegle introduced the Senate bill on the floor, noting that "[HUD regulations] have been too weak and often have not been enforced. So the bill creates better standards with specific enforcement tools that will require the GSEs to increase their efforts to provide financing for those who need it most" (Senate 1992, S8,607). Others, such as Senator Alan Dixon (D – IL), were more strident:

> Congress must send a strong message to the GSEs that they have important public purposes which must be fulfilled. Their responsibilities are not just to their shareholders, who have benefited handsomely from the GSEs' unique relationship to the Federal Government. Their responsibilities are also to the public: to maintain their financial safety, but also to assure that our housing finance markets work for the benefit of all Americans – not just the affluent. (Senate 1992, S8651)

The affordable housing provisions of the bill were solidified and specified, effectively adding enforcement provisions and force of law to existing HUD housing goals.

Fannie Mae and Freddie Mac were reluctant to express opposition to housing goals in principle and, in fact, endorsed the Senate legislation after extensive negotiation. Groups sympathetic to the GSEs resisted the housing goals, testifying that such goals were unnecessary and potentially damaging to the enterprises. As one Treasury staffer who worked on the legislation recalled, "Fannie would make a phone call and all of a sudden fifty letters would arrive on the Hill. And the letters all pretty much looked the same because Fannie would draft it and send it out" (interview 102). Representatives of the National Association of Realtors, the Mortgage Bankers Association and the National Association of Home Builders visited members en masse and warned against the dangers of stretching the GSEs. Overly ambitious housing goals, they claimed, could jeopardize their safety and soundness and cost taxpayers billions.

On this issue, the advocates of safety and soundness were in the swing position. Initially, Treasury resisted the goals, fearing that they might pose a threat to safety and soundness, but this position was never taken publicly. Treasury officials recognized that, without the support of housing interests that demanded the affordable housing goals and, more importantly, the Senators who agreed with them, the bill would never pass and the safety and soundness portion would die with it. Although the Treasury Department's reports on GSE regulation and testimony before Congress made it clear that safety ought to be the paramount regulatory concern, the housing goals could be approved with confidence that safety and soundness would not be jeopardized.

Fannie Mae and Freddie Mac argued that the programmatic goals were poorly defined and difficult to meet, yet they could not attack them on principle. Thus the only mechanism available was to enlist the third node: safety and soundness. Treasury's unwillingness to endorse the argument that safety and soundness was threatened by the affordable housing goals diluted the strength of this approach. The GSEs argued that they were already working to expand lending to low- and moderate-income families, but without the support of the safety and soundness node the GSEs could not eliminate the goals.

The inclusion of affordable housing goals was not an overwhelming defeat of Fannie Mae and Freddie Mac. The deletion of the rent subsidization program demonstrated that Fannie Mae and Freddie Mac *could* influence the crafting of the goals and avoid their most disliked designs when alliances among interests were not formed. The GSEs' political muscle was utilized effectively to mobilize sympathetic interest groups in the housing and financial sectors. As the testimony on the subject of the Affordable Housing Program subsidy indicates, a range of groups lobbied against the requirement. Most importantly, Treasury's antipathy towards this provision was never in doubt. It was dropped from the conference version of the bill.

Furthermore, critics point out that the goals did not force the GSEs to finance significantly higher levels of affordable housing than Fannie Mae was funding at the time of the bill's passage. Also the enforcement mechanisms are either extremely weak or so strong as to be practically unusable. HUD can effectively do little more than admonish the GSEs if they do not meet goals. Finally, HUD may be reluctant to damage the productive working relationship it has established with Fannie Mae and Freddie Mac.

Epilogue It is still too early to pass judgment on the efficacy of the new regulatory regime. OFHEO has finalized and applied the minimum capital standards (both companies have complied) and published the risk-based capital regulation following a contentious period of negotiation and gamesmanship with the GSEs, Congress and the administration (OFHEO 1997, Connor 1999). During the comment period, which closed March 10, 2000, OFHEO received more than two thousand pages of comments from 39 individuals and organizations (interview 102). Even as the regulations neared final approval from the Office of Management and Budget, the GSEs were urging the Bush Administration to delay finalization (Rehm 2001). The new regulations became officially enforceable in the fall of 2002.

The housing goals passed by Congress had a three-part requirement with interim goals in the "low-income", "central cities" and "special affordable" categories. Although there has been some controversy regarding HUD's interpretation of the law, both Fannie Mae and Freddie Mac met most of the interim targets (failing in the central cities category).

HUD published its final regulation raising the target for loans to low- and moderate-income families from 42 percent to 50 percent of loans purchased by the GSEs by 2001 (Day 1999). Despite some misgivings regarding the new objectives, Fannie Mae and Freddie Mac have met the goals. Still, there has been tension between HUD and the GSEs. HUD officials have expressed disappointment with the performance of Fannie Mae and Freddie Mac, particularly in comparison with the FHA (Day 2000a, 2000b). Fannie Mae chairman Franklin Raines responded aggressively in a *Washington Post* opinion article that his company has, in fact, "led the market" in providing financing to low-income and minority home buyers (Raines 2000).

In recent years, there has been quite a bit of discussion regarding reform of the regulatory structure for the GSEs. Led by Congressman Richard Baker (R – LA), chairman of the House committee responsible for Fannie Mae and Freddie Mac, critics of the two companies have argued that OFHEO is not sufficiently strong to rein them in (Garver 2001, Heller 2001, Kulish 2001). It is certain that the GSEs will resist any legislation that, for example, moves regulation to the Treasury Department. Arguments regarding any structural changes – such as arguments against the new capital rules and housing goals – will likely conform to the patterns described in this chapter. The third node – programmatic concerns in the case of safety regulations, financial safety in the case of programmatic regulations – will inevitably be invoked to tilt the scales towards the outcome desired by the GSEs.

Implications

This legislative history of the FHEFSSA indicates the dramatic political consequences that can result from structural variation. That is not to say that in all respects Fannie Mae and Freddie Mac are typical hybrid organizations. Not every hybrid wields the influence that Fannie Mae and Freddie Mac display. The two companies are among the most aggressive and influential organizations in Washington. Still, the story examined is important to this study of hybrid organizations as it provides useful insight into the relationship between an organization's design and its influence on the political system.

The hybrid form creates the potential for political influence by endowing organizations with many of the advantages possessed by private companies and government agencies. In extreme cases, such as this one, the idea of bureaucratic control can be turned on its head. The bureaucratic *agent* may, in fact, be able to influence the *principal.*

Organizational structure as feedback loop

As Terry Moe would expect, interest group influence in the legislative process provides a partial explanation for the creation of a regulatory infrastructure for Fannie Mae and Freddie Mac that is saddled with contradictions and ambiguities (Moe 1989, 1990). In each component of the FHEFSSA, the GSEs were able to dilute or obfuscate the objectives promoted by Members of Congress and the Bush Administration. However, an account that focuses on interest groups glosses over the ability of Fannie Mae and Freddie Mac to shape and manipulate those interest groups' preferences. This suggests the need for refinement of Moe's argument.

The previous section illustrated that the triangular arrangement of interests rewarded actors who maintained alliances between interest group nodes. Fannie Mae and Freddie Mac were able, in the view of first-hand observers, to design their own regulation because they mobilized both eager and reluctant allies, many of whom had little self-interest in helping the GSEs. Models of interest group participation in institution building ought to account for organizations with the ability to manipulate preferences of other groups for their own self-interest. Without accounting for such behavior, organizations may be wrongfully depicted as passive subjects of the governmental process rather than active, perhaps dominant, participants.

In this case, the politics of structure could be represented as a "feedback loop." By exerting influence on the crafting of the FHEFSSA, Fannie Mae and Freddie Mac effectively influenced their own regulatory structure. This, in turn, guaranteed their future influence by building into the new structure congressional review of the regulators' yearly appropriations and ambiguous language that invites dispute. The limits of this loop are unclear. Fannie Mae and Freddie Mac, for example, have agitated for congressional charter amendments to broaden the scope of potential activities. However, this has engendered serious opposition from formidable opponents and the organization of FM Watch, a well-financed entity created by companies concerned about competition from Fannie Mae and Freddie Mac.

With a single case, it is difficult to specify when such feedback loops might arise. Certainly many government agencies also influence the political actors ostensibly overseeing them. However, the structure of government-sponsored enterprises is a key factor explaining the distinguishing influence of Fannie Mae and Freddie Mac. It endows the GSEs with resources for political influence and results in an arrangement of interest groups that allows and rewards strategic manipulation. Although greater specification is required, the point is noteworthy. Like genetic mutations, some hybrid organizations may continue to change – sometimes in ways neither foreseen nor desired by their creators.

Hybrid organizations: out-of-control or self-control?

Lloyd Musolf and Harold Seidman warned that government-sponsored enterprises are governmental institutions beyond the control of government (Musolf and Seidman 1980). This proposition offends ideals of popular sovereignty and government accountability. And while it does appear that principals do exercise some measure of control over Fannie Mae and Freddie Mac, this study suggests a more complicated truth.

The appearance and infrastructure of control may exist, but GSEs have the resources, ability and position effectively to control their own controllers. In a remarkable letter to their colleagues, Representatives J. J. Pickle (D – TX) and Willis Gradison (R – OH), who began the drive toward passage of the FHEFSSA by inserting the GSE report requirement into the savings and loan bill, urged that Fannie Mae's influence be resisted: "We believe that Fannie Mae should not possess a veto over the form of its own supervision. The primary concern of Congress in drafting this legislation should be to protect the taxpayer by requiring all GSEs to be capitalized adequately. Public policy on such a serious issue should not be stalled, perhaps permanently, by lobbying efforts that put the private interest of a single enterprise above the broader public interest" (Pickle and Gradison, 1992). They emphatically concluded, "The time has come to protect the public purse, not Fannie Mae's profits."

The regulatory agencies created by the FHEFSSA have now issued regulations but it is too soon to pass judgment on the new regulatory infrastructure. Even if the current arrangement proves ineffective, one could hardly conclude that these types of hybrids cannot be regulated. Alternative proposals for the regulation of Fannie Mae and Freddie Mac might provide more stringent oversight. For example, a proposed super-regulator for all government-sponsored enterprises might be more independent and less prone to capture than a single-purpose quasi-independent office of HUD (GAO 1997). The more vexing question is whether implementation of such a scheme is theoretically possible given the power of the GSEs.

Thus, this case provides a crucial lesson for those considering creation of hybrid organizations to address public policy needs – a lesson echoing the sentiments of David Truman. "Although the effect of structural arrangements is not always what its designers intended," Truman observed, "these formalities are rarely neutral" (1993, 322). Few would have anticipated that Fannie Mae and Freddie Mac would grow into political heavyweights; now they are dominant players in American housing. Designers of future hybrids should not be surprised if hybrid organizations acquire unusual political influence due to their unique combination of public- and private-sector advantages.

6

The limits of congressional control: agent structure as constraint

Successful congressional control is more elusive with respect to hybrid organizations than to traditional government agencies. The difference is a function of the interaction between the prerequisites of effective oversight and the organizational structure of hybrids. There is no indication that this outcome was intended; nor does it appear to satisfy the preferences of any enacting coalition. It is, it seems, an unforeseen consequence of the turn to quasi-government.

Whether one envisages Congress in a purely altruistic fashion, with Members seeking only the greatest public good for the nation as a whole, or as a collection of individuals with an overriding self-interest in re-election, the ability to compel bureaucratic agents to satisfy preferences is critical. Without effective oversight, the capacity of Congress to govern is reduced.

For any Congress the prerequisites of control are the same. Congress requires the timely acquisition of data regarding performance, regular opportunities for review, unlimited access to information and the power to shape and reshape the legislation governing the budget, priorities and operations of the overseen entity. This chapter explains why key features of hybrid organizations blunt the tools utilized by Congress to satisfy these requirements.

Tools of congressional control

Congress has multiple tools available to control its bureaucratic agents. Of course, it has the power to rewrite law thus altering the structure of agents as well as the procedural requirements with which they must comply and the substantive ends they are charged with achieving. Congress also carries out regular oversight of its agents. This involves the collection of information, hearings, inquiries and constituent-related casework. A review of these tools, described briefly in chapter 3, sets the stage for discussion of the control challenges posed by hybrid organizations.

Legislation

Congress can alter the structure, powers and status of any federal entity. The restructuring or creation of new organizations is not a costless, predictable process. To accomplish direction (or redirection) by legislation involves numerous treacherous steps, each requiring negotiation and compromise. Most problematically, the ability of any Member or group of Members to control the outcome of a legislative initiative is quite limited. Thus, as a tool, legislation is difficult to wield (Dodd and Schott 1979).

Congress attempts to effect control through legislation pertaining to the structure, substantive purpose and authority of bureaucratic organizations (Ripley and Franklin 1980). A structural constraint, for example, is a requirement that leadership include representation of particular interest groups (Seidman and Gilmour 1986, 305–308). Procedural constraints include guaranteed opportunities for judicial review, requirements for congressional review of proposed regulations and mandatory waiting periods before decisive action (McCubbins, Noll and Weingast 1987).

Oversight

Non-legislative tools of congressional control are here lumped into the broad category called oversight. These tools are used every day and do not require the same expenditure of resources required to achieve control by initiating and managing the process of passing new legislation. Thus, as a practical matter, oversight is a more accessible mechanism for control, available to individual Members and Congress as a whole.

Budget process The cornerstone of congressional oversight is the budget process in general and the authorization and appropriations processes in particular. The budget process is included in the oversight category (despite the obvious fact that budgets are, of course, legislative) because it is part of the day-to-day activities of Congress. It is not an extraordinary event and thus Members need not expend any resources to initiate this activity even though they still must expend resources to achieve their objectives. Some agencies require periodic reauthorization, giving Members an opportunity to threaten the entity's existence without passing a piece of legislation.

The annual budget process allocates financial resources for the coming budget year. It also provides a forum for members to question representatives of federal agencies and gather detailed information regarding previous performance, allocation of resources, current activities, future objectives, etc. Members have the opportunity to make clear – in both a formal and informal manner – their preferences regarding the activities of the agency under review. Thus, the budget process not only shapes the mission of executive agencies, it maintains linkages between Congress and the bureaucracy and gives Congress an opportunity to signal its expectations (Wildavsky 1992).

Hearings Congressional hearings fall into two categories: periodic and timely. Periodic hearings are most frequently associated with the budgetary and appropriations process described above. There are also perennial issues that get attention on a regular basis (e.g., human rights violations in China). In the Senate, review of presidential nominations produces a regular stream of hearings related to almost every federal entity.

Timely hearings are typically held in response to a developing or pressing policy matter (e.g., television violence, Internet crime, Enron) or pending legislation. Both types of hearings provide opportunities for Members to state their preferences and their evaluation of current agency performance. When testifying before congressional committees, bureaucrats also can express their concerns about the obstacles they are encountering and the limitations under which their agencies must operate.

Reporting Congressional oversight generates an ocean of paper in the form of reports. Agencies prepare annual reports to Congress that require the collection and organization of data. There is also a wide range of reports required by various management statutes. Perhaps the most significant new report requirement is that created by the Government Performance and Results Act, passed in 1993. GPRA obliges every federal agency to develop a set of goals with measures and annually report on their achievement.

Congressional agencies such as the General Accounting Office and the Congressional Budget Office also conduct regular studies of federal agencies (many agencies are by statute subject to periodic examination by the GAO) in addition to the irregular reports ordered by Congressional committees or individual Members. Even if read by a small audience, these reports keep federal agencies aware of congressional interest and represent a means by which Congress reminds executive branch personnel that it is watching (Mosher 1979, Weiss, Gruber and Carver 1989).

Constituent service Constituent service provides another opportunity for Members to reinforce their oversight role. Congressional staff interact regularly with federal bureaucrats on behalf of constituents who are experiencing difficulty of some sort. Such "casework" not only benefits the constituent (and, by extension, the Member, for whom the assisted constituent is likely to vote), it keeps Congress informed regarding the performance of key constituent-related agencies (Fenno 1978). It also provides Members an opportunity to communicate preferences to agencies (Balla 2000).

Interest groups Congress relies upon the large community of interest groups that monitor the activities of federal agencies to report difficulties, areas of concern and other developments to Members and their staff. This informal network of overseers allows any Member of Congress to direct attention to oversight at critical moments when his or her interests (personal or political) are in jeopardy. Thus, interest groups are effectively a set of "fire alarms" that supplement the congressional "police patrols" of regular hearings and reports (McCubbins and Schwartz 1984).

Interest groups can also help Congress compensate for the information asymmetries that exist with government bureaucracies. Interest groups collect and gather data that can be useful to Members interested in evaluating the claims of agencies without relying upon information produced by the agency under review.

Hybrids are more difficult to control than agencies

This study of hybrids and agencies in three policy areas revealed that hybrid organizations are less likely than traditional government agencies to satisfy congressional preferences. A brief review of the findings presented in chapters 3 and 4 serves as a precursor to this discussion of the relationship between hybrid structure and reduced congressional control.

Housing Fannie Mae and Freddie Mac appear less responsive than HUD to congressional desire for more home lending in low- and moderate-income communities. Following a lengthy battle, Congress passed legislation in 1992 that created a new regulatory infrastructure for Fannie Mae and Freddie Mac (see chapter 5). Congress divided regulatory responsibility between HUD and a new semi-independent agency, the Office of Federal Housing Enterprise Oversight. HUD's responsibility is programmatic regulation intended to guarantee that the two GSEs serve neglected communities. OFHEO is responsible for regulation of the GSEs' financial safety and soundness.

Although Fannie Mae and Freddie Mac increased their allocation of credit to low-income borrowers following the clear statement of preferences by Congress and the President, their improvement did not match HUD's performance. The differences in performance for the housing organizations are detailed in chapter 4. Moreover, Fannie Mae and Freddie Mac have both resisted the efforts of Members of Congress and the administration to raise the levels of expected performance while HUD embraced the objectives (Nitschke 1998).

The safety and soundness regulation performed by OFHEO has been more effective. Both Fannie Mae and Freddie Mac have met the minimum capital requirements (largely spelled out in the 1992 legislation). As OFHEO prepared the final risk-based capital regulation, tensions increased between the regulator and GSEs. The companies publicly criticized the agency's rule-making process and actively lobbied Congress for relief. Still, Fannie Mae and Freddie Mac moved to meet the capital requirements stipulated by OFHEO's regulation just as they did with respect to the programmatic goals.

Export promotion The Department of Commerce and two government corporations, the Export-Import Bank and the Overseas Private Investment Corporation, carry out different activities aimed at increasing international activity of American business with the ultimate objective of creating (or protecting) jobs domestically. The responses of these three organizations to four policy preferences – cessation of trade promotion activities in China following the Tiananmen Square massacre, emphasis on environmental technology exports, emphasis on small business exports and emphasis on exports to Africa – were compared.

The record shows that the sanctions desired by Congress against China were indeed imposed by all three agents. The Commerce Department curtailed activities in China and overall exports to the country declined following implementation of the sanctions. OPIC activity in China was curtailed quite dramatically (see figure 4.1). ExIm's total authorization for exports to China were down to nearly zero percent by 1991 (figure 4.2).

But this highly visible preference proved to be more the exception than the rule. When President Clinton took office, he and his appointees declared a desire to promote small business, environmental technology and African markets, all previously neglected by export promotion agencies (Bradsher 1993, Beamish and Lane 1993, TPCC 1997). Members of Congress and, more importantly, the relevant oversight committees endorsed all three of these preferences. In fact, Congress passed legislation intended to bolster the export promotion efforts consistent with the President's objectives.

With respect to all three preferences the Department of Commerce was more responsive than ExIm or OPIC. In the years following Clinton's inauguration, the Department of Commerce, under the leadership of Secretary Ron Brown, worked aggressively to emphasize environmental technology, Africa and small business in export promotion. Commerce staff attributed this dedication to the close relationship between Brown and senior White House staff, including the President (interview 47).

In the area of environmental technology this paid noticeable dividends. American environmental technology exports have increased from $9.4 billion to $22.4 billion (figure 4.4) as the market for environmental technology has expanded. The American share of the non-US market has increased from 3.6 percent to 6.9 percent during the same period (figure 4.4). Neither ExIm nor OPIC has registered significant improvement in the area of environmental technology. Even the apparent increase in ExIm activity can be accounted for (according to ExIm officials) by the refinement of measurement (interviews 37, 78). (See the more detailed discussion of export promotion activities in chapter 4.)

According to interview subjects within and outside the organization, the Department of Commerce has devoted energy and attention to improvement of exports to Africa and from small businesses (interviews 46, 48, 55, 56). However, there is little evidence of increases in exports in either category (figure 4.3). The two hybrids examined also claimed an increased dedication to these objectives (with the stronger case being made with respect to Africa) but have little to show for it.

International market development Two sets of government-backed venture capital funds – Enterprise Funds and OPIC investment funds – were compared with some reference to the US Agency for International Development. Both programs consist of multiple funds; USAID oversees the Enterprise Funds and OPIC runs its investment funds program.

The most obvious congressional preference expressed regarding both sets of venture capital funds is the prevention of financial malfeasance. There are opportunities for each fund to squander resources (both by intention and incompetence) that could prove embarrassing to Members of Congress and a waste of public resources. Rep. David Obey's investigation of misuse of funds by the Hungarian American Enterprise Fund led to changes in the management of the Enterprise Fund program. USAID overseers, caught off guard by the controversy, pressured the Funds to submit to more meaningful supervision, including more required reports and the possibility of investigation by the USAID Inspector General (interviews 19, 13). Thus the preferences for better reporting and oversight have been gradually satisfied despite the persistence of problems such as petty theft (revealed in Enterprise Fund reports to USAID). The OPIC investment funds seem to have done a good job policing the management of the investment funds. This is aided by the supervision of private investors in the funds.

Congress has had some success in placing substantive restrictions on fund investments. For example, both sets of funds are prohibited from investing in companies that produce armaments. More conventional American aid programs, such as those funded by USAID, also comply with such constraints.

Congress has had less success with goals articulated in legislation singling out certain types of investments for emphasis by the Enterprise Funds. This includes emphasis on a particular sector of the economy, a particular region or a particular type of business. This is discussed in greater detail in chapter 3.

The same limitation exists for the OPIC investment fund program. The West Bank and Gaza investment fund created by OPIC at Congress' behest had a difficult time raising capital and identifying investment (US State Department 1999). Fearing a similar outcome, OPIC has resisted for years pressure from the chairman of their oversight committee to create an investment fund dedicated to maritime construction industries (interviews 31, 28, 23).

Challenges posed by hybrid structure[6]

Despite the heterogeneity of hybrid organizations, observation of this diverse group reveals complications for congressional oversight that are linked to the hybrid structure. First, measuring the costs and benefits of hybrid activities is particularly difficult. Second, the off-budget status of some hybrids increases the cost of carrying out congressional oversight. Third, the necessity of using intermediaries to monitor and regulate hybrids adds complexity to the oversight process. Fourth, the conflict among the goals of hybrid organizations creates unique control challenges. Finally, some hybrids possess resources that allow them to influence Congress and limit oversight.

None of the general challenges to congressional control are unique to hybrids. Still, the obstacles tend to be more profound in their case.

Uncertainty in evaluating costs and benefits

Analysis of the costs and benefits of the programs carried out by government bureaucracies is central to congressional oversight and control. Thus the difficulty in estimating costs and benefits associated with hybrids and their activities is particularly problematic. The indirect method by which many hybrids receive public resources to carry out congressional objectives creates this complication. Although traditional government programs also have uncertainty associated with their attainment of congressional goals, the degree of uncertainty is higher and more intractable for hybrids.

---

[6] This section draws upon a paper co-authored with Ron Feldman, "Congressional oversight of Fannie Mae and Freddie Mac: does their GSE structure matter?" presented at the American Enterprise Institute (Feldman and Koppell 1999).

Uncertain costs In order to maintain control over hybrid organizations, Congress needs to determine the total cost of relying upon these agents. This requires calculating any direct appropriations, the size and beneficiaries of any subsidies that pass through the hybrid and the probability and expected cost of bailing out a hybrid in the event of failure. Of course, Congress performs similar analysis of government agencies (particularly focusing on outlays).

Outlays can be known with a degree of certainty (at least retrospectively) but analysts cannot determine a hybrid's subsidies or potential losses with a high degree of confidence. Without certainty regarding the cost of a particular program, Congress cannot formulate appropriate demands or even assess whether the benefits produced by that organization justify its existence.

Subsidy costs. Techniques used to estimate the size of the subsidy received by hybrids produce results with a high degree of uncertainty and sensitivity (Feldman 1999). For example, Fannie Mae and Freddie Mac receive a large subsidy in the form of their "agency status," which allows them to borrow at rates preferable to the most highly rated companies. To determine the economic advantage of agency status (i.e., the net reduction in borrowing costs) analysts compare the yields on Fannie Mae and Freddie Mac debt to yields on debt with similar characteristics – except for GSE status. The problem is that there are very few legitimate comparisons available, and even these cases present differences other than the borrowing organization's legal status.[7] Even the Treasury Department conceded that its calculations give only a "rough estimate" of the financial benefit of GSE status (US Department of the Treasury 1996, 32).

The cost of a subsidy is critical information for Congress. Without reliable estimates of the costs of supporting Fannie Mae and Freddie Mac, Congress has difficulty formulating proportionate demands. The GSEs are able to blunt calls for higher levels of programmatic performance by contesting the estimates put forth by government agencies and offering lower estimates of the subsidy. For example, the Congressional Budget Office published an estimate of the federal subsidy to the GSEs that prompted criticism from Fannie Mae. CBO director Dan Crippen accused Fannie Mae of making "misleading" claims in response to his agency's argument that the GSEs retained some $3.9 billion of the federal subsidy – estimated at $10.6 billion – they received in 2000 (Connor 2001).

---

[7] The total subsidy received by a GSE exceeds the reduction in borrowing costs it receives. In addition, there are usually tax advantages as well as exemptions from certain fees (e.g., registration fees). Moreover, federal sponsorship also allows, for example, the GSEs to issue certain types of debt in amounts that a purely private organization could not. Finally, GSE debt can be purchased by organizations that are restricted to government markets.

Determining the "value" of government-guaranteed loans to OPIC's investment funds can be equally tricky. The guaranteed loans are used to attract private capital and provide "leverage" so that the return on a dollar invested reflects the return on two dollars of capital. The value of this subsidy to the investor cannot be known until the fund is completely invested and dissolved. It depends entirely on the fund's performance. Thus Congress cannot reliably know whether it is "getting enough" in return for the advantage it is bestowing upon private market participants who are profiting with the assistance of government-guaranteed loans.

Bailout costs. Estimates of the likelihood and size of a bailout of a hybrid are crucial. A bailout can cost millions, even billions of dollars. It would require funding cuts in other areas and it would tar the reputations of Members running for re-election. This reality was underscored by the savings and loan crisis and subsequent bailout.

The seemingly harmless guarantee extended by the Federal Home Loan Bank Board to the thousands of customers who entrusted their savings to poorly managed savings and loan associations ballooned into hundreds of millions of dollars in real federal outlays (Kane 1989). Tellingly, there is still no agreed-upon price tag for the bailout. As a consequence of this mess, attention turned to the huge liability created by the government's implicit backing of Fannie Mae and Freddie Mac.

Estimating the likelihood of a bailout of the two GSEs is an inherently difficult task. The implicit (or explicit) guarantee on a hybrid's debt ensures that its pricing will not accurately reflect the risks being incurred. That is, the usual measure of an organization's creditworthiness, the market-determined rate charged on that organization's debt, is not reliable in the case of hybrids precisely because of the government guarantee. Thus alternative approaches are required.

The risk-based stress test to be applied to Fannie Mae and Freddie Mac as per the 1992 law estimates the capital required to withstand a financial calamity but it is based on extrapolations from historic data. This approach has been criticized by Fannie Mae and Freddie Mac for its complexity and underlying assumptions (Collins 1999). Indeed, determining what a reasonable model of financial market behavior is during events that have a low probability of ever occurring is quite difficult (Kupiec 1995).

Smaller, privately held entities such as the government-backed venture capital funds are even more difficult to assess. First, the risk is spread out among many organizations, raising monitoring costs significantly. Second, overseers would have to acquaint themselves with the business models of each firm to assess that organization's risk management adequately. This would be extraordinarily time-consuming and, given limited resources, not worth the effort.

Government corporations are subject to the Credit Reform Act, which establishes a baseline accounting standard for their risk. Still, that is primarily an accounting tool, providing a means to "score" loan guarantees on the budget rather than an evaluation of the underlying risk associated with particular products on a hybrid's total book of business (Meyers 1988). The risk of failure and resulting costs of a bailout are essentially unknown.

Certain and uncertain benefits Determining the benefits provided by hybrid organizations can be as difficult as determining the costs. For example, Fannie Mae and Freddie Mac have admitted that calculating the amount by which they reduce mortgage costs is "more art than science" (Cotterman and Pearce 1996, 155). It is also quite difficult to determine how many more members of a targeted group (e.g., racial minorities or central city dwellers) are able to purchase a house because of Fannie Mae and Freddie Mac's activities. This effort requires estimates of homeownership costs, the relationship between the cost of homeownerhip and the demand for housing, and rates of homeownership more generally (assuming that Fannie Mae and Freddie Mac did not exist).

Recent econometric analysis of a similar question found that such estimates are "not precise" because of the assumptions required (Wachter et al. 1996, 355). Without a grasp on such benefits, Congress is unable to determine if Fannie Mae and Freddie Mac are meeting goals of improving housing opportunities that are proportionate to the benefits the companies receive by virtue of their GSE status. Indirect forms of oversight do not help Congress in the case of Fannie Mae, Freddie Mac or most hybrids. Hybrids are often one or two stages removed from the constituent's experience. Thus constituent feedback does not help Congress gauge the benefits of Fannie Mae and Freddie Mac because the companies' behind-the-scenes role is inscrutable to most consumers.

This problem is common across hybrid forms. The venture capital funds were created with the difficult-to-measure goal of contributing to the development of market-based economies in post-communist and developing countries. Assessing the general development of a market economy is difficult. Characterizing the contribution of one venture capital firm is almost impossible. As a result, focus has turned to financial performance. This is easier to measure but skews the organizational objectives of the Enterprise Funds. Generating substantial return on capital may require an investment strategy that does not maximize the developmental impact of the fund (see "Conflict among goals" below).

In general, Congress' difficulties in ascertaining the costs and benefits hinders its control by leaving the principal without the information necessary to determine if preferences are being satisfied. On the other hand,

Congress could realize an *advantage* from uncertainty concerning hybrids' costs and benefits. If Congress were receiving political advantages from a high-cost program with limited public benefit, ambiguity would certainly be preferable. Members might also prefer to obscure the costs of a program they supported as a means of minimizing electoral penalties in the event of failure.

Off-budget status

Many hybrids are "off-budget." That is, their expenditures (and revenues) are not included in the annual calculation of the federal budget. This is one of the attractions of the hybrid model for Congress; moving a hybrid off-budget creates opportunities for spending in other areas. But the decision to move a hybrid off-budget raises the costs of congressional oversight in at least two ways. First, it reduces the information flow and financial control available to Congress. Second, it prevents Congress from benefiting from economies of scope that it enjoys monitoring other governmental organizations.

Fannie Mae and Freddie Mac were the only off-budget hybrids that received significant attention as part of this study. Thus the following observations regarding the implications of this organizational attribute are based largely on these two organizations.

Financial autonomy   The off-budget status of Fannie Mae and Freddie Mac deprives Congress of the benefits of the budget process (e.g., the information and control already discussed).[8] In fact, it is Fannie Mae and Freddie Mac that control the amount of public resources they consume, by adjusting, for example, the amount of risk they assume (CBO 1996). This results from the circuitous method by which Fannie Mae and Freddie Mac receive and redistribute their public support.

Recall that the primary subsidy enjoyed by Fannie Mae and Freddie Mac is their preferential borrowing status. This provides the companies

---

[8] Although the budget is required to include analysis of the financial condition of the GSEs and the exposure they create for the federal government, the quality of this analysis varies. The FY 2000 budget does not provide an empirically based estimate of the risk and potential GSE costs to the government. The detailed financial data and description of the GSEs is received from the GSEs and put into the budget document without review (Feldman and Koppell 1999). See "Analytical perspectives," *Budget of the United States government,* FY 2000, pages 188–189 and page 202, as well as pages 1,227 through 1,238 of the *Budget appendix of the United States government FY 2000.* In contrast, the FY 1992 budget reported the results of a stress test conducted by budget staff and discussed the total subsidy transmitted to the housing GSEs (*Budget of the United States government,* FY 1992, page 229), while the FY 1993 budget estimated the government's exposure via an options pricing model (*Budget of the United States government,* FY 1993, pages 268 and 279).

with relatively inexpensive capital. The question, then, is how much of the "savings" resulting from the GSEs' preferential borrowing status is passed on to American homebuyers. The answer is determined not by Congress but by Fannie Mae and Freddie Mac. Thus, in a very real sense, each company determines its own subsidy. This is inherent in the structure of these two government-sponsored enterprises.

Higher monitoring costs There are fixed costs for a congressional committee or Member to become involved in the budgeting process. They must develop a level of expertise for their area of responsibility and establish relationships with various stakeholders in the programs under review. They must also become proficient in the appropriate congressional rules and procedures and develop systems for receiving and analyzing data in their area of interest. In addition, the budget process provides opportunities for interest groups in a particular policy area with a regular method for interacting with Congress. Those involved with the budget process can conduct additional monitoring or review with minimal additional cost after this initial investment. Of course, attempting to *alter* the budget in a manner to suit personal preferences requires significant allocation of resources.

A committee or Member interested in the oversight of an off-budget hybrid such as Fannie Mae or Freddie Mac cannot exploit the cost advantage of regularly scheduled budget-related hearings. Any attempt at monitoring an off-budget hybrid requires initiation of proceedings for that purpose alone. Scholars have found that, when the costs of gathering information are higher, principals enjoy less control (Banks and Weingast 1992). Similarly, those affected by Fannie Mae and Freddie Mac's activities do not have routine opportunities to engage Congress, thereby raising *their* cost of congressional interaction. In theory, this problem is mitigated by budgetary hearings of the hybrids' regulators as well as the oversight agenda of the committees with legislative jurisdiction. But this oversight is indirect and, in practice, the focus is frequently shifted from the GSEs to the regulator. Indeed, OFHEO is lobbying Congress to exempt the agency from the appropriations process, as bank regulatory agencies are (Julavits 2000, OFHEO 2002).

Benefits of off-budget status across programs Congress may be willing to give up control and oversight in exchange for the federal spending made possible by shifting some programs off-budget. The activities of Fannie Mae and Freddie Mac that benefit Congress directly (including ample campaign contributions from GSE executives and post-political employment opportunities with the two high-paying companies) might also receive less scrutiny under the off-budget regime. Also the semi-private status of the GSEs provides Congress with "plausible deniability" in the event of failure.

There are other programs where Congress receives less than full information or control via the budget process. Entitlement and insurance programs provide limited and sometimes misleading information that hinders congressional control. However, in both of these cases the budget provides more oversight, and considerable resources are currently devoted to analyzing and improving budgetary treatments. Even tax expenditures, which escape all form of budgetary control, are included as substantive informational items in the budget. Fannie Mae and Freddie Mac are extreme cases where the budget provides a limited sense of the federal resources they consume. Most hybrids are closer to government agencies in terms of budget treatment.

Use of agents

Congress often relies on executive branch organizations to monitor government agencies and hybrids. These regulatory agencies are, in turn, overseen by Congress. For example, the Occupational Safety and Health Administration examines the behavior of other federal agencies (and private companies) for violations of workplace safety rules. Thus, Congress is made aware of safety problems in the agencies it oversees.

In rare cases, however, Congress has created agencies dedicated to the oversight of another creature of the government, often a hybrid. The Farm Credit Administration, for example, oversees the Farm Credit system and "Farmer Mac" – GSEs that provide loans to farmers and agricultural enterprises. The Office of Federal Housing Enterprise Oversight was created to regulate the safety and soundness of Fannie Mae and Freddie Mac.

The delegation of monitoring to agents does not indicate a lack of congressional interest in hybrids but it does introduce an additional level of complexity in oversight. The regulator may have incentives to engage in behavior that runs counter to congressional desires. The Department of Housing and Urban Development, for example, which also has regulatory responsibility for Fannie Mae and Freddie Mac, may not be eager to challenge the two companies because HUD frequently relies upon the two companies in programmatic partnerships. This dynamic did affect the rule-making process at HUD (interviews 82, 85).

Even when the regulatory agency enjoys some independence within the executive branch, reliance on such an agent increases the potential involvement of the administration. This may undermine the pursuit of preferences articulated by Congress. Thus, the principal and agent problems that Congress faces with regard to hybrid organizations also hold true for the regulators. This is a second principal-agent problem embedded within a principal-agent problem; it is explored more deeply in the next chapter.

There can also be problems of transparency introduced by inserting a regulatory agent between Congress and the hybrid. While OPIC collects information from the investment funds it supervises, it is reluctant to share that information, even with Members of Congress. In this case, OPIC argues that divulging most information regarding the funds would violate their legal obligation to keep business secrets private (interviews 87, 88, 89). While members who press OPIC for information are eventually satisfied, the resistance increases the costs of information.

The use of agents, as with all the other challenges discussed, could also serve to further certain congressional objectives. In particular, the existence of the regulator allows Congress to assign blame to it even for actions that Congress took in the first place, while allowing Congress to take credit for safeguarding public funds. OFHEO, for example, has been blamed for aspects of its stress test that were mandated by Congress. USAID was blamed for problems experienced by Enterprise Funds. Additionally, the creation of a regulator creates opportunities for Congress to satisfy interest group demands by directing the regulator to do something. For example, members of Congress can earn the gratitude of Fannie Mae and Freddie Mac by "calling off" OFHEO or HUD.

Conflict among goals

A central challenge for Congress is reconciliation of conflict among the multiple goals pursued simultaneously by hybrid organizations. It is not unusual for Congress to have contradictory public policy objectives. For example, the federal government spends millions of dollars on anti-smoking campaigns while subsidizing tobacco growers. But Congress generally assigns contradictory missions to separate agencies. For example, one agency tries to maximize high-tech exports while another limits such activity for security reasons. Hybrids are unique inasmuch as they usually have multiple, internally conflicting objectives.

Programmatic objectives The hybrids studied were created to perform different policy functions. Fannie Mae and Freddie Mac were created in part to bring liquidity, stability and improved spatial allocation of credit to residential mortgage markets. The United States Export-Import Bank was designed to facilitate American exports by guaranteeing loans to foreign purchasers of American goods. The Overseas Private Investment Corporation was established as a separate entity outside the US Agency for International Development to develop markets for American goods abroad. The two sets of government-backed venture capital funds studied (Enterprise Funds and

OPIC investment funds) were created to facilitate the development of stable, liquid markets in less developed countries.

Often the organizational objectives of hybrids, like government agencies, evolve over time. This has been the case with the hybrids examined in this study. Fannie Mae and Freddie Mac, for example, have in recent years been directed to focus on segments of the market underserved by private lenders. This is, in part, a function of the organizations' successful development of a robust secondary mortgage market that serves middle-class Americans well. In many cases, however, there is disagreement regarding the appropriate substantive mission of hybrids.

Safety and soundness   Every year federal revenues (tax receipts, fees, debt) are allocated to federal programs and agencies. Some hybrids receive appropriations as part of this process. However, many hybrids operate not on appropriated dollars but on funds generated through their own activities, including fees for services and/or debt. By incurring financial obligations, these hybrids thus create a financial liability: a risk to which the federal government is exposed. Thus Congress has an interest in ensuring that this risk does not translate into real losses by monitoring the financial safety and soundness of hybrid organizations.

One of the challenges in maintaining safety and soundness is the problem of moral hazard. That is, under circumstances where the party bearing risk is not the party managing risk, there is an increased danger that the risk of financial loss will be greater (particularly if the amount of risk is inversely related to profitability, as is often the case). The government's guarantee of Fannie Mae and Freddie Mac securities in a sense encourages the two companies to take on more risk than they would otherwise (Weicher 1999). The significance of this off-budget liability and moral hazard problem was underscored for Congress by the savings and loan crisis (Kane 1989).

Thus Congress has a significant interest in the financial health and risk management practices of hybrids. It has expressed such interest through, for example, charter limits on their activities (e.g., on the loan-to-value ratio of mortgages they can finance). This concern is not limited to profit-seeking hybrids such as Fannie Mae and the OPIC investment funds. Government corporations, which are not profit-seeking, create a significant financial liability for the federal government by virtue of the explicit federal guarantee on their debt securities.

Profitability   Profit-seeking hybrids are in business to make money. Indeed, the goal of earning an economic return is enshrined in the GSEs' charters (12 USC 1716). The compensation of a profit-seeking hybrids' management is, at least in part, a function of stock performance (or asset valuation), giving them a strong incentive to operate the firms in a manner which maximizes profits.

While not directly concerned with the profitability of any hybrid, Congress must consider profitability when it reviews hybrid behavior. Investors who have placed their capital in the hands of hybrids with the expectation of profitability would have a legitimate grievance if Congress were to saddle the organization with obligations that made profitability impossible. The need for profitability constrains the degree to which hybrids can pursue competing public policy objectives.

Even hybrids that are not profit-seeking face similar pressure to cover expenses with self-generated revenue. Government corporations, for example, are expected to break even and risk severe criticism in the event of failure. Moreover, the federal government depends on the revenue generated by some hybrids; thus, meeting the bottom line is of more than cosmetic significance.

Unfair competition Hybrid organizations generally participate in private market places. Because their governmental connections endow them with business advantages, the scope of hybrids' mission is a sensitive concern. A subsidy to a hybrid that permits this organization to serve a market ignored by companies with traditional sources of financing could also permit that hybrid to underprice existing businesses in other areas.

The definition of markets that are fair and unfair game for hybrids has proven tricky. Congress sought to protect firms without government sponsorship from competing with Fannie Mae and Freddie Mac, for example, by prohibiting the GSEs from originating mortgages. But both companies have edged ever closer to this activity through technological innovations, which have aroused fears in the mortgage industry.

Conflict and control The conflicting nature of hybrid objectives complicates congressional control by making it difficult to set coherent goals and evaluate performance. Defining the "bottom line" for a mix of trade-offs among goals poses a very serious challenge for Members of Congress, and an "out" for the agent when any preference appears to be unsatisfied. Although many government agencies have multiple programmatic objectives that may compete for resources within the organization, they are rarely at functional odds.

This is certainly the case with the GSEs studied. Both Fannie Mae and Freddie Mac argue that they have done as much as possible to meet Congress' goal of increased availability of credit in underserved areas. Doing more, they argue, would conflict with Congress' *other* goal of maintaining financial safety and soundness. And, usually argued *sotto voce*, the profitability of the two corporations could also be threatened, undermining the confidence of shareholders and purchasers of debt. As discussed previously, assessment of such claims is somewhat subjective and thus difficult to rebut.

The same dynamic accounts for the control difficulties with respect to the government corporations. Both ExIm and OPIC are reluctant to increase risk exposure because Congress has made its preference for less risk clear. The imperative to increase exports to markets in Africa, for example, may be at odds with this goal. Similarly, promotion of exports from small businesses requires greater expenditure of resources for every loan dollar guaranteed. Thus, emphasis on this objective would negatively affect the ability of the two government corporations to "break even."

Although not as powerful as the profit motive, the pressure for hybrid organizations to break even is significant. This objective is enshrined in OPIC's charter (22 USC §2,191(a)) and it motivates the leadership of most hybrids. For example, following the success of the Polish American Enterprise Fund, other Enterprise Funds endeavored to find investments that would return enough money for them eventually to repay their total appropriated capital. To date, no Fund other than the PAEF is in that position. Still, this objective has, by all accounts, slowed the flow of capital into businesses despite the fact that many of the Enterprise Fund program originators say they never had any intention of getting a return on the funds (interviews 80, 8). As a consequence, the Funds resist preferences they fear will damage the bottom line.

Compounding the inherent conflict among goals is their vagueness. The CBO noted that tasks such as "responding appropriately to the private capital market [were] subject to such varieties of interpretation and reinterpretation that it is difficult to determine if and when they have been met" (CBO 1996, 34). Even the clearest-sounding preferences leave gray area. As noted above, Congress clearly prohibited both Fannie Mae and Freddie Mac from originating mortgages. But both GSEs have extensive "automated underwriting" programs that shift some activities of mortgage originators, and presumably their profits, to Fannie Mae and Freddie Mac (OFHEO 1995, 5). The companies argue that automated underwriting is crucial to meeting programmatic objectives by reducing costs paid by homebuyers.

Assigning hybrid organization contradictory objectives *does* serve congressional objectives in at least one respect. Multiple goals allow Congress to receive credit for favorable activities when those objectives are achieved (e.g., increased homeownership) and provide cover when outcomes are less attractive (e.g., protecting the US Treasury from unmanaged risk).

Hybrids and the politics of oversight

Hybrids can be politically powerful players in their own right. The GSE form, for example, gives Fannie Mae and Freddie Mac a unique combination of resources – both public and private – and an extremely strong incentive to influence congressional oversight (see chapter 5). At the same time, and as is the case with many other federal programs, the diffuse nature of GSE costs has traditionally provided little rationale for others to call for enhanced GSE oversight.

Fannie Mae and Freddie Mac have more political resources than are available to a purely private firm or to government agencies. These resources include money, activity in almost every congressional district, the ability to hire former Members and congressional staff at relatively high salaries, and a host of private-sector firms with similarly aligned interests. They also have access to public resources, including the goodwill associated with carrying out pro-housing activities and expertise in government procedures, policies and personnel with regard to housing.

At the same time, Fannie Mae and Freddie Mac have an extremely strong incentive to use these resources to influence congressional behavior. Not surprisingly, stockholders place great importance on the public support for the agencies. A roughly 10 percent recent decline in the GSEs' stock price was attributed to "higher political risk" (Brockman 1999a).

This combination of resources and incentives has led several observers to argue that Fannie Mae and Freddie Mac are able to exert unusually significant influence on the nature of congressional oversight. Government agencies obviously also interact with Congress to reduce oversight that they find detrimental. However, these agencies cannot bring the same resources to bear as Fannie Mae and Freddie Mac. They do not have the financial wherewithal of the GSEs or the legal right to lobby Congress independent of the administration.

The resources available to Fannie Mae and Freddie Mac may present Members of Congress with an opportunity to maximize personal gain. Members have been known to ring the bells of Fannie Mae and Freddie Mac staff when looking for contributions. The fund-raising chief for Senate candidates of one party, for example, was reported to have asked the GSEs to increase their financial contributions during a time of congressional hearings on privatizing Fannie Mae and Freddie Mac (Prakash 1996).

While hybrids may have resources and incentives to influence congressional oversight, the diffuse and obscure nature of their public support reduces the incentive that others have to challenge them. The cost to a taxpayer to examine GSE public support is greater than the "extra" tax she would have to pay in the event of a government bailout. The nature of

Fannie Mae and Freddie Mac's activities – a step removed from the ordinary homebuyer – also makes the chances of a constituent complaint remote.

Diffusion of costs characterizes many federal programs but the lack of routine financial reporting on subsides and the absence of other tools of routine oversight, for example, raise any citizen's costs of getting involved and mobilizing support for additional oversight.

Costs can, of course, change over time. The savings and loan crisis increased the perceived risk of GSE failure sufficiently to make regulatory reform possible notwithstanding Fannie Mae and Freddie Mac's political influence. If a hybrid's activity threatened a defined group rather than being spread across all taxpayers, that group would have the incentive to monitor and resist the GSEs. The recent increase in complaints about the GSEs' activities by mortgage-sector companies that fear the expansion of Fannie Mae and Freddie Mac activities reflects this phenomenon.

Conclusion

Hybrid structure poses special challenges for congressional oversight and control: (1) difficulty in measuring both costs and benefits of hybrid program; (2) hybrids' off-budget status; (3) Congress' reliance on regulatory agents; (4) conflict among hybrids' objectives; and (5) the political influence of hybrid organizations. All five factors constrain Members of Congress as they attempt to use hybrids to satisfy their preferences.

Additionally, there is no evidence suggesting that the hybrid organizations' resistance to control satisfied the preferences of some congressional minority or past enacting coalition. In theory, the creators of these hybrids fully understood the sacrifice being made in terms of control. It has been argued that many bureaucratic organizations are so constructed as a means of locking in the preferences of the enacting coalition in Congress (Moe 1989, Horn and Shepsle 1989). In the cases studied for this research, however, Congress seems only frustrated by their agents' intransigence.

The applicability of these findings to quasi-government in other contexts is obviously mixed. The separation of powers between the Congress and the executive branch in the American system creates different imperatives from, say, a parliamentary system. Moe and Caldwell explored this difference (1994). They concluded that the parliamentary system provides less incentive for legislators to craft institutions that will hinder administration in the future. As noted in the previous paragraph, however, Moe's explanation is not especially compelling with respect to the control challenges Congress experiences with hybrids. Thus it is ironic that analysts of quangos in the United Kingdom suggest that policy-makers do, in fact, employ this type of hybrid as a means of protecting policy decisions from future politics (Flinders 1999).

Studies of legislative control in any setting clearly must take agent structure into account. The heterogeneous class of institutions referred to here as hybrids introduces only a sample of the myriad other variations among bureaucratic agents that could account for differences in congressional influence. For example, regulatory agencies may be more or less conducive to effective control than non-regulatory agencies. Certain policy areas (by virtue of interest group participation or substantive considerations) may be more or less hospitable to congressional control. Thus greater attention to agent structure is but a single step towards better understanding of the dynamic relationship between Congress and the bureaucracy.

7

Regulating hybrids: structure and control

Quasi-government does not merely transfer policy responsibility from a traditional executive agency to a hybrid organization. It effectively splits responsibility between two entities: an implementer and a regulator. The "implementer" is the deliverer of goods and services. Fannie Mae and the Hungarian American Enterprise Fund are examples of implementers discussed in this book. Hybrid implementers generally utilize market-oriented mechanisms such as loan guarantees or direct investment to accomplish public policy goals. Unlike government agencies, many hybrid implementers also have explicit non-public objectives (e.g., profitability) and create financial liability for the government.

The "regulator" exists to maintain the hybrid organization as an effective substitute for a government agency. The Office of Federal Housing Enterprise Oversight and the Agency for International Development are regulators considered in this study. As seen through the cases examined in previous chapters, the regulators must ensure that implementers address the public policy needs for which they were created and guarantee that implementers do not abuse their quasi-governmental status. That is, they must see that hybrids pursue the objectives determined by policy-makers, operate in a fiscally prudent fashion and abide by procedural requirements laid out by Congress.

Note that the function of the regulator under such an arrangement is substantially different from a traditional regulatory agency. As discussed in chapter 3, regulation is traditionally justified by a feature or deformation of the market that requires intervention in the name of public interest. For example, were it not for government regulation, manufacturers could release harmful pollutants with resulting costs to be borne by society as a whole.

In contrast, regulation of hybrid organizations is intended to ensure that a quasi-public entity pursues the goals set by elected representatives and does not in so doing endanger the financial well-being of the government. Thus quasi-government tests the adaptability of regulation in addition to experimenting with alternative mechanisms for the delivery of public goods and services.

For most of this book, Congress and the President are referred to as the principals while hybrid organizations are the agents. This is an accurate representation but it simplifies the picture by downplaying the dual roles of the hybrid regulator.

The regulator, when acting as an intermediary between the principal (i.e., Congress or the President) and the agent (i.e., the hybrid organization), is effectively both a principal *and* an agent. The regulator is a *principal* with respect to the hybrid as it crafts and enforces regulations to compel the desired behavior from its agent. The regulator is an *agent* with respect to Congress and the President as it is expected to satisfy their preferences by regulating the hybrid organization. In chapters 3, 4 and 6, principals' reliance upon regulatory agents is identified as an obstacle to reliable control over hybrid organizations. This was termed the embedded principal–agent problem of quasi-government.

Although the bulk of this book examines the implementers (i.e., the hybrid organizations) to determine which traditional ties between principals and agents can be shed without sacrificing control, this chapter focuses on the regulators to examine the consequences of reliance on quasi-government. Specifically, the ramifications of variation in the structure of regulatory agencies are considered in light of the adaptation of regulation required to make quasi-government work.

The chapter has two major sections. First, the general challenges of intra-governmental regulation are fleshed out. It has been suggested that government is incapable of regulating itself (Wilson and Rachal 1977). If true, this assessment might doom any of the institutional frameworks associated with quasi-government. But it may be that hybrid organizations, because they function more like private organizations than most government agencies, can be regulated effectively.

Second, variation in the structures of hybrid regulators is examined in an effort to answer key questions. How do different types of regulatory agencies approach the challenges of hybrid regulation? How do alternative organizational designs affect the relationship between hybrid and regulator? Are there superior and inferior structural arrangements?

This chapter is more speculative than previous chapters because the entities considered in this study – Fannie Mae, Freddie Mac, the Enterprise Funds, OPIC investment funds – did not provide sufficient variation in the structure of regulators to investigate the relevant hypotheses fully. Moreover, OPIC and ExIm, the two government corporations studied in the export promotion policy area, are among the hybrid organizations *not* regulated by an outside organization at all (although both are governed by multi-member boards that, in some sense, serve this function).

Still, the available data allow for informed speculation about the critical dimensions on which regulatory agencies vary and the laying of a theoretical foundation for future research. This in turn permits identification of key concerns to be considered by policy-makers designing hybrid organizations as alternative policy tools.

Can government regulate itself?

Research on regulation generally begins with the presumption that the regulator is the government and the regulated entity is a private individual or organization. Relatively few discussions of regulation consider regulated organizations in the public sector – Durant is an exception (1985) – despite the fact that government agencies are among the most regulated institutions in the United States. Federal agencies must adhere to a laundry list of rules that govern personnel practices, contracting, the public availability of information and even the procedures for making additional regulations. Such regulations apply *only* to government agencies. Agencies are also subject to many regulations that apply to private- and public-sector organizations: work safety rules, anti-discrimination rules, environmental protection rules and so on. Finally, as described in chapter 3, hybrid organizations are subject to federal regulations that define their public mission. For example, Fannie Mae and Freddie Mac are regulated by the Department of Housing and Urban Development to ensure that a minimum percentage of their business benefits homebuyers in low-income communities. This is equally true of governments and other levels, in the United States and in nations around the world.

The Wilson and Rachal argument

In a brief article entitled "Can the government regulate itself?" James Wilson and Patricia Rachal argue that regulation of public institutions is more difficult than regulation of private organizations (1977). In the years since the article's publication, the effectiveness of intra-governmental regulation has gained importance for at least two reasons. First, federal reliance on state and local government for program implementation has increased (Kettl 1983). Thus the ability of federal regulators to ensure adequate performance by state government agencies has become a critical skill of federal bureaucrats.

Second, use of hybrid organizations has placed a premium on government's ability to ensure performance through regulation because otherwise public policy goals may go unmet (Seidman and Gilmour 1986).

Drawing upon examples to illustrate the distinctive challenges associated with regulating governmental organizations, Wilson and Rachal offer the following four reasons why government cannot regulate itself. Note that Wilson and Rachal implicitly include hybrids within the class of organizations they call "governmental." These four points are summarized and then examined critically.

Can't cut off funds – Regulators do not have the power to terminate funding of non-compliant government agencies. The authors note that, through Medicare and Medicaid, the government has "powerful tools it could use to control the behavior of private hospitals." No federal agency has equivalent tools with respect to the independently appropriated Department of Veterans Affairs. Thus the VA hospitals are more difficult to control. The authors also cite the Tennessee Valley Authority, a government corporation, which "finances itself . . . from retained earnings and revenue bonds" and thus puts up strong resistance to interference.

Competing goals – Any regulatory enforcement directed at governmental organizations could jeopardize public policy objectives. Again Wilson and Rachal cite the TVA, which has a poorer record on environmental protection than most private utilities. This is, in part, due to TVA's mission: to provide inexpensive power to poor Americans. Should TVA's pollution problem be addressed at the expense of such citizens? Similarly, the Boston Housing Authority has an abysmal record on housing code violations. When challenged on this failing, it points to its primary goal of keeping rents low and not passing increases in operating costs on to tenants.

No means of control – Regulators lack the tools to exact compliance from government agencies. Discussing the failures of the Office of Federal Contracts Compliance to improve government employment practices and use of minority contractors, for example, Wilson and Rachal cite the regulator's lack of control over "the budget, personnel or structure of any other agency" (12). With private companies, on the other hand, the government can terminate contracts or go to court in pursuit of compliance.

Mutual independence – Separate entities within the government are ill-suited to "command" other entities. Each entity is capable of political maneuvering and "mobilizing allies elsewhere in government" to undermine adversaries (10). Also, courts cannot resolve disputes between agencies because, "in the opinion of most constitutional scholars, [that would] violate the doctrine of the separation of powers" (10).

There are reasons to regard these observations skeptically. First, the notion that federal agencies can simply "cut off" funds to offending private institutions is simplistic. Consider Wilson and Rachal's example. The Department of Health and Human Services' option to withhold funds from hospitals is a blunt instrument; its use is self-defeating and politically improbable. Donald Kettl's study of relationships between government agencies and contractors demonstrates that government rarely enjoys the ability to bark orders and expect compliance even from private-sector agents (1983).

Second, regulators of private organizations must also routinely weigh competing public policy goals, as discussed in chapter 4. Consider the Federal Aviation Administration's difficulty in balancing safety regulation with airline industry promotion (Wald 1996b). The Department of Transportation faces a similar challenge as fuel efficiency concerns conflict with safety demands (Weidenbaum 1984).

Still, the article is useful, for it suggests that the nature of the regulated entity is a variable that may affect the efficacy of regulation. Assuming for a moment that Wilson and Rachal's claims about the inherent difficulties in intra-government regulation are correct, it is reasonable to hypothesize that variations in the structure of regulated and regulating entities might mitigate (or exacerbate) these problems. Thus application of the claims to hybrids is informative.

Applying the argument to hybrid organizations

Evaluating the applicability of the Wilson and Rachal argument to hybrid organizations is best done by taking each point in turn.

Can't cut off funds – Regulators of hybrid organizations certainly do not have the power to "cut off" funds to the organizations they regulate. But regulators rarely have this power. Thus Wilson and Rachal overstate the comparative difficulty of regulating public-sector institutions. There are numerous regulators of private-sector organizations that have demonstrated effectiveness while relying upon tools that fall short of the ability to cut off funds.

And regulators of hybrid organizations also have tools. As argued in chapter 3, the most effective hybrid regulators are those with a coherent set of regulatory tools, including the ability to write clear, comprehensive regulations and the power to enforce those regulations (or contractual agreements). Thus, while this point does apply to hybrids, it is not especially compelling in any case.

Competing goals – The vexing problems of competing objectives are certainly operative with respect to hybrids. As the discussion in chapters 4, 5 and 6 indicated, these problems can be exacerbated when hybrids or other interested parties manipulate the conflict among goals to the advantage of their own interests.

The problem may be more severe with hybrid organizations than with government agencies because the competing goal is frequently profitability or the need to "break even" financially. This creates strong incentives for the hybrid organizations to resist more onerous public policy objectives. Indeed, the examples cited by Wilson and Rachal (the TVA and the Boston Housing Authority) are both hybrid organizations. Durant discusses the contradictory objectives of regulators and the TVA and notes the importance of the conflict (1985).

No means of control – This claim does not seem to apply very well to hybrids (which is not to say it applies well to governmental entities). Some regulatory agencies *do* have tools of control that, to some extent, allow them to compel desired behavior from regulated organizations. For example, OPIC can invoke the loan agreements it negotiates with its investment funds if a regulated fund does not live up to its legal commitments. Both OFHEO and HUD have legal recourse if Fannie Mae and Freddie Mac do not abide by the regulations issued by the two agencies. Although imperfect, these control tools do exist.

In fact, purely governmental entities may be *more* difficult to regulate than hybrids precisely because these regulatory tools are generally absent and the administrative ties are ineffective. This conclusion is obviously consistent with the argument of chapter 3, although not substantiated by this research. In any event, the blanket pronouncement that government self-regulation is *impossible* certainly does seem an overstatement with respect to hybrids.

Mutual independence – The notion that agencies cannot regulate one another because the regulated entity can always outmaneuver the regulator is supported by this book. Principals' reliance on regulatory agencies *does* provide opportunities for influence and manipulation by interest groups, including the hybrid organizations. And, as described in some detail in chapter 5, some hybrid organizations are uniquely structured to take advantage of these opportunities because they have significant financial resources and almost no restrictions on their political activity. Durant describes similar complex politics in his study of environmental regulation and the TVA (1985). He noted that the Environmental Protection Agency's attempts to control pollution by the federal entity resulted in wide-ranging political maneuvering.

Any regulator seeking to control a hybrid organization is likely to face resistance from the regulated entity and a political struggle.

Hybrids do not seem easier to regulate

If the Wilson and Rachal argument is true with respect to government agencies, it would follow that hybrid organizations might be even more difficult to regulate. The problem of *competing goals* is arguably more acute for hybrid organizations, most of which are either profit-seeking or concerned with "breaking even" financially. The *mutual independence* problem appears to be more serious in the case of hybrid organizations due to their potential political power. Hybrids are better equipped to influence the political process and thereby undermine their regulators. Only the *means of control* problem seems worse with respect to government agencies. Regulators of some hybrids do have tools, typically regulatory in character, available to encourage compliance.

Thus, with respect to two of the four claims made by Wilson and Rachal, hybrids appear to be more vulnerable to the difficulties of intragovernmental regulation. On one count, the regulators of hybrids may be in a better position. The relative superiority of regulatory tools available to some hybrid regulators (as noted in chapter 3) gives them a comparative advantage. And, in the fourth area, it appears to be neutral with respect to organizational type of regulated entity.

Moreover, there may be benefits to the division of implementer and regulator. This is Durant's somewhat surprising conclusion after he documents the TVA's repeated flouting of the Clean Air Act. He notes that conflict among agencies is consistent with the Madisonian notion of ambition countering ambition. Durant concludes that "federal government activities and public regulation are not incompatible; adversary bureaucracies can hold other public agencies accountable to the law" (1985, 144).

Structural variation in hybrid regulators

Bureaucratic structure is rarely if ever neutral. As the case study described in chapter 5 illustrated, battles over structure can be pitched and critical. McCubbins, Noll and Weingast have hypothesized that Congress utilizes structure and procedural requirements effectively to control administrative agencies such that Members of Congress (and their constituencies) are satisfied (1987, 1989). These authors – and others who have connected structure with congressional interest in control – have not considered the implications of structure with specific reference to hybrids.

There is no standard design for the regulatory agencies charged with overseeing hybrid organizations. Indeed, just as each hybrid is *sui generis*, each hybrid regulator is unique. There are at least three dimensions on which variation in the structure of the regulator seems to affect the relationships among the principal (i.e., Congress, the President), the regulator and the regulated hybrid:

○ *Concentration of regulatory authority* – Some hybrids are overseen by a single entity in which all regulatory authority is vested. Other hybrids are regulated by multiple entities, each with responsibility for different types of regulation (e.g., programmatic or financial safety and soundness).

○ *Structure of regulatory agency leadership* – Many regulatory agencies are led by multi-member commissions or boards. Typically such commissions are composed of an odd number of appointees with statutory stipulations of mixed composition (in terms of partisanship) and terms of office that do not correspond with presidential administrations. In contrast, some regulatory agencies are led by single individuals appointed by the President.

○ *Scope of regulatory agency authority* – Some hybrids are regulated by offices or staff located within large executive agencies with multiple purposes. Other hybrid organizations are overseen by smaller, single-purpose organizations that focus almost exclusively on regulating one or more hybrid organizations. Whereas "concentration" concerns the number of regulators to which a hybrid is answerable, "scope" concerns the number of responsibilities the hybrids' regulating agency must fulfill.

Some of the distinctions are highly correlated. Independent agencies are generally led by multi-member boards and, more often than not, are vested with all regulatory authority over hybrid organizations. In contrast, regulatory agencies located within Cabinet agencies are typically led by individuals, not multi-member boards. These tendencies notwithstanding, the three structural variations are differentiated because (1) each has independent explanatory power in predicting the nature of the relationship between hybrid organizations and their regulators; and (2) there is not perfect correlation among any of the variables – thus there are cases where only one of two frequently correlated structures exists.

For each structural variation the consequences are discussed for the regulatory agency as both a principal (with respect to the hybrid organization) and an agent (with respect to elected representatives).

Concentration of regulatory authority

Hybrids, like all private and public organizations, are subject to a wide variety of regulations. Among them are laws and rules that apply to all kinds of organizations. For example, hybrids must adhere to fire codes that prohibit locked exit doors and require sprinkler systems. They are not permitted to discriminate on the basis of race or religion. Various federal, state and local agencies are responsible for enforcing such laws and regulations. To the extent that they are subject to this oversight, hybrid organizations, like all organizations, face diffuse regulatory authority. This type of regulation is

Table 7.1 *Summary table of key variations in regulatory agency structure*

Dimension	Type	Example
Concentration of regulatory authority	*Unified*	The FEC is the sole executive agency with responsibility for enforcing federal election laws.
	or	
	Divided	OFHEO and HUD divide regulatory responsibility with respect to Fannie Mae and Freddie Mac.
Structure of agency leadership	*Single-headed*	The Federal Aviation Administration, regulator of the nation's airlines and airports, is led by a single administrator.
	or	
	Multi-headed	The SEC is led by five commissioners, one of whom serves as chairman.
Scope of regulatory authority	*Single-purpose*	The Office of Thrift Supervision's sole responsibility is overseeing the nation's savings and loan associations.
	or	
	Multi-purpose	USDA is a large Cabinet agency with numerous tasks, one of which is regulating the nation's meat and poultry producers.

extremely broad and is not specifically related to the activities of a regulated entity, the nature of its mission or the manner in which it pursues its objectives. As such, this type of "generic" regulation is set aside so the focus can remain on regulation that is specific to a particular organization – or type of organization.

As discussed previously, most hybrid organizations are subject to at least two types of regulation. Mission-related regulation defines the public policy goals to be pursued by the hybrid organization. The clearest example is HUD's regulation of Fannie Mae and Freddie Mac. Non-mission-related regulation is less substantive in character, including regulation intended to guarantee adherence to specific procedural requirements. Examples include reporting requirements, to which all the hybrids examined in this project are subject. Does it make a difference whether non-mission and mission-related regulation is performed by one or multiple entities? That is the question addressed in this section.

Many hybrid organizations are overseen by a single entity in which all regulatory authority is vested. For example, the OPIC investment funds are overseen only by OPIC. No other government agency has regulatory responsibility for the OPIC investment funds. Similarly, the Farm Credit Administration is the sole entity with regulatory responsibility for the organizations that make up the Farm Credit system, a network of hybrids resembling the Federal Home Loan Bank system.

Both OPIC and the FCA are responsible for mission-related regulation. In the case of OPIC, this means reviewing proposed investments for compliance with the substantive requirements of the loan agreement (e.g., the formula for the distribution of investments among multiple countries). For the FCA this requires monitoring lending to ensure that adequate provision of credit to small farm owners is in place.

Both organizations also carry out non-mission regulation. OPIC ensures that procedural requirements are fulfilled, such as the required review of all potential investments for their environmental impact. The FCA monitors regulated entities to ensure that fair lending practices are employed.

In contrast, other hybrid organizations face divided regulatory authority. Fannie Mae and Freddie Mac are regulated by the Office of Federal Housing Enterprise Oversight and the Department of Housing and Urban Development. Sallie Mae, a hybrid organization that helps finance education by purchasing student loans in the same manner that Fannie Mae purchases home loans, is undergoing a transformation from government-sponsored enterprise into a fully private corporation (Crenshaw 1997). As a GSE, Sallie Mae is regulated by the Departments of Education and the Treasury. The Education Department has mission-related responsibilities while the Treasury Department is concerned with financial safety and soundness.

The Enterprise Funds are a special case. They are overseen by both the Agency for International Development and the State Department. In this case, regulatory authority is not neatly divided. Both agencies essentially share all regulatory authority, with USAID taking the lead.

Consequences of regulatory authority concentration   The concentration of regulatory authority is most relevant when multiple regulatory objectives are in conflict. For example, the regulator charged with ensuring the financial safety of a hybrid may object to requirements imposed by the programmatic regulator. Such conflicts occur even when all regulatory functions are assigned to a single entity. The manner in which conflicting regulatory objectives are resolved, however, varies with the concentration of regulatory authority.

When hybrids are regulated by multiple agencies, resolution of conflicts can be public, highly contentious affairs. This is an accurate description of the TVA case (Durant 1985). Concentration of regulatory authority in a single organization may allow the reconciliation to take place internally, for the most part, behind closed doors.

Regulator as bureaucratic principal. When authority is divided among two or more organizations, the competition among regulators may make them all less effective as principal (i.e., unable to compel satisfactory behavior from the hybrid).

The case of Fannie Mae and Freddie Mac indicates why this is true. The division of regulatory authority among multiple agencies creates an open process for negotiating competing demands: achievement of programmatic objectives and maintenance of financial safety and soundness. The separate, concomitant rule-making processes for the programmatic and financial safety regulations provide Fannie Mae and Freddie Mac with opportunities to play the two objectives against each other. The company's representatives have already argued that the programmatic regulations being promulgated by HUD endanger their safety and soundness and, conversely, that the safety and soundness requirements undermine their ability to meet programmatic goals (*National Mortgage News* 1999, Kosterlitz 2000a). This echoes the arguments made by the GSEs during consideration of the FHEFSSA (see chapter 5).

This example reinforces the "mutual independence" argument made by Wilson and Rachal. They claim that governmental entities, including hybrids, are able to manipulate the regulatory process from the inside. Divided regulatory authority simply increases the opportunities for manipulation. The more players there are involved in the process, the more opportunities there are for the political maneuvering that makes the job of the regulator more difficult.

Thus far the two regulatory agencies responsible for Fannie Mae and Freddie Mac have maintained a united front. Neither OFHEO nor HUD has supported claims by the regulated hybrids that the other regulator's actions jeopardize their objectives. This is not altogether surprising; the two agencies assumed their current regulatory responsibilities under the Clinton Administration. In the future, however, when OFHEO is led by an individual appointed by a President who has since left office (the term of the OFHEO director is five years), conflict with a HUD secretary appointed by the sitting President is more likely.

Oversight of the Enterprise Funds has also been made more complicated by the division of responsibility between USAID and the State Department.

Although USAID has taken the leading role in administering the program, the required involvement of the State Department SEED coordinators can make interactions cumbersome (interviews 9, 14, 72).

There is a lesson for designers of hybrid regulatory structures: concentrating regulatory authority tends to reduce the difficulties for regulators arising from the "mutual independence" problem described above.

Regulator as bureaucratic agent. The regulator is a principal with respect to the hybrid organization but it is, in fact, acting on behalf of the President and/or Congress. Thus the regulator is also a bureaucratic agent. The division of regulatory responsibilities among multiple agents affects *this* principal–agent relationship as well.

The division of regulatory authority may provide Congress with the benefit of transparency as the competing regulatory objectives are negotiated. When regulatory authority is concentrated within a single entity, the resolution of competing claims occurs hidden from view. For example, OPIC investment fund managers determine when an investment is justified by its programmatic contribution despite its financial risk. This makes it difficult for Congress to oversee the reconciliation of competing objectives and ensure that its preferred outcome is achieved.

Note that the concentration of regulatory authority does not necessarily benefit one interest group or another. There *could* be a bias associated with the partisanship of the regulatory agency's leader or simply her personal opinion. But the persons responsible for reconciling competing claims may also be "honest brokers," open to the arguments of all interested parties. If the leadership and personnel of the regulatory agency who must reconcile competing positions *do* have preferences regarding the proper prioritization of competing objectives, however, the concentration of regulatory authority clearly amplifies their power. In such circumstances, without equal opportunities for participation afforded by the relatively public reconciliation of objectives when authority is divided, the concentrated structure could advantage one interest group at the expense of another. In some instances, this may be exactly what some Members of Congress desired. In other cases, the regulator may not be a "good" agent in the sense that it does not seek the objectives preferred by its principals.

In the mid-1980s, the Farm Credit system suffered significant fiscal difficulties. At that time, the Farm Credit Administration's board was dominated by individuals representing the regional banks and associations that make up the Farm Credit system. The financial failure was attributed to the board's inclination to stress the credit needs of American farmers rather than the fiscal soundness of the Farm Credit system. When Congress bailed out the Farm Credit system it radically restructured the board to avoid similar "capture" by a group with clear bias in its priorities.

The division of regulatory authority among multiple entities *could* be explained by those scholars who argue that inefficient bureaucratic arrangements satisfy the preferences of certain legislators (McCubbins, Noll and Weingast 1989, Moe 1989). First, by involving multiple parties in the regulation of any hybrid, Congress has created a unique type of "fire alarm." In this case, Congress need not depend on an interest group to make noise in the event of some undesirable regulatory activity. It has empowered a federal agency to perform that function. Second, conflict among agencies will certainly slow the regulatory process considerably. Third, the likelihood of conflict among agencies will facilitate the intervention of Congress to settle controversial disputes in a satisfactory manner.

To some extent, these arguments are applicable in the case of Fannie Mae and Freddie Mac. The development of regulations by both OFHEO and HUD was time-consuming, although it is not clear that the division of regulatory authority contributed to the delays. The separation of the functions did allow Congress to hear from two entities with respect to all proposed regulations. That is, HUD could comment on the programmatic implications of capital regulations while OFHEO could be questioned on the fiscal implications of housing goals.

This analysis suggests an important lesson about the "competing goals" problem raised by Wilson and Rachal. Hybrids' conflicting objectives create a never-ending competition for organizational emphasis. Principals interested in ensuring the pre-eminence of their preferred reconciliation of competing objectives may be wary of designs that vest complete authority in a single organization.

Structure of regulatory agency leadership

Traditionally, federal agencies are led by individuals appointed by the President and confirmed by the Senate. Many hybrid organizations are regulated by organizations that conform to this model. For example, Fannie Mae and Freddie Mac are overseen by HUD (led by the secretary of Housing and Urban Development) and OFHEO (headed by its director). Enterprise Funds are monitored by two executive agencies, the State Department and the US Agency for International Development, each of which has a single appointed chief executive.

There are, however, many federal entities with regulatory responsibilities that are not headed by single appointed executives. For example, the Securities and Exchange Commission and the Federal Trade Commission have multiple members. These commissions are ostensibly structured to reduce "political influence" on agency decision-making, based on the normative judgment that regulation should be carried out in a neutral fashion (Moe 1982, Wood 1990).

To keep regulatory decision-making apolitical, Congress has created agencies that enjoy some independence from the executive branch by virtue of leadership by multi-member commissions and separation from executive departments (Seidman and Gilmour 1986). Congress requires that commissions be mixed in terms of partisanship. Thus, although some commissions are composed of an odd number of appointees, the discrepancy in party representation is not greater than one member. The term of appointments is typically five years – a length intended to limit domination by individuals selected by the same President. The President is denied the power to remove commissioners.

Hybrids regulated by these types of commissions or boards include the Federal Home Loan Bank system and the Farm Credit system. The United States Postal Service is subject to a complex arrangement including two different oversight commissions. Other commissions with oversight responsibility for private-sector organizations include the Commodity Futures Trading Commission, the Consumer Product Safety Commission and the Federal Communications Commission.

Consequences of leadership structure Putting the leadership of an organization in the hands of a group of people that is, by law, divided along party lines is clearly an invitation for disagreement. In practical terms, this presents a significant obstacle to efficient management and decision-making. Mixed composition of boards does not necessarily frustrate congressional principals. Indeed, it may serve their purposes by protecting interests that benefit from a lack of vigorous regulation.

The regulatory commission is an oft-criticized bureaucratic form. Commissions are frequently described as "independent" but it is never entirely clear from what or whom the organization is independent. Shapiro concludes that the significant "independence" is not a commission's placement outside a Cabinet-level agency (1997). Commissioners are generally appointed by the President and have ties to the administration with respect to overarching policy, if not particular cases (Shapiro 1997, Brigman 1981). "Independence" also does not indicate lack of congressional oversight; commissions are subject to hearings and budget treatment. Rather, Shapiro points to the insulation of the commission from party politics, as embodied in the typical requirement that there be representation of multiple parties in a multi-member board.

In the context of quasi-government, however, the idea of insulating the regulatory agency from the political parties is quite striking. American political parties serve a crucial function in the policy-making process. They are aggregators of preferences; institutions that help shape policies such that multiple constituencies are satisfied (Schattschneider 1942, Hofstadter 1969). Therefore, the independence of regulatory commissions is criticized by those who believe critical decision-making ought never to be removed from the people's representatives and their political parties (Cushman 1941, Scher 1961). The Supreme Court has found that the insular commission design is justified when the regulatory agency administers a quasi-judicial function (Seidman and Gilmour 1986).

Even if one accepts the logic of the Supreme Court in differentiating agencies that have a judicial function, delegation of regulatory authority over a *hybrid* organization is problematic. The regulator of the hybrid organization is charged with transmitting principals' preferences and compelling the hybrid to satisfy them. This is clearly not a judicial function. Only the financial safety and soundness regulation of hybrid organizations is of a character that could justify the "independent" commission structure.

The other frequent critique of commissions is quite different from the charge that they are too removed from the political process. Regulatory bodies are often described as being "captured" by the very industries they regulate. Bernstein's classic work on commissions sets forth the idea that regulatory bodies have a natural "life cycle," during which they gradually become servants of the entities they are supposed to regulate as a means of maintaining political support (1955). Noll argues that commissions are, in fact, more susceptible to industry capture than traditional agencies (1971). Although the universality of this observation has been questioned, the basic notion of capture is widely accepted (Meier and Plumlee 1978).

The capture critique is obviously relevant to the regulators of hybrid organizations. Indeed, the desperate situation of the Farm Credit system was commonly explained by the failure of the system's regulator, the Farm Credit Administration (Schneider 1985, Gulino 1985, Sinclair 1987). Thus, in the discussion of the consequences of leadership structure for the regulators of hybrids, the questions of insulation and capture must remain in the forefront.

Regulator as bureaucratic principal. Students of bureaucratic control have argued that Congress purposively selects designs that may make effective administration *more* difficult (Moe 1989). This analysis is, in fact, based on a study of regulatory commissions. Perhaps the most dramatic example, not cited in Moe's article, is the Federal Election Commission. The FEC has a six-member board equally divided between the two major parties. This almost ensures organizational paralysis and very little threat of rigorous campaign law enforcement.

Even when the divisions among board members do not occur along partisan lines, the multi-member design may lead to paralysis. As interest groups affected by the relevant regulatory agency agitate for representation on the board or commission, substantive "gridlock" is likely. McCubbins, Noll and Weingast make the important point that inaction may be precisely what the creators of the regulator sought – an unfortunately plausible hypothesis in the FEC case; thus this outcome may not indicate a failure of control (1989).

The paralyzing effect of leadership by commission can be seen in the aforementioned case of the Farm Credit Administration. Even in the face of impending financial disaster for the Farm Credit system, the large, interest-driven board of the FCA was functionally immobile (interview 58, Rauch 1989). The post-mortem of the savings and loan debacle also assigned blame to the multi-member Federal Home Loan Bank board (Kane 1989).

Decisive, politically bold policy decisions are more likely to come from a single-headed regulatory organization. If the President is willing to expend political capital to take a position that will alienate an important group, the single-headed agency is a much more facile instrument. It can be mobilized with the assistance of the presidentially-appointed head of the regulatory agency. Convincing the collection of individuals comprising a commission, many appointed by another President, to follow a new path is more challenging. A recent example is the Food and Drug Administration's attempt to classify tobacco as an addictive substance within the regulatory agency's jurisdiction (Neikirk 1996). This action reflected the willingness of President Clinton and FDA administrator David Kessler to take on the tobacco industry and its supporters. Had the FDA been led by a multi-member commission, it is unlikely that such an approach would have been attempted. The President would have been hard-pressed to win the support of a bipartisan board or commission.

The same dynamic is likely for hybrid regulators. OFHEO's willingness to issue a proposed regulation that antagonizes Fannie Mae would result from its leadership by a single individual. Were OFHEO governed by a commission, that collection of individuals would very likely include some people sympathetic to the interests of the regulated hybrids. Of course, an individual agency leader *may* be as disinclined to confront regulated organizations as a multi-member board, but an organization led by an individual does not have the commission's high level of structural inertia.

There may be circumstances that create either consensus or non-partisan majorities on commissions and multi-member boards. At such times, often moments of crisis, commissions could be as effective in the role of principals as agencies led by a single individual. In fact, at such times the multi-member structure might provide *more* flexibility than a single appointed leader. This is because the multi-member design provides "cover" to the individual commissioners. An unpopular decision by a single-headed agency can draw heavy fire from any adversely affected constituency upon the leader of that organization, the administration *writ large* and the political party affiliated with the administration. Indeed, anticipating such a reaction may deter the action in the first place. However, a multi-member commission would be able to act, confident in the knowledge that, under our two-party system, the aggrieved group would not have anywhere to turn.

Regulator as bureaucratic agent. The structure of a regulatory agency's leadership also affects the likelihood of its satisfying the President and/or Congress. As noted above, an individual leader is more likely to move an agency in a desired direction than a multi-member commission because he does not have to contend with dissenting commissioners. On the other hand, if Congress seeks an agent that is not active, the commission structure is desirable (McCubbins, Noll and Weingast 1989). With consensus difficult to reach, the regulatory agency may be unable to act and the regulated entity will be essentially free to follow its own course. Moe and others utilize this logic to explain the existence of regulatory agencies that are "designed to fail" from the moment they are created (1989).

Whether intentional or not, the commission structure creates tremendous institutional inertia. As a consequence, one should not expect the regulatory organization led by a multi-member board or commission to prove a particularly malleable instrument of control for Congress or the President if they attempt to influence the regulated hybrid. For an enacting coalition interesting in preserving the substantive autonomy of a hybrid, such a regulator would be an appealing agent.

Comparing the Federal Home Finance Board (FHFB, the entity responsible for overseeing the Federal Home Loan Bank system) with HUD illustrates the consequences of the structural variation. According to a former senior HUD official who served ex officio as a member of the Federal Home Finance Board, the department is far more representative than the FHFB of the administration's views with respect to the hybrids it regulates (interview 85). The FHFB is constantly divided and often unable to act – a problem that also undermines its performance as a principal.

Scope of regulating agency authority

There is tremendous variation in the breadth of activities performed by agencies responsible for regulating hybrids. Some agencies perform a wide variety of functions. For example, the Department of Housing and Urban Development not only regulates Fannie Mae and Freddie Mac, it finances public housing, runs lead abatement programs, promotes development on Indian reservations and even fosters housing development outside the United States.

Some regulatory agencies have broad authority in a different sense. Although they only carry out regulatory functions, they have jurisdiction over a large number of individuals and/or organizations. The Occupational Safety and Health Administration is an example. OSHA has regulatory jurisdiction over thousands of private companies and government agencies all over the United States.

In contrast, some organizations have narrow authority in one or both senses. The St Lawrence Seaway Corporation, for example, has a single task: joint regulation of the important shipping corridor with its Canadian counterpart. OFHEO regulates only two organizations: Fannie Mae and Freddie Mac.

The scope of authority enjoyed by the agencies responsible for overseeing hybrids reflects the full spectrum described above. Hybrid regulators frequently perform functions other than regulation. Like HUD, USAID carries out numerous programs in addition to overseeing Enterprise Funds. As these examples suggest, regulators of hybrid organizations that have multiple tasks are large Cabinet agencies and independent agencies.

Regulators with the relatively narrow responsibility of hybrid regulation are typically small independent or semi-independent entities.[9] OFHEO is such an agency. The Federal Home Finance Board is another. The Farm Credit Administration, discussed above, oversees only the Farm Credit system and Farmer Mac, a government-sponsored enterprise.

Whether carried out by an independent or semi-independent agency or an office within a large executive agency, the scope of actual *regulatory* authority over hybrids is typically limited to a small number of organizations. Like OFHEO, which has as its sole function regulation of Fannie Mae and Freddie Mac, OPIC regulates only its investment funds. The exceptions to this observation are the two "systems" of hybrids that are regulated by federal agencies: the Federal Home Loan Bank system and the Farm Credit system.

---

[9] Regulatory agencies that are not part of Cabinet departments fall into two subcategories: "arm's length" agencies and independent agencies. "Arm's length" agencies are affiliated with executive departments but operate with significant substantive independence in terms of decision-making, rule-making and oversight. The most prominent examples are the financial regulatory agencies of the Treasury Department: the Office of the Comptroller of the Currency (OCC) and the Office of Thrift Supervision (OTS). The relationship of OFHEO to HUD is modeled on the relationship between OCC, OTS and the Treasury Department. Independent agencies operate without supervision from Cabinet secretaries although many have departmental representatives as ex officio members of their boards. Independent agencies that regulate hybrids include the FHFB, the FCA and the Postal Commission.

These two national networks of organizations are monitored by the Federal Home Finance Board and the Farm Credit Administration, respectively.

Consequences of agency scope   Interest groups historically have agitated for "their" agency to be elevated to departmental status (or at least an independent agency), based on the belief that an organization embedded within a Cabinet agency has lower "status" than other entities. By this rationale, the relegation of a regulatory organization to a position buried on the organizational chart of a large Cabinet agency would appear to be negative. In practice, however, placement within a large bureaucracy might enhance the regulator's performance.

Regulator as bureaucratic principal. Influential hybrids obviously pose a significant control challenge to the regulatory agencies that oversee them. Hybrid organizations, as demonstrated in chapter 5, may have the ability to influence Congress or the administration and thus turn the principal-agent relationship on its head. Regulatory agencies with broader scope are better equipped to resist the political influence of hybrid organizations. Thus they may be more effective principals.

Studies of regulatory capture note that regulatory agencies overseeing a single industry – say, coal mining – are more susceptible to capture than an organization that has responsibility for a host of different industries (Lewis-Beck and Alford 1980, Macey 1992). Cabinet departments and independent agencies with broader portfolios than single-purpose regulators are expected to have greater ability to resist the influence of interested parties, including regulated hybrid organizations.

The General Accounting Office compared proposed designs of GSE regulators in anticipation of the 1992 legislation that would reshape GSE regulation. Its conclusion was consistent with the academic literature. The report suggested that a "super-regulator" responsible for all government-sponsored enterprises, spanning substantive policy areas, would be best equipped to avoid capture (GAO 1991). This proposal never received serious consideration because, as discussed earlier, it would have concentrated congressional oversight of the new regulatory agency in the banking committees of Congress. Such an outcome would deprive members of, say, the education and agriculture committees the opportunity to influence hybrids operating in their areas of substantive interest.

While it is premature to brand OFHEO a captive of Fannie Mae and Freddie Mac – Bernstein's life cycle theory would lead us to expect such an outcome in the future – the new office has been roundly criticized. Proponents of further regulatory reform have argued that, at the very least, OFHEO is hamstrung by the limitations inserted into the FHEFSSA at the behest of Fannie Mae (Sanghera 2000, Stanton 1999). The Farm Credit

Administration, before its reorganization, was highly deferential to the Farm Credit system, leading to lax regulation. Similarly, the Federal Home Loan Bank Board that oversaw the savings and loan industry became dominated by the organizations it regulated. Suggested reforms intended to address OFHEO's diminutive stature include transferring its function to the Treasury Department, or even the Federal Reserve.

Regulator as bureaucratic agent. Independent regulatory agencies are relatively easy to observe and follow if a Member of Congress or interest group has an interest in so doing. This can expose agencies to intense monitoring and even attack. A relatively small agency, such as OPIC, can receive inordinate attention. Rep. John Kasich's attack on OPIC was facilitated (and perhaps prompted) by its visibility as an independent, stand-alone entity. Had it been buried within another large agency, as it once was, it might have made a less appetizing target. Eliminating an office within USAID would make a significantly smaller splash than eliminating a whole agency. As a consequence, independent agencies may be more cautious and careful to keep their principals satisfied.

Policy-makers overseeing large Cabinet departments or independent agencies are likely to be more interested in an agency's programmatic activities than its oversight of hybrid organizations. The consequences of an agency's hybrid regulation are less apparent to constituents than the caliber of services delivered by that agency. Thus Members of Congress are likely to focus less on regulatory function. As a result, the regulatory personnel may face less monitoring and interference from Congress than other government agencies. A regulatory office within a large bureaucracy can potentially be redirected more quietly than a highly visible independent organization. Although this is a potential advantage to the President, it may frustrate Members of Congress or interest groups concerned with the regulation of the hybrid organization.

There are ways to reduce congressional influence over the activities of a hybrid's regulator. The Bush Administration recently recommended that OFHEO be moved "off-budget" such that it is no longer included in the annual appropriations process (*National Mortgage News* 2002). This would remove a structure intended to guarantee congressional influence over the regulator of Fannie Mae and Freddie Mac (see chapter 5). The chess game in pursuit of bureaucratic control is never over.

Conclusion

Principals' reliance on regulators to compel preference satisfaction from hybrid agents creates an embedded principal-agent problem that is not easily avoided or solved. Hybrid organizations present many of the same challenges that regulators confront when overseeing government agencies. This chapter suggests that the structure of the regulatory agency does not present an obvious mitigation for the challenges of hybrid regulation.

Still, there are indications that variation in the structure of the regulatory agency affects the nature of the relationship between the regulator and the hybrid. Looking at the three dimensions of variation identified in this chapter, one can identify elements of the model hybrid regulator that are most likely to be effective.

Concentration of regulatory authority – Regulators of hybrid organizations are better poised to overcome the problem of "mutual independence" when all regulatory responsibility is concentrated in a single entity. That is, an agency with all regulatory authority over a hybrid would not be as vulnerable to strategic manipulation by hybrid organizations and other interest groups.

Structure of regulatory agency leadership – Agencies led by a single individual are more likely to take decisive action and challenge an influential hybrid organization than a regulatory agency led by a multi-member commission. This is an important advantage for the hybrid regulator as a principal. Although the quality of tools available to the regulatory agency is not a function of the leadership structure, the individual-led agency is better suited to utilize the same tools more effectively than a commission. As an agent, however, the commission structure is likely preferable to a principal that fears independence or greater responsiveness to the President than Congress.

Scope of regulating agency authority – Regulatory agencies that are large, multi-purpose organizations are more resistant to capture than limited-scope, independent agencies. This makes them somewhat more effective as principals. However, as agents, particularly congressional agents, regulatory offices within large departments may be less responsive. Independent regulatory agencies are easier to monitor and thus easier to influence from a congressional perspective.

The preponderance of evidence suggests that an individual-led agency with all regulatory authority concentrated therein is most likely to prove an effective regulator of hybrid organizations. Such a regulator would have the institutional gravity to resist the political influence of hybrid organizations and function as an effective principal. It would have the flexibility to utilize its regulatory authority without being paralyzed by a divided commission or board. These are particularly important considerations with respect to the regulators of hybrid organizations. A regulator that is ineffective as a principal undermines quasi-government inasmuch as it leaves in doubt attainment of the public policy goals for which hybrids were created.

The problem with designs that make regulators of hybrid organizations more effective principals is that they might make them less effective as agents. Members of Congress would be understandably reluctant to grant authority to a regulator that cannot be relied upon to pursue their preferences. And yet, reliable regulatory agents are less likely to prove effective as regulators in compelling the desired performance from hybrids. This is a conundrum of quasi-government.

8

Conclusion

Hybrid organizations are less likely than traditional government agencies to satisfy the policy preferences of their principals – Congress and the President. That is, hybrids are more difficult to control than agencies. This conclusion is not intended nor should it be read as a searing indictment of quasi-government. It is simply a neutral observation.

This observation does have significant implications. Although hybrids are not bad or inappropriate policy tools in all situations, they clearly pose novel challenges that ought to be addressed by policy-makers before they dive head first into the waters of quasi-government. Can a hybrid be regulated effectively? Is the achievement of a policy goal critical or merely desirable? Most fundamentally, what are the political costs of quasi-government?

This book has demonstrated that part of the price is a loss of control over public policy. Hybrid organizations can do many things and have contributed to the public good of the United States. However, it is clear that, as instruments of elected officials, they are unwieldy and unpredictable. This conclusion alone does not close the door to quasi-government. Control is but one aspect of accountability. Indeed, critics of government bureaucracy argue that reducing the control wielded by elected principals is the key to improving the performance of public agencies! The creation of additional hybrid organizations (and other novel institutional arrangements) in the public sector needs to be accompanied by a reconsideration of our notions of accountability – a key concept at the foundation of American public administration.

Therefore, in addition to summarizing the findings and discussing the implications of this book for students of bureaucratic control and policy-makers interested in quasi-government, this chapter considers alternative conceptions of accountability that may prove more appropriate than "control" for our times. A brief review of the many conceptions of accountability is offered, with the suggestion that those who see hybrid organizations as the model for government in the future must argue for a definition of accountability *other* than control.

Summary of findings

In chapter 3, it was shown that hybrids are generally less reliable as bureaucratic agents than traditional government agencies. Fannie Mae and Freddie Mac, for instance, were less responsive than HUD to the congressional and presidential preference for an increased allocation of credit to underserved Americans. A similar condition was evident in the study of government-backed venture capital funds – programs that demonstrated limited ability to pursue and/or achieve clearly articulated policy objectives.

The most straightforward explanation for the relative lack of control experienced by principals with respect to hybrids is the inadequacy of the control tools. Principals rely upon a set of "regulatory" control tools that are unwieldy compared with traditional "administrative" control tools. The transmission of preferences by regulation requires the translation of broad objectives into specific legal requirements that can be enforced. Organizational performance must be measured and judged against some benchmark. This is all quite difficult.

Inferior control tools, however, are only part of the explanation of the difficulties principals have in realizing their preferences when they rely upon a hybrid agent. Hybrid organizations are, by nature, resistant to control, for two basic reasons. One, the typical hybrid relies upon private organizations that respond only to economic incentives. If the hybrid cannot compel the private organization to undertake the activity necessary to satisfy the hybrids' principal, the hybrid has no means to satisfy the principal. For example, the OPIC investment fund created to channel capital to the West Bank seems to have accomplished very little because private investors were not interested. Two, many hybrid organizations have objectives that compete with public policy goals. Fannie Mae and Freddie Mac, for example, are trying to provide financing to low-income homebuyers *and* earn a healthy return for shareholders. Hybrids will resist preferences that might have a negative impact on financial performance.

These two impediments to principal control do not affect all preferences equally. Including the nature of principal preferences in the bureaucratic control model is essential because there is an interaction effect between organization type and preference type. Principal preferences are differentiated on two dimensions in chapter 4. "Positive" preferences are distinguished from "negative" preferences and "mission-related" are separated from "non-mission-related" preferences. Positive preferences require the bureaucratic agent to undertake some new activity in order to satisfy the principal whereas negative preferences require the agent to cease some activity. Mission-related preferences require the agent to alter its objectives substantively to satisfy principals whereas non-mission preferences do not concern an organization's core objectives.

Hybrid organizations are less likely to satisfy positive, mission-related preferences than negative, non-mission-preferences. This accounts for much of the disparity between hybrids and government agencies. Hybrids are *much* less likely than traditional organizations to satisfy positive, mission-related preferences. For example, OPIC and ExIm demonstrated little improvement in boosting exports to Africa even after this preference was made clear by Congress and the President. The differences in the likelihood of preference satisfaction between hybrids and traditional government agencies are far less pronounced when preferences are negative, non-mission-related.

All three explanations of hybrids' resistance to principal control – less effective control tools, ceding control to the market, competing considerations – reflect the interaction between organization type and preference type.

Tools of control. As described in chapter 3, principals rely upon regulatory control tools rather than administrative control tools to transmit their preferences. These tools lend themselves better to negative preferences than positive preferences because negative preferences, unlike positive preferences, are easily translated into clear, enforceable regulations. For example, articulating the prohibition on investment in armaments companies (negative preference) was fairly easy. Defining a potential investment company as worker-intensive (positive preference) was difficult. As a result, the venture capital funds have satisfied the negative preference but struggled on the positive preference.

Ceding control to the market. Most hybrids depend to some extent on the cooperation of market participants to satisfy principal preferences. Thus, if they are unable to induce private agents to assist in satisfying policy preferences, they are unable to follow their orders. This constraint does not affect negative preferences. For example, OPIC and ExIm were able to stop funding projects in China, without having to cajole their market partners, when that was the clear principal preference. But the lack of interest in African markets made the fulfillment of the preference for increased exports to Africa almost impossible.

Competing considerations. Hybrids often have objectives that compete with the preferences of political principals for attention and resources. Most prominent among these considerations is profitability. Hybrids are often reluctant to satisfy preferences if they believe it will reduce their ability to be profitable. This more frequently affects mission-related preferences. For example, Fannie Mae and Freddie Mac were particularly resistant to programmatic regulation calling for more low-income lending because it threatened their profitability. Even hybrids that are not profit-seeking can behave similarly because there is a strong presumption that such entities will at least break even; thus, taking on unprofitable objectives would present an obstacle to satisfying *that* preference.

The implications of hybrid structure for the dynamics of the governmental process were also considered. In chapter 5, the immense political power that has been acquired by Fannie Mae and Freddie Mac, two government-sponsored enterprises, was described and explained. The crafting of the Federal Housing Enterprises Financial Safety and Soundness Act, passed in 1992, provided a demonstration of that power. Fannie Mae and Freddie Mac were able to exert a tremendous amount of influence over the course of several years, resulting in a final law that reflected many of the companies' preferences.

The political influence of Fannie Mae and Freddie Mac is not merely a coincidence or the result of their leaders' savvy. It is a function of the hybrid structure of government-sponsored enterprises. As hybrids, Fannie Mae and Freddie Mac have all the advantages available to both private- and public-sector organizations and none of the disadvantages. They have immense stores of wealth and no restrictions on political lobbying. But they are also congressionally chartered with a public purpose and the ability to "wrap themselves in the flag" for strategic purposes. Perhaps most important, because the GSEs' interests are often affected by legislative decisions, the two companies have a strong incentive to cultivate and wield this power.

This political influence poses a unique challenge to congressional control. Indeed, it turns the concept on its head. Conventional thinking on bureaucratic control holds that an agent carrying out activities that satisfy congressional preferences is "controlled" by Congress. But the GSE case introduces another possibility: Congress' preferences may, in fact, reflect the agent's influence over its principal!

Even for hybrids that do not wield the political influence of Fannie Mae and Freddie Mac, there are structural obstacles that make oversight of hybrid organizations particularly difficult for Congress. In chapter 6, the broader implications of hybrid structure for congressional control are revealed. Among the aspects of quasi-government that make congressional oversight more difficult are hybrids' conflicting goals, uncertainty in measuring the costs and benefits of their activities, off-budget status (which increases the costs of oversight by making any supervision supplemental to the ordinary oversight accomplished through the appropriations and authorization process) and the reliance on agents (such as OFHEO, and OPIC in the case of investment funds) to carry out monitoring and the transmission of preferences.

This does not mean that the President or executive branch appointees have more influence than Congress with hybrid organizations. The structure of hybrid government also erects barriers to executive control that make the satisfaction of presidential preferences less likely with respect to hybrid organizations. Delegation of public policy responsibilities to hybrids generally facilitates a division of tasks. Implementation of a policy program is carried out by a hybrid. But responsibility for monitoring that hybrid and ensuring performance is usually delegated to another institution. In chapter 7, the significance of the wide variation in structure among the regulators of hybrid organizations is considered.

The reliance on regulatory bodies to monitor and transmit preferences to hybrid organizations raises an important if understudied question: can government regulate itself? If the answer is no, as has been suggested, then the quasi-government model is deeply flawed, for it presupposes the efficacy of such regulation as the means of ensuring attention to public policy objectives. Although there is no definitive evidence to support this damning conclusion, in chapter 7 three dimensions on which the structure of hybrid regulators vary are identified. Each variation offers strengths and weaknesses for the regulator.

The three dimensions are: *concentration of regulatory authority* (is the hybrid regulated by one or more entities?); *structure of agency leadership* (is the regulator led by a single individual or a multi-member board?); and *scope of regulatory authority* (does the regulatory agency have multiple functions in addition to regulation of the hybrid?). Regulatory agencies led by individuals, as opposed to commissions, with concentrated regulatory authority are more likely to be effective principals. Such agencies may, however, frustrate congressional principals by pursuing objectives not consistent with Congress' preferences.

Implications

Beyond the immediate conclusions discussed above, there are two sets of implications of this research. First, this study of hybrid organizations illuminates aspects of the governmental process that are frequently ignored but help explain why principals enjoy control in some situations and not others. Second, there are multiple lessons for those considering hybrid organizations as public policy tools.

Building a better theory of bureaucratic control

The complexity and unpredictable nature of politics makes distillation of the key ingredients of bureaucratic control a significant challenge. The reasonable response to this challenge has been to focus on particular elements of the bureaucratic dynamic, isolating specific institutions and exploring variables that theory suggests are pivotal, such as congressional partisanship and legislative/executive agreement. This is a sound research strategy – one that has resulted in many interesting and informative findings.

The danger of this approach lies in our tendency to overlook the simplification part of the process when drawing conclusions. Investigation of rather narrow elements of an equation yields rather narrow findings, from which more sweeping conclusions are inevitably extrapolated. This book demonstrates the intuitive truth: that such extrapolation fails to take into account important variables that were excluded from the research; variables that undermine the sweeping conclusions to which most social scientists aspire. The findings presented in this volume will contribute to a more nuanced theory of bureaucratic control by pointing out some crucial excluded considerations.

Addressing measurement challenges In previous chapters, simplifications that led to misunderstanding or ambiguity in most bureaucratic control research were enumerated. Perhaps most important is the conflation of inputs and outputs in the discussion of control. Even the most sophisticated students of bureaucratic control measure organizational performance by examining the results of an organization's activities, here called outputs. Unmeasured are inputs, the time, effort and resources devoted by the staff of bureaucracies. While outputs measure the organization's success in satisfying a principal's preference, they do not measure the organization's attempt to satisfy the same preference.

This is a crucial distinction. From the perspective of democratic theory, we may be *more* concerned that bureaucratic agents are attempting to carry out the popular will (as expressed by their elected representatives) than by their efficacy. The degree to which the bureaucracy is *successful* may be as much a function of the feasibility of the preference as it is related to the responsiveness of the agent.

Another logical flaw in typical analyses of bureaucratic control relates to the assumption that correlation between preference and performance indicates control. This is highly problematic. First, the agent might have performed in precisely the same fashion regardless of the principal's preference. This is particularly true if the principal's preference is related to an apparent need that could have been concomitantly recognized and prioritized by the leaders of the bureaucratic organization. Second, the correlation could result from the bureaucracy's influence over the principal. That is, the "principal" only declared the preference because the "agent" exercised influence. To call this control would certainly turn the concept on its head. At the very least this would indicate bureaucratic autonomy not control.

Finally, the dangers of relying upon fixed events as interruptions in time series data are pointed out. The problem with equating a change in presidential administration or committee leadership with a change in preference is that it can cause flawed interpretation of data. The inauguration of a new President may not alter presidential preferences on a host of policy matters. Thus, if we were to look at bureaucratic performance before and after the change, we might conclude no control. This would be a false negative. A better approach, employed in this study, is to rely instead upon explicit statements and acts that indicate preferences.

All control is not created equal An additional complexity in the control story arises from the fact that some types of preferences are easier to secure than others. As argued in chapter 4, for example, it is easier to stop an action than it is to prompt an action. This is but one dimension on which preferences can vary. Another, mission versus non-mission, is recognized but there could be a host of others including specificity, resource-sensitivity, policy area, etc.

Research in organizational theory has pointed out that organizations buffer "core technology" from outside interference (Thompson 1967). Thus one might expect principals to find satisfying some preferences – those related to core competencies – more difficult than satisfying other preferences. Still, studies of bureaucratic control generally ignore variation on the preference part of the equation. This project demonstrates that the simplification of bureaucratic control models glosses over variation that helps explain outcomes.

Excluding preference type from the analysis of control over hybrids would have led to a misinterpretation of the findings. The differences in control tools for hybrids and traditional government agencies provided only a partial explanation for the difficulties encountered by principals in satisfying positive, mission-related preferences. It could not account for the fact that OPIC and ExIm proved more resistant to principal control *in some instances.* These two hybrids – both are government corporations – are subject to most of the administrative control tools identified in chapter 2. These proved effective with respect to negative, non-mission preferences. Only when examining variation in preference type did the significance of their reliance on private, market-oriented organizations and their competing financial objectives become clear. Thus the inclusion of preference type in this study resulted in more accurate interpretation of the findings.

Agent structure matters A more glaring problem is the reliance upon a single type of agent – the regulatory agency – that is predominant in the bureaucratic control literature. This is understandable for methodological reasons: regulatory agencies produce easily interpretable time series data of outputs – for example, the number of violations cited per month. But differences between regulatory and non-regulatory agents may be a crucial variable in explaining bureaucratic control. Indeed, the very availability of data that facilitates such research may also facilitate control! There is also research suggesting that Presidents do not care much about regulatory policy, potentially inflating congressional control (relative to executive control) in this area (Wilson 1980, Weingast 1981).

The underlying hypothesis of this project was that hybrids, as a consequence of their structural differences, present distinctive control challenges to political principals. There is clearly evidence supporting this hypothesis. Of course, additional research on more hybrid organizations would add considerable weight to these findings.

More importantly, the manner in which structural variation translated into reduced control was unveiled. First, the tools of control available to principals made some preferences more attainable than others. Second, hybrids' reliance on private market participants and competing objectives erected barriers to the satisfaction of certain types of preferences. The interaction effect with preference type was unanticipated. This is the type of finding, however, that leads to a more complete understanding of the consequences of structural variation.

Control was lost in ways that were not anticipated. It is true that creators of bureaucratic organizations do not always have control as their principal objective. Sometimes, Members of Congress may create an agency that is beyond control as a means of reducing their adversaries' influence – even if this tactic risks damaging their own influence (Moe 1989, McCubbins, Noll and Weingast 1989, Horn and Shepsle 1989). Unfortunately, there is a circular logic to this claim that makes it extremely difficult to disprove. Any evidence of non-control is interpreted as an indicator of the enacting legislature's lack of interest in control.

In this study, the principals struggled with the limitations on control created by the structure of hybrid organizations. There was no evidence that these difficulties reinforced the preferences of an enacting coalition or interest group. Rather the cases observed point to an *unanticipated* alienation of control. This is the greatest danger posed by the reckless creation of hybrid organizations.

Understanding the realities of quasi-government

Putting aside the bureaucratic control debate, this book provides a much needed evaluation of hybrid organizations as public policy tools. Specifically, the political implications of delegating public policy functions to quasi-governmental organizations are considered. There are multiple lessons for policy-makers contemplating the use of hybrids.

Focus on regulation Control of hybrid organizations depends more on sound regulation than on traditional tools of control. The comparison of the government's two venture capital fund programs best demonstrates this point. Enterprise Funds, which have more administrative ties in place, are more difficult to control than the seemingly independent OPIC investment funds because the OPIC funds have a superior regulatory infrastructure in the form of legally binding, specific loan agreements. The administrative ties to the Enterprise Funds are essentially vestigial and provide less wieldy control tools.

Emphasis on the number and function of administrative control tools is misplaced with respect to hybrid organizations. Policy-makers concerned about control should concentrate their efforts on developing a sound, comprehensive regulatory infrastructure including clearly articulated objectives, defined measures of performance and defined rights and responsibilities. Consider the two housing government-sponsored enterprises. The directors of Fannie Mae and Freddie Mac, who are appointed by the President of the United States, provide little in the way of influence or leverage because they are in an overwhelmingly minority position on the board and, furthermore, they have no special responsibility to represent the interests of the President (Musolf 1983). The success or failure of attempts to satisfy preferences depends entirely on the two regulatory entities, HUD and OFHEO, as well as the legislation that is the basis of their regulatory authority.

Define objectives carefully at the outset As a consequence of the limitations on control, it is important to define a hybrid's mission and strategic objectives at its inception; more important than for government agencies, which can be more easily redirected during the course of their lifetimes. Revising and adapting the goals of hybrid organizations once created is difficult because parties with an interest in the extant configuration of the hybrid develop quickly and are endowed with resources to defend their economic interests from the imposition of new policy responsibilities. As described in chapter 5, principals may find their own discretion circumscribed by the alignment of powerful interests arrayed around hybrids. Thus, at the time of inception, policy-makers should have a clear idea of the hybrid organization's purpose, the means by which it should accomplish that purpose and the standard by which performance will be measured and judged.

The findings presented in chapter 4 suggest that this lesson is especially significant for positive, mission-related preferences. This is because principals appear more likely to satisfy preferences that restrict the hybrid from certain activities and preferences that do not relate to the hybrids' mission. Thus there is more room for refinement regarding such concerns after the hybrid is up and running. Hybrids can be stopped from doing business with countries that support terrorist organizations, for example, but it is more challenging to compel business with nations that have good records on human rights.

Law of unintended (political) consequences   One of the most surprising developments for policy-makers who create a new organization to accomplish some public policy purpose may be that, once translated from abstract concept into actual entity, the organization takes on a life of its own. It has its own interests and the means to pursue them. Of course, this is true for government agencies as well as hybrid organizations. But many hybrids are, by structure, capable of generating significant political support and influencing the legislative process – to a far greater extent than almost any agency. For example, Fannie Mae and Freddie Mac have considerable financial resources at their disposal and a compelling public mission they can emphasize when lobbying Congress.

Hybrid organizations may even be able to use their influence to reshape themselves in ways that the original designers had neither intended nor desired. Fannie Mae and Freddie Mac, for example, have agitated for Congress to amend their charters to permit expansion into new lines of business. Therefore, while it may not be possible to foresee all the ramifications of creating a hybrid with potential political power, policy-makers should try to anticipate the possibility of hybrids' evolving into their own interest groups. This would suggest including restrictions on the political activities of hybrid organizations.

Accepting unsatisfied preferences   Perhaps the most fundamental instruction for those considering hybrid organizations is that they should understand what they are getting. The hybrid *may* be less "governmental" in the sense that it is more efficient. But, in exchange for this anticipated benefit, the principal must accept a higher likelihood that his or her preferences will not be satisfied. This is a classic case of not being able to have one's cake and eat it too.

Thus the hybrid model is most appropriate where the likelihood of preference satisfaction is not required to be high or exacting. So, for example, a venture capital fund may be a perfectly acceptable tool for international market development but not for the development of key defense technology. A government-sponsored enterprise may be entirely suitable in the housing arena but not appropriate to ensure the financing of primary schools. This is the bottom-line calculation required when new hybrids are proposed.

Reinventing accountability in the reinvention era

Principals' ability to control their bureaucratic agents is the focus of this volume. In the previous chapters, as in most bureaucratic control research, a significant normative judgment is implicit: bureaucratic control is good.

This conclusion is neither obvious nor incontestable.

From its earliest days, the field of public administration has been concerned with the proper relationship between the bureaucracy and elected officials. Some have argued that elected officials should always retain control over the unelected bureaucracy; at least as many have argued that bureaucratic discretion is a requirement for good governance. In much scholarship, however, this debate gets papered over by the conflation of control and "accountability."

Accountability is good. There is little disagreement on this point. Complaints that an organization is "too accountable" are rarely heard. Congressional oversight committees do not excoriate bureaucrats for excessive accountability. And yet, while everyone agrees on its desirability, the meaning of accountability remains elusive.

The Public Administration Dictionary defines "accountability" as "a condition in which individuals who exercise power are constrained by external means and by internal norms" (Chandler and Plano 1988, 119). This definition provides a sense of the word and hints at its many meanings. Within the notion of "external means," for example, one could include the preferences of principals (legislatures, elected and appointed executives, citizens and courts) as well as institutions such as laws, regulations and moral principles. Is an organization accountable only if it is constrained by *all* such "external means?" What if, as is often the case, there is conflict among principals? What if a principal's demand conflicts with an organization's legal mandate? The answers to such questions depend on one's understanding of accountability.

One's conception of accountability, in turn, is intimately tied to one's beliefs regarding the nature of democratic government. Specifically, defining accountability is ultimately about defining the place of bureaucracy in a democratic state. This is not necessarily a static definition. As our expectations for government organizations evolve, our conception of the bureaucracy and accountability may change as well. For example, there is increasing sentiment that public organizations should pay their own way by charging user fees. This may render reliance on the control notion of accountability obsolete; the organization focused on its bottom line now has a new master that also demands attention.

Scholars have offered typologies of accountability to help us articulate the value emphasis underpinning approaches to public administration. Consider a small sample. Barbara Romzek has written extensively on accountability in different contexts (1996). Her operating understanding of accountability is consistent with this book's emphasis on control. For instance, she and Dubnick describe what they call "accountability relationships" (see Romzek and Dubnick 1987). Their typology is based on a characterization of the degree of control (low *v.* high) over individuals within organizations. This system does not account for situations in which control is not the paramount value.

Gruber defines the "terrain" of accountability by focusing on the degree of constraint on organizational behavior in both procedural and substantive arenas (1987). In this framework, organizational autonomy – from tight to loose constraint – is linked to underlying beliefs about the capability of the citizenry. Thus, for example, one would expect an agency operating in a complex, technical area to find itself in the loose constraint area because citizens' (or elected representatives') ability to make reasoned judgments is quite limited. Gruber's framework thus demonstrates how practical considerations – the complexity of the policy domain – moderate our insistence on bureaucratic control.

In discussions of accountability, however, rejections of bureaucratic control are often based not on technical considerations or citizen capability. They are derived from alternative visions of accountability. For example, the "reinventing government" sentiment that gained popular acceptance in the 1990s substituted "responsiveness to citizen demands" as the core objective of bureaucracies rather than "obedience to political principals."

Most recently, Behn divvies disparate cries for accountability into four categories: accountability for finances, accountability for fairness, accountability for abuse of power and accountability for performance (2001). He notes that these types of accountability can sometimes conflict, creating a dilemma for those held accountable: which poison shall be picked? And Behn argues that there is an "accountability bias" born of the relative ease in holding one accountable on fairness or finances. These two types of accountability offer the highest probability of a "Gotcha!" – the ultimate payoff for one seeking to hold others accountable.

Behn's typology is useful but, in focusing on what an organization is accountable *for*, he actually gives limited attention to accountability itself. What makes an organization accountable for finances? That it managed finances as instructed? That it managed finances such that a surplus was generated? Does it mean that the organization managed finances in accordance with accepted procedures? Or that it managed finances in an open and reviewable fashion? The answers to these questions help define the many meanings of accountability.

The purpose of the following section is to organize notions of accountability in an effort to determine which conception, if any, is most consonant with quasi-government. There is no need for a new, all-encompassing definition of accountability. An inventory of existing approaches is more helpful.

Five dimensions of accountability (transparency, liability, controllability, responsibility and responsiveness) are offered. These categories are not mutually exclusive; that is, organizations can be accountable in one or more senses. Indeed, the first two senses of accountability (transparency and liability) can be thought of as foundations, underpinning accountability in all its manifestations. There is, however, tension between different types of accountability, as shall be discussed below.

Transparency

"Transparency" is the literal value of accountability; the idea that an accountable bureaucrat and organization must explain – account for – his, her or its actions. Thus an accountable organization cannot hide its mistakes or obfuscate its actions to avoid scrutiny. The scandal regarding the Federal Bureau of Investigation's handling of the post-Waco investigation – the agency seemed to cover up questionable decisions – essentially concerns a violation of this type of accountability. The availability of information is not an end in itself but it facilitates evaluation of an organization's controllability, responsibility or responsiveness and it is crucial if an organization is to be liable for its performance.

Transparency requires the subjection of bureaucrats to regular hearings and periodic review as well as the investigation of alleged wrongdoing or perceived failure. More generally, an answerable organization maintains a high degree of openness. This includes access to the public, the press, interest groups and other parties interested in an organization's activities. Such openness has been institutionalized in the form of freedom of information requirements, "sunshine" laws and other regulations that open up the governmental process to review. In the private sector, transparency requires the presentation of truthful information to stockholders, creditors, analysts, customers and regulators.

Thus the standard for this dimension of accountability is straightforward: did the organization reveal the facts of its performance?

Transparency goes hand in hand with other values of accountability. Controllability, responsibility and even responsiveness (described below) are reinforced by frequent evaluation and the potential for public exposure of

failure. Moreover, the requirement to explain actions and decisions theoretically forces a degree of internal review and judgment that might not
take place in its absence. Thus organizational transparency has intrinsic and
instrumental value.

Liability

Some conceptions of accountability include a vision of more concrete reinforcement than transparency. This conception attaches culpability – and
attendant consequences – to accountability. In this view, individuals and
organizations should be held liable for their actions. Note that this includes
but is not limited to punitive reinforcement. Rewarding public managers
with remuneration based on their individual or agency performance is consistent with the liability vision of accountability. For example, five states
were "rewarded" for their achievement in reducing the number of births to
single mothers; the federal government granted each $20 million under a
provision of the 1996 welfare reform law (Healy 1999).

This idea of accountability, alien in the abstract, is quite familiar as applied
to elected officials. Elected representatives are said to be accountable because
voters can "punish" them by removing them from office. It is in this sense that
bureaucrats and judges are sometimes said to be unaccountable. Of course,
the more stark vision created by this view of accountability can also involve
punishing employees for failure. This is the case with acts of malfeasance
and other misdeeds. Bureaucrats are criminally liable for stealing funds,
misappropriating resources or abusing their authority.

This logic could be extended to failures of judgment or bias in policy-
making. Note that the negative consequences do not have to involve criminal
penalties to fulfill the liability vision. Negative performance evaluations with
consequent impact on compensation are intended to achieve this type of
accountability. Proposals for reforming education have suggested cutting
funds to schools that do not meet performance standards (Scales 1999).

The animating principle of liability as an element of accountability is that
forcing an individual or organization to acknowledge wrongdoing or failure is not enough. Consequences must be attached to performance in the
form of professional rewards/setbacks, added/diminished budget authority, increased/limited discretion or reduced/increased monitoring. The key
question, then, in assessing this type of accountability is: does the organization face consequences for its performance?

Controllability

The dominant substantive conception of accountability emphasizes control.
If X can command the behavior of Y, it is said that X controls Y – and

that Y is accountable to X. Although few relationships between political principals and bureaucratic agents are so straightforward, this notion of accountability is a starting point for many analyses of organizations in the governmental context, including this one. The reality of such authority has been the subject of debate from the early days of public administration to the present (Barnard 1938, Pennock 1941, Selznick 1957).

This traditional line of analysis extends from the work of Wilson (1887) and Goodnow (1900), who offered the normative ideal of a politics/ administration dichotomy. In their vision, elected officials should reach consensus on public policy objectives and rely upon bureaucrats for implementation. By determining the organizational goals, elected leaders control the bureaucracy.

Herman Finer, in a seminal dialogue with Carl Friedrich, laid out the case for indirect popular control of government bureaucracies as the critical element of accountability. Without control, bureaucracies rob citizens of their authority and render elections meaningless. In contrast to Friedrich's position that effective bureaucrats must be given latitude to make substantive policy determinations and act upon them, Finer argued that the role of government bureaucracies was to carry out the will of the people as expressed through their elected representatives. An accountable government, Finer held, is one in which the people possess "the authority and power to exercise an effect upon the course which the latter are to pursue, the power to exact obedience to orders" (1940, 337). Thus the accountability of an organization depends on the answer to this key question: did the organization do what the principal (e.g., Congress, the President) desired?

Recent debate has centered on congressional control of the bureaucracy. Utilizing formal models, several scholars have argued that Congress enjoys a high degree of control over federal bureaucracies (Weingast and Moran 1983, Ferejohn and Shipan 1990). Other studies, whether in the rational choice, social choice or transaction costs mode, address the control aspect of accountability (McCubbins, Noll and Weingast 1987, Robinson 1989, Horn and Shepsle 1989, Hill and Brazier 1991).

The ability of Presidents (and their appointees) to control bureaucrats has also been assessed (Beck 1982, Moe 1982, Golden 1992, Krause 1994). Recent work has sought to demonstrate quantitatively a connection between changes in presidential administrations and policy shifts (Aberbach and Rockman 1988, Eisner and Meier 1990, Wood and Waterman 1994). Some such studies have focused on the competition for control between the President and Congress, interest groups and career civil servants (Heclo 1978, Wilson 1989, Hammond and Knott 1996). The courts have also been described as significant players in the determination of bureaucratic behavior (Melnick 1983, Mashaw 1994). Others have argued that the bureaucrats utilize informational asymmetry and other advantages to enjoy a large measure of autonomy (Moe 1982, Riley 1987, Miller 1992, West 1995).

This book follows in the path of these and many other studies. Hybrids are evaluated herein on the basis of their "controllability." Their shortcomings on this dimension of accountability, however, beg consideration of at least the following two alternative notions of accountability.

Responsibility

One alternative conception of accountability emphasizes constraints on bureaucrats in the form of rules and norms. This can be called "responsibility." Responsibility can pertain to internal standards of behavior and performance *not* set by legislators. For example, Bernard Rosen outlines responsibilities to "make laws work as intended," to "initiate changes in policies and programs" and to "enhance citizen confidence in the administrative institutions of government" (1989). These general responsibilities differentiate the accountability of a public bureaucrat from the accountability of a private bureaucrat. Sometimes these moral obligations are implicit, sometimes, as in the case of oaths, they are explicit. For example, all federal employees pledge to "support and defend the Constitution of the United States." A private-sector analogy can be drawn with the fiduciary obligation of corporate directors to shareholders.

Moe and Gilmour urge a return to public law principles in public administration (1995). This entails strong legal responsibility, incorporation of policy and program objectives into legislation, and elimination of plural executives (commissions, committees, etc.) that confuse lines of authority. By this account, adherence to the law is a more desirable ideal for bureaucracy than allegiance to a principal.

Responsibility can also relate to professional standards. Such professional standards may encourage better behavior and set norms against which bureaucrats can be evaluated (Kearney and Sinha 1988, DiIulio 1994). This was essentially the alternative notion of accountability articulated by Carl Friedrich (1940) in his debate with Finer. Accountable bureaucrats cannot simply follow orders, Friedrich argued; they must utilize their expertise constructively in line with professional and moral standards. Not surprisingly, some have argued that professional standards can, in fact, hinder control by substituting professional interests for public concerns (Tullock 1965, Piven and Cloward 1971, Mladenka 1980, Hummel 1987).

An agency being judged on the basis of its responsibility faces a different question from one being judged on the basis of controllability. Did the organization follow the rules?

It should be noted that several scholars have argued that Congress can structure seemingly procedural features to produce desired outcomes (Epstein and O'Halloran 1994, 1996, McCubbins, Noll and Weingast 1987, Bawn 1995). For example, requiring cost-benefit justifications for environmental regulations can effectively circumscribe potential regulations. In such instances, responsibility to the law collapses into control. This complicates the notion of responsibility as an independent conception of accountability. Laws that are instruments of control may not present an alternative to control. Wood and Waterman make the interesting point, however, that bureaucracies, by remaining true to laws enacted by the previous legislature *until* new law is passed, are performing an important function (1994). They preserve the importance of formal expressions of policy and keep policy-making in the congressional realm.

Responsiveness

Notions of control that descend from the Finer perspective do not capture influences on bureaucratic action that are not hierarchical. Such influences are critical in the democratic context and they suggest the responsiveness conception of accountability. In contrast to the control conception of accountability, responsiveness emphasizes an organization's attention to direct expressions of needs and desires rather than the preferences of elected intermediaries. This element of accountability is emphasized in the "customer-oriented" approach suggested by recent reforms aimed at "reinventing government" (Sensenbrenner 1991, Osborne and Gaebler 1992). Responsiveness turns accountability outward rather than upward.

There is room for multiple interpretations within the responsiveness conception. For example, an organization can be responsive to the *demands* of its clientele. This can be accomplished in different ways. An organization might poll "customers" to determine their preferences, solicit input through focus groups or establish advisory councils with the representation of key constituent groups. Profit-seeking organizations also carefully track consumer preferences through analysis of the market and allocate resources accordingly.

Another way of expressing the responsiveness idea emphasizes substantive accomplishment. That is, an organization is accountable if it meets a particular *need*. Note the difference in emphasis. Under the control conception, if a bureaucratic agency receives a command, its accountability is judged on the basis of the extent to which it carried out that order. If bureaucrats are responding to popular preference, their accountability is a function of consumer satisfaction. An emphasis on substantive expectations (e.g., reduce poverty, increase economic activity) shifts the standard of accountability to

Table 8.1 *Conceptions of accountability*

Conception of accountability	Key determination
Transparency	Did the organization reveal the facts of its performance?
Liability	Did the organization face consequences for its performance?
Controllability	Did the organization do what the principal (e.g., Congress, the President) desired?
Responsibility	Did the organization follow the rules?
Responsiveness	Did the organization fulfill the substantive expectation (demand/need)?

need. Organizations are responsive (accountable) if they meet the need that they were created to address. This is sometimes described as a "bottom-line" vision of accountability.

The two different shades of responsiveness – one focused on demand, the other on need – share a common standard of evaluation: did the organization fulfill its substantive expectation? The difference lies in the determination of that expectation. The *demand* approach looks at citizen or constituent preferences while the *need* approach relies upon an objective assessment of the public policy goals that the organizations ought to be pursuing.

Responsiveness is more consistent with responsibility than control. Indeed, the combination of strong formal and/or informal norms with performance-based evaluation presents an alternative vision of accountability to hierarchical control. Without the ability to make discretionary decisions, a bureaucrat cannot be responsive *or* responsible because her focus is on satisfying the principal. Thus a relaxation of demands for hierarchical control is required. A responsive, responsible bureaucracy can function only where "spheres of discretion and non-discretion" are clearly differentiated (O'Laughlin 1990).

Accountability in the reinvention era

Distinguishing these dimensions of accountability is a necessary prior step before making any judgment on the accountability of any organization. That is, whether one thinks an organization is accountable depends a great deal on what one means by accountability. Comparing the fundamental question at the heart of each conception of accountability makes this point quite clearly (see table 8.1).

The core conclusion of this book is that reliance on hybrid organizations does result in a loss of control. It is a finding that should give pause because controllability is deeply embedded in most theories of democratic government. However, it is not a conclusion that renders the idea of quasi-government inimical to democracy.

Equating loss of control with loss of accountability would require a narrow interpretation of accountability – one that excludes four other conceptions of accountability outlined above. Other notions of accountability may be more consistent with reliance on hybrid organizations. Given the expectations now placed upon public-sector organizations, it may be necessary to abandon controllability as the dominant notion of accountability for government organizations.

Indeed, a bureaucracy that was accountable *only* in the sense that it could be controlled by elected representatives would not appeal to many students of democracy or public administration. This vision precludes the possibility of direct relationship between the bureaucracy and the citizenry. It places an unrealistic burden on the legislature and elected executive to transmit citizen demands and needs to the multitude of bureaucratic organizations that serve the population. Wood and Waterman point out that the growth in size and scope of the bureaucracy, in addition to its professionalization, make the control idea less appropriate than it once was (1994).

The question, then, is what conceptions of accountability might be more consistent with quasi-government than controllability. Although this book reveals that elected principals lose some measure of control when public policy activities are delegated to hybrid organizations, the observations hint at accountability in other forms.

The resistance of Fannie Mae and Freddie Mac to preferences that were not in the organizations' economic interests (e.g., finance more loans to low-income borrowers) could be seen as a form of *responsibility*. The unwillingness of government-backed venture capital funds to invest in unprofitable sectors or regions could be seen in the same light. This type of fiscal restraint is a type of responsibility that is, in some respects, more confining than control. Of course, in these examples, the responsibility of the organization is in line with private interests while principals seeking control are pursuing public objectives.

This is not always the case. As chapter 3 explains, hybrid organizations do generally adhere to legal mandates and regulations, especially those that are "negative" in character. Recall that the venture capital funds did not invest in prohibited industries and the export promotion organizations were quickly in compliance with restrictions against business in China. Thus one can think of hybrid organizations as potentially quite accountable in the responsibility sense.

Hybrid organizations might also be seen as being accountable on the *responsiveness* dimension as well. Export promotion organizations did not seem to boost exports to Africa despite the clear articulation of a preference for this outcome. However, this could be explained by the lack of interest in such programs. Given the lack of demand for assistance in exports to Africa, one *could* see this as a type of accountability. The organization did not try to satisfy a demand that did not exist. Similarly, the Enterprise Funds' failure to invest in telecommunications (despite the congressional instruction to do so) could be seen as this form of responsiveness. There was no market for telecommunications investment so the Enterprise Funds directed capital where it was demanded.

This perspective is more problematic. The very lack of demand may be the problem the hybrid was created to address. It simply confirms the rationale of the policy and does little to address the underlying objectives. As discussed in chapter 4, this dynamic is likely to occur when hybrids are reliant on the cooperation of market-oriented organizations to carry out their missions. If the demand existed, there would be little reason for any government intervention at all.

In the context of quasi-government, then, the critical question is *whose* demand or need is being satisfied. Consider the two housing GSEs. Fannie Mae and Freddie Mac could be characterized as responsive to shareholders if they eschewed less profitable loans to low-income borrowers. Yet this seems a strange metric by which a governmental entity should be judged. One would likely want to ask if the companies were responsive to the demand and need of potential borrowers.

Expansion of quasi-government requires a conscious restatement of accountability expectations. Without this accompanying change, hybrid organizations will inevitably leave some people dissatisfied and shocked by their lack of "accountability." As the previous paragraphs indicate, there is no reason that hybrids cannot be accountable in the responsibility or responsiveness senses as here defined. In order for these types of accountability to prove meaningful as substitutes for control, however, the public objectives of the hybrid organization must be translated into the language of responsibility or responsiveness. As the discussion above indicates, this is a challenging project.

The promise of quasi-government

There can be little doubt that hybrid organizations will remain attractive to policy-makers at the local, state, national and even international levels of government. In the current political environment, proposals for new government agencies are greeted with skepticism. Hybrids, in contrast, receive limited scrutiny. The oft-repeated argument in favor of hybrid organizations – that organizations modeled on those from the private sector are more disciplined and efficient – has been neither challenged nor substantiated.

Determining the desirability of quasi-government requires analysis of a complex set of questions, each of which poses significant hurdles. First, it must be determined whether hybrid organizations do, in fact, produce goods more efficiently than traditional government agencies. Second, it must be determined that the *public* goods produced by a hybrid organization exceed the goods produced by a traditional government agency. That is, the mere fact that the hybrid produces more goods does not indicate that it is a more efficient producer of *public* goods (i.e., goods that otherwise would not be produced by the market). This poses a more complicated problem. Essentially, this is an evaluation of the effectiveness of the hybrid organization *and* the regulatory agency assigned responsibility for the hybrid. Can the regulator "extract" more public goods from the hybrid than can be produced by the government agency?

If the amount of public goods extracted from the hybrid organization's total outputs exceeds the total goods produced by the government agency for the same cost (per unit) then the hybrid mechanism is an efficient mechanism for producing that public good (see figure 8.1 for illustration). Note that the cost of production for the hybrid must include the cost of operating the regulatory agency.

Still, this is not the end of the evaluation required. It must be determined that the political costs of relying upon hybrid government are less than the marginal benefit of employing a hybrid organization rather than a traditional government agency. This final question, of course, revolves around the issues raised in this book. Despite the fact that the logically prior questions remain largely unexamined, this matter is quite urgent because policy-makers have

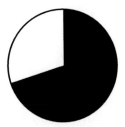

Total output of
government agency
(public goods in black)

Total output of
hybrid organization
(public goods in black)

Figure 8.1 Can regulation of a hybrid organization extract greater public good than a government agency can produce?

already made the leap. Nevertheless, there is ample room and need for additional research on all three fronts.

Hybrid organizations offer immense promise as public policy tools. They allow government to harness the power of markets. They are capable of steering private, profit-seeking organizations into arenas improved by their presence. And they offer innovative solutions to vexing governance challenges that are sure to multiply in the future.

More to the point, hybrids are sure to play a prominent role in future governance. Technological development, including the growth of the Internet, is increasing the number of human activities that span political borders. Governments worldwide are being forced to delegate responsibilities to a new set of institutions and organizations – entities that collect taxes, set technical standards and coordinate law enforcement.

Much will be demanded of these organizations operating outside the confines of traditional public bureaucracy. They will be expected to start quickly, to act decisively and to run efficiently. In short, these organizations will likely be hybrids. And so the vexing problems of defining accountability for a new era are not likely to go away. Rather, they will multiply and take on new significance as quasi-government moves from the shadows to center stage.

Appendix

Background of organizations studied

As described in chapter 2, the research design called for comparison of federal hybrids and government agencies within three policy spheres: housing, export promotion and international market development. This facilitated comparison of organizations with different structural features as they undertook similar tasks, responded to similar sets of preferences and interacted with similar sets of interest groups. This appendix describes the organizations studied in more detail than the main text of this book, providing an understanding of the history and operations of the hybrids and agencies.

Housing

Hybrid organizations are vital to federal housing policy, particularly in the realm of housing finance. The organizations studied include a large federal agency, a government corporation and three government-sponsored enterprises. Table 2.1 (page 28) summarizes the structure of these entities according to the key dimensions identified in chapter 1: ownership and funding.

Not only does the housing domain offer a diverse population of organizations, but it has been the subject of intense interest from the legislative and executive branches. Congress has revamped regulation of the housing hybrids and proposals for additional changes are pending (Guerrero 2000). The Clinton Administration demonstrated sustained interest in housing policy. Thus there is an available record of preferences and outputs of the federal housing organizations.

Department of housing and urban development

Although the department was only created in 1965, HUD's history extends back to housing programs initiated to accommodate workers mobilized for World War I. These temporary programs were revived during World War II. In the 1950s and 1960s, Congress restructured the federal government's disparate housing agencies, consolidating several agencies and creating the Department of Housing and Urban Development in 1965.

Within the department there exists a government-owned corporation, the Federal Housing Administration. With its origins as a Depression-era agency, the FHA long predates HUD. Although, in name, the FHA is a government corporation it is in practice a part of HUD. It is led by an assistant secretary of the department, who participates in departmental meetings and activities. Indeed, the FHA is a core component of HUD. It provides mortgage insurance to first-time homebuyers and also underwrites loans on multi-family housing. In the 1960s and 1970s FHA programs were expanded, targeting low-income areas with slum clearance and improvement programs.

The FHA can be differentiated from other government corporations by its reliance on appropriated funds to operate. Unlike OPIC, described below, the FHA does not generate enough fees to cover the cost of its operations. The amount appropriated for FHA programs typically exceeds the revenue generated through the organization's insurance activities (GAO 1995). Because the FHA exists within the Department of Housing and Urban Development, and runs one of the core HUD programs, its decision-making is not independent but integral to departmental strategy.

Fannie Mae and Freddie Mac

Known formally as the Federal National Mortgage Association and the Federal Home Loan Mortgage Corporation, Fannie Mae and Freddie Mac are government-sponsored enterprises. They are private, profit-seeking corporations created by Congress to serve a public purpose: increasing the availability of credit to American homebuyers while bringing stability and liquidity to the financial sector.

As quasi-public entities, they are endowed with advantages that distinguish them from purely private companies. Fannie Mae and Freddie Mac are exempt from state and local taxes, exempt from the registration requirements of the Securities and Exchange Commission, and have a $2.25 billion line of credit with the United States Treasury.

Although they receive no direct subsidy from the federal government, securities issued by GSEs are implicitly backed by the full faith and credit of the United States government. That is, investors believe that, if Fannie Mae or Freddie Mac were to go broke, the federal government would make good on their outstanding obligations. Despite the fact that all GSE securities carry an explicit disclaimer that they are not guaranteed by the federal government, the perception is powerful because the government has done nothing to discourage it. As a consequence, Fannie Mae and Freddie Mac pay lower interest rates on their debt than even the most well regarded corporations – those rated "AAA" by private rating firms.

Fannie Mae and Freddie Mac are profitable "Fortune 500" companies owned by private shareholders. Their combined net income in 2001 was more than $10 billion (OFHEO 2001). In terms of assets, Fannie Mae and Freddie Mac rank second and sixth, respectively, among American corporations (*Fortune* 2002). Fannie Mae and Freddie Mac stocks, traded on the New York Stock Exchange, consistently outperform the Standard & Poor's 500 average and are considered good, safe investments. Their executives earn multi-million dollar salaries comparable to Fortune 500 peers.

Despite their connections to the federal government and their unique advantages, Fannie Mae and Freddie Mac are not considered agencies of the United States government. They are *not* subject to the regulations that govern the activities of federal agencies and their employees. They are, however, subject to two sets of regulations that pertain only to them.

Fannie Mae and Freddie Mac are both governed by eighteen-member boards of directors. The President of the United States appoints five of the eighteen board members. The presidentially-appointed directors are not distinguished from the other members by a statutory obligation to represent the President or the administration (Musolf 1983). The president and officers of Fannie Mae and Freddie Mac are selected by the boards of directors. Their management answers to the board, not the United States government.

A brief history. Prior to the Great Depression, most Americans financed their home purchases with loans from savings and building societies. Borrowers made yearly interest payments and repaid the principal at the end of a short loan period, typically five years. Frequently, borrowers renewed their loans several times without repaying the principal.

When the Depression hit, banks and thrifts found themselves in an illiquid position: without the cash to pay depositors seeking their money. They refused to renew home loans that were due and foreclosed on the mortgages to raise what cash they could by selling the properties. Many argued, therefore, that the "real cause" of the ensuing wave of foreclosures was the lack of a credit source for the banks and thrifts. With no one to borrow from, cash-short savings institutions had to foreclose on borrowers.

This prompted several types of federal intervention (Fish 1979). Congress first created a system of federal Home Loan Banks (described below) that existed to loan federally borrowed money to cash-strapped lending institutions. These institutions were successful forerunners of Fannie Mae and Freddie Mac.[10]

Congress also wanted to lift the United States out of the Depression by stimulating the housing market. The National Housing Act of 1934 created the Federal Housing Administration to insure lenders against borrower default. This would prompt home sales, construction and economic activity.

Private mortgage associations were expected to purchase the mortgages from the lenders and hold them as investments. Such associations never materialized. In 1938 an office within the Reconstruction Finance Corporation was created to fill the role (Fish 1979).[11] This office, eventually named the Federal National Mortgage Association (FNMA), purchased FHA-insured loans from private lenders. The federal government thus created a secondary mortgage market – a place for lenders to sell loans – thereby increasing the supply of money for yet more loans.

After World War II, the end of the wartime production boom raised fears of a renewed Depression. So Congress expanded the role of home finance institutions to keep the economy humming. In addition to the FHA guarantee program, veterans were offered a federal loan guarantee (with no down payment required).[12] These loans, also purchased by the FNMA, fueled the great suburban expansion of the 1950s (Jackson 1985).

Because of budget pressures, the FNMA was first changed into a government corporation and gradually sold to private owners. In 1968, Fannie Mae was chartered as a fully private government-sponsored enterprise (Moe 1983). This raised revenues and moved the expenditures of the growing agency "off-budget." At the same time the Government National Mortgage Association (Ginnie Mae) was created as a smaller government-*owned* corporation – a part of HUD. Ginnie Mae (described below) was created to handle unprofitable subsidization programs that Fannie Mae could not undertake in accordance with its new GSE charter. The separation of Fannie Mae from Ginnie Mae clarified Fannie Mae's status as a private, profit-seeking corporation.

In 1970, Congress created the Federal Home Loan Mortgage Corporation (Freddie Mac) to purchase loans made by institutions that were part of

---

[10] The Home Owners Loan Corporation (HOLC), for example, was originally capitalized by Treasury notes and made answerable to the Home Loan Bank Board. By the time it was liquidated in 1951, it had made a profit (Fish 1979, 185).

[11] The Reconstruction Finance Corporation (RFC) was created in 1932 to lend money at 3 percent interest in an effort to revive the economy. Congress appropriated $300 million to the agency. It also issued debt and bonds to raise money (Fish 1979, 195).

[12] In this book, loans described as FHA-insured also include loans insured by the Department of Veterans Affairs.

the Federal Home Loan Bank system. Although technically owned by thrifts through the Federal Home Loan Bank Board, Freddie Mac, like Ginnie Mae, functioned more like a government agency than a private company. When the savings and loan crisis precipitated the restructuring of the savings industry in 1989, Congress transformed Freddie Mac into a private ownership, government-sponsored enterprise modeled on Fannie Mae as part of the restructuring of the Federal Home Loan Bank Board.

Fannie Mae and Freddie Mac are considerably more removed from the federal government than other federal housing entities. The Home Loan Bank system is managed by the Federal Housing Finance Board, an entity led by five presidential appointees. Both the president of Ginnie Mae and the commissioner of the FHA are appointed by the President and answer to the secretary of HUD. This is in stark contrast to the leadership of Fannie Mae and Freddie Mac, selected by the corporations' boards of directors.

In 1992 Congress restructured the oversight of Fannie Mae and Freddie Mac, splitting regulatory authority between HUD and a new quasi-independent agency of HUD, the Office of Federal Housing Enterprise Oversight. The legislative process culminating in the current regulatory arrangement is detailed in chapter 5.

How they work. Fannie Mae and Freddie Mac do not lend money or insure individual mortgages but act as conduits. They purchase loans originated by private institutions (banks, thrifts or mortgage bankers). After selling loans to Fannie Mae or Freddie Mac, lenders have money to make additional loans or investments (see figure A.1 for an illustration of the GSEs' role in the housing finance system). By "buying the loan," Fannie Mae or Freddie Mac is entitled to the monthly payments made by the borrower.

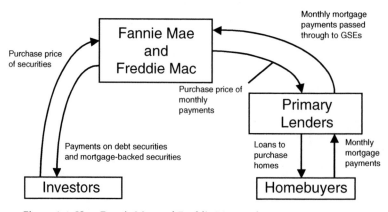

Figure A.1 How Fannie Mae and Freddie Mac work

Fannie Mae and Freddie Mac either keep the loans and receive the monthly mortgage payments or bundle many loans together and resell shares of the monthly payments as "mortgage-backed securities." These are sometimes called "pass-throughs" because the monthly mortgage payments pass through Fannie Mae or Freddie Mac to the holder of the security.

Securities sold by Fannie Mae and Freddie Mac are free of credit risk. That is, even if a homebuyer defaults on his loan, Fannie Mae or Freddie Mac will pay the holder of the mortgage security all the money to which she is entitled.

The most significant business advantage Fannie Mae and Freddie Mac enjoy by virtue of their status as government-sponsored enterprises is their low cost of funds (described above). Not only do GSEs pay low interest rates on debt, but the prices of their mortgage securities reflect the safety of the investment. As a result of the government-provided advantages, Fannie Mae and Freddie Mac enjoy an effective duopoly over the secondary market for home loans.[13] This, in turn, creates a tremendous volume of loans handled by Fannie Mae and Freddie Mac, resulting in significant financial obligations – approximately $2.8 trillion (OFHEO 2001).

Other housing organizations

There are two other governmental organizations that are involved in federal housing policy. Reference is made to these organizations but they are not central to the research. Both are hybrids but their operational differences make comparison with Fannie Mae, Freddie Mac and the Federal Housing Administration difficult.

Ginnie Mae. The Government National Mortgage Association was created when Fannie Mae was transformed into a government-sponsored enterprise. In order for Fannie Mae to attract private investors and generate revenues to cover costs and return profits, it had to be relieved of its obligation to operate unprofitable programs. This essentially translated into allowing Fannie Mae to reject some loans as overly risky.

Still, the Federal Housing Administration and the Department of Veterans Affairs were offering guarantees on such loans. Thus, in order to keep the flow of mortgage credit to borrowers eligible for FHA/VA loans intact, Ginnie Mae was created to fulfill essentially the same function performed by Fannie Mae (and now Freddie Mac). Ginnie Mae purchases mortgages and pools them together, then issues mortgage-backed securities to investors, who receive guaranteed income streams from the mortgage payments. Ginnie

---

[13] Not all home loans are eligible for purchase by Fannie Mae and Freddie Mac. There is a ceiling on the dollar value of loans that they can purchase plus standards that all loans must meet for purchase. Loans that meet these requirements are called conforming loans.

Mae securities are explicitly backed by the full faith and credit of the US government.

Ginnie Mae is structured as a government corporation within HUD. The president of the corporation and its senior employees are appointed by the President of the United States with the advice and consent of the Senate. A staff of civil servants (and many contract employees) carry out organizational functions. Ginnie Mae is physically located in the HUD building and its president generally works closely with the secretary and other senior appointed HUD officials. In recent years, proposals concerning the restructuring of Ginnie Mae have surfaced frequently. For example, the Clinton Administration considered selling the corporation to create a GSE similar to Fannie Mae and Freddie Mac.

Federal Home Loan Bank system. As described above, one of the causes of the Depression was the illiquidity experienced by financial institutions. In addition to the programs described above, the federal government responded by creating a network of banks that would lend only to banks. The Home Loan Bank system, created in 1932, consisted of twelve district banks that provided a stable source of credit and imposed regulatory discipline on the member savings institutions. Cash-strapped thrifts used their outstanding mortgage portfolios as collateral for cash advances. These could, in turn, be used to finance home purchases (generating mortgage payments for the banks and economic activity that would help pull the country out of the Depression).

The Home Loan Banks were financed by debt issued through the Home Loan Bank Board. The notes issued by the Board had "agency status." That is to say, the Home Loan Banks are able to borrow at preferential rates because their debt is implicitly guaranteed by the federal government – just like Fannie Mae and Freddie Mac (Moe 1983).

The Home Loan Bank system was not enough, however, to stem the massive tide of foreclosures, so Congress also created agencies to purchase home loans in danger of default from the lenders. Borrowers were given the opportunity to repay the federal government over a longer term.[14] The growth of Fannie Mae, Freddie Mac and private companies that perform the same function for loans that do not fit the GSE eligibility requirements has effectively eliminated the risk of such a credit crunch occurring again.

---

[14] The Farm Credit Administration and Home Owners Loan Corporation were each appropriated $2.3 billion to buy loans from creditors on which they would otherwise foreclose. The FCA focused on agricultural properties and farms and the HOLC worked on standard home loans. The FCA reported to the Department of Agriculture and the HOLC was responsible to the Home Loan Bank Board. In operation, the FCA was an agency of the federal government while the HOLC functioned as a government-owned corporation (Fish 1979, 185).

Export promotion

Trade policy generally has a low public profile but it was emphasized by the Clinton Administration. This took the form of support for international treaties such as NAFTA and GATT. It also included renewed interest in government promotion of American exports as a tool for domestic economic growth. Commerce Secretary Ron Brown brought a high profile to this activity before his death in 1996 (Lawrence 1996, Crutsinger 1996).

This policy area features comparison of the Department of Commerce, a government agency, and two government corporations: the Export-Import Bank and the Overseas Private Investment Corporation. In addition to these organizations of principal interest in this study, other entities were also considered. These organizations are all represented on the Trade Promotion Coordinating Committee, established within the Commerce Department, which exists to coordinate policy across the multiple agencies that have trade-related functions. Table 2.2 (page 30) provides basic information on these organizations.

Department of Commerce

The Commerce Department includes a variety of bureaus with disparate missions: the Census Bureau, the National Oceanographic and Atmospheric Administration and the Patents and Trademark Office. Of interest in this study are the department's export promotion activities, housed primarily in the International Trade Administration (ITA).

The ITA is overseen by an Under-Secretary of Commerce and includes the Foreign Commercial Service (FCS), which helps promote American business abroad, as well as research branches dedicated to providing American firms with information on foreign markets and monitoring imports from other countries.

A brief history. Established in 1903, the Commerce Department has expanded over the years to include a host of seemingly unrelated functions. Indeed, in recent years, the department has been targeted for dissolution. Even a former Commerce Secretary noted that the department had become "nothing more than a hall closet where you throw in everything that you don't know what to do with" (Chrysler 1995).

The department's role in promoting American businesses abroad has expanded in recent years with the growth in international commerce. Governments are highly competitive in their efforts to boost exports. In addition to the Commerce Department's activities, the US government promotes agriculture exports through programs operated by the Department of Agriculture.

How it works. The ITA promotes exports with a few core activities. First, agency staff analyze economic activities in potential markets and provide advice to American exporters regarding potential opportunities and marketing strategies. They also identify obstacles to American exports and work to reduce such impediments. Second, the department organizes trade missions to countries that are identified as potential markets for US goods and services. Trade missions introduce American suppliers to potential consumers and help establish the basis of a working relationship.

Third, the department operates the Foreign Commercial Service, which functions in the United States and abroad. American offices assist small and medium businesses as they attempt to get into the export sector. Abroad, the FCS operates as a commercial diplomatic corps, gathering information, making contacts and laying the groundwork for American businesses. These services help American exporters create appropriate strategies for different markets, price their products appropriately and generally enter new markets more smoothly and successfully.

Export-Import Bank of the United States

The Export-Import Bank of the United States is another governmental entity with its origins in the Depression era. The name is a misnomer; ExIm has nothing to with imports and everything to do with exports. Utilizing a variety of tools, ExIm endeavors to support American exports and keep American companies competitive with non-American corporations supported by their national export credit agencies. ExIm charges fees that typically cover its operating costs but it also receives government appropriations, primarily in the form of budgetary allotments made to cover the risk represented by ExIm guarantees.

ExIm is a uniquely structured government corporation. It is independent of all cabinet departments and governed by a five-member board of directors. The president of the bank serves as chairman of the board; the first vice-president serves as vice-chairman. All five board members are appointed by the President of the United States with the advice and consent of the Senate. Only three of the directors may be from the same political party. In recent years, Congress has designated directors with specific responsibilities (e.g. environmental policy, small business). ExIm is subject to most federal management laws in addition to the Government Corporation Control Act.

A brief history. In 1934, two Export-Import Banks were created. One was dedicated exclusively to financing exports to a key ally, the Soviet Union. The second was dedicated to exports to other nations and was envisioned as a mechanism to protect and cultivate American jobs through exports while stabilizing international markets. The banks were merged two years later.

ExIm became an instrument of the United States' policy of assisting the Allies in Europe before the American entrance into World War II. And, following the war, the Export-Import Bank became a central component of the early reconstruction policy for devastated nations. With international institutions and the creation of the Marshall Plan, ExIm returned to its original mission of financing US exports. It has operated under revised versions of the organizing legislation passed in 1945 for the past fifty-five years (Emery et al. 1984).

In recent years there has been conflict regarding the degree to which ExIm decisions should be influenced by political considerations. Two large projects, one in Russia and another in China, generated significant disagreement. The Russian project concerned financing for Gazprom, an energy company. Members of Congress objected to American assistance for Gazprom because the company was also developing natural gas fields in Iran (Abruzzese 1997). Annoyed by the controversy, Gazprom ultimately withdrew its application for financing (Gordon 1997). ExIm's plans to help finance construction of the massive Three Gorges Dam project in China also drew criticism. Environmentalists (among other critics) who assailed the project found sympathetic ears in the Clinton Administration. Despite howls from Republican critics who argued that ExIm decisions should not be influenced by environmental considerations, the administration convened a meeting of environmentally concerned officials and appeared to urge ExIm to reconsider the deal's environmental impact (interviews 52, 40). Ultimately, China opted not to comply with ExIm's requests for additional information, thus ending ExIm's consideration of the application for financing.

Similar controversies added fuel to the fire when critics attacked ExIm in the 1990s as a form of "corporate welfare" and attempted to eliminate the organization. This was not the first time ExIm had come under attack. In 1953 it was nearly phased out by President Eisenhower, who felt ExIm was unnecessary. ExIm has survived because of support from the export community and the compelling argument that the United States must match the similar export support programs operated by every industrialized country (Levine 1998).

How ExIm works. ExIm has multiple programs to facilitate American exports. The principal activity is the extension of loan guarantees that allow foreign purchasers to acquire American goods. For example, ExIm will guarantee a loan to a Brazilian airline that allows it to purchase a Boeing jet. Thus buyers who may not be able to secure credit elsewhere are able to purchase American goods (generally very expensive American goods that take a significant period of time to pay for). ExIm charges fees based on the amount, duration and risk associated with the loan. ExIm also makes a limited number of direct loans to foreign buyers of American goods. The borrower pays a fixed rate that is competitive with private financing.

ExIm also helps American exporters directly in two ways. ExIm provides guarantees on working capital loans to small- and medium-sized American businesses that are producing goods and/or services for export. A fee is paid for this guarantee based on the amount covered. ExIm also provides insurance against political and commercial risk. That is, ExIm insures the American exporter against losses that result from political turmoil in the importing country or general default on the part of the buyer. These guarantees are generally short-term (less than a year).

Overseas Private Investment Corporation

Unlike the other export promotion agencies, OPIC has an interest in the development of foreign countries, not just American business. These two objectives are pursued concomitantly through three programs: political risk insurance for American companies investing in developing countries; guaranteed loans to businesses involved in large, capital-intensive initiatives in developing countries; and guaranteed loans to venture capital funds focusing on developing countries.

These programs are intended to serve American businesses in the short and long term. In the short term, they encourage infrastructure projects and other large public works that require American knowledge and technology. In the long term, new markets for American goods and services are cultivated that will support exports in the future. The third program, OPIC-backed venture capital funds, is considered in this study's comparison of agencies and hybrids in the field of international market development (described below).

OPIC is overseen by a board of directors that includes six ex officio members of the administration – the administrator of the Agency for International Development and representatives of the Office of the US Trade Representative, the Department of Commerce, the Department of the Treasury, the Department of the State and the Department of Labor – as well as seven other presidential appointees. The board is not intimately involved in the day-to-day activities of OPIC, functioning like a corporate board that reviews major policy decisions (interviews 22, 34). The OPIC president (who also serves as a corporate director) and senior management are appointed by the President of the United States and confirmed by the Senate.

Unlike ExIm, OPIC is considered a foreign policy agency of the United States government. This has several implications. First, congressional oversight of OPIC is vested in the foreign affairs committees. ExIm is overseen through the banking committees. Second, OPIC is, by default, subject to the same limitations that affect other foreign policy instruments (i.e., sanctions against countries restrict OPIC activities). Finally, unlike ExIm, OPIC is not regarded as somewhat apolitical; it is expected that OPIC will undertake activities for policy reasons rather than simply responding to market demand.

A brief history. Once an office of the Agency for International Development, OPIC was created as a government corporation in 1974. Its origins lay in the economic assistance aimed at rebuilding Europe after World War II. The Investment Guaranty Program was established in 1948 as part of the Economic Cooperation Act. Over the course of the next twenty years, the administration of the program moved several times. Responsibility shifted from the Foreign Operations Administration to the International Cooperation Administration of the State Department amidst criticism that the Investment Guaranty Program was not being administered in a manner consistent with US foreign policy (Brennglass 1983). Critics argued that the program was subsidizing investment in countries that required no subsidy.

President Kennedy reorganized much of the foreign policy bureaucracy and created the Agency for International Development. The Investment Guaranty Program was moved into the new agency with its creation in 1961. Potential investments to be guaranteed under the program were judged on their potential contribution to economic development in the target country. Risk management and the impact on American business were notably absent from considerations (Brennglass 1983, 17).

This institutional arrangement proved short-lived. Senator Jacob Javits (R – NY) was leading a movement among Members of Congress to create a "Peace by Investment Corporation" at the same time that Lyndon Johnson was reorganizing USAID. Although the Johnson Administration consolidated the guarantee programs in an Office of Private Resources within USAID, Nixon Administration officials and some Members of Congress shared the idea that USAID was not doing an adequate job developing market economies in the developing world (interviews 32, 17, 19). They concluded that a less governmental entity would be better suited to develop market institutions and monitor investments. They endorsed the Javits idea and essentially transferred the Investment Guaranty Program from USAID's Office of Private Resources to a new government corporation, the Overseas Private Investment Corporation. At that time some Members of Congress expressed concerns that the government would lose control over a tool of foreign policy (Brennglass 1983, 24).

As American interest in foreign policy waned and the strategic importance of cultivating allies in the Cold War environment evaporated, OPIC's defenders emphasized its contribution to the health of American businesses and, by extension, American workers (interview 33). Ironically, this rationale proved a liability when OPIC was targeted as a form of "corporate welfare" by Rep. John Kasich (R – OH) in the budget-cutting fervor of the 1990s (Doherty 1996). OPIC narrowly survived a bruising reauthorization battle by rallying support not from the development community but export-oriented businesses and trade groups with influence on Capitol Hill. In fact, OPIC was reauthorized through the appropriations committee – an unusual back-door tactic made necessary by the authorizing committee's refusal to do the same (Lawrence 1997).

How OPIC works. OPIC has two major programs. First, it insures against political risk as a means of encouraging investment in developing countries. OPIC will insure investments up to $200 million against currency inconvertibility, expropriation and political violence. Essentially, OPIC provides a guarantee that the risk associated with investment in a developing country is limited.

Companies or individuals do not receive OPIC insurance free of charge. There is a schedule of premiums related to the risk of the investment and the type of insurance. OPIC charges different rates for different types of coverage. For example, businesses would pay 60 cents for every $100 insured against property loss to political violence.

The second major OPIC program provides financing for major projects through direct loans and loan guarantees. Such ventures must have significant equity and/or management participation by American companies. These loan guarantees and/or direct loans are also capped at $200 million.

Again, OPIC judges investments on the quality of the project and the soundness of the business plan. Loan recipients pay interest on the loans that is comparable to those of other US government-guaranteed issues of similar maturity. OPIC also charges a guaranty fee related to the outstanding principal amount and the commercial and political risk.

Both of these programs encourage development by underwriting economic activity in countries that are shunned by private financial institutions. OPIC's programs have been justified in recent years by their value as export promotion programs. Projects financed through OPIC loans, loan guarantees and insurance often result in exports of American goods and services.

Businesses interested in participating in OPIC programs must apply through a formal process. The organization does advertise and organize conferences to educate American companies regarding OPIC and its programs but it relies upon private-sector organizations to accomplish its mission.

It does not make direct investments in developing countries. The closest OPIC comes to such direct investment is its third major program, OPIC investment funds. These are described in detail in the international market development section of this appendix.

Other export promotion organizations

Trade and Development Agency (TDA). The TDA also has its origins in USAID. It finances feasibility studies and informational trips for projects in developing countries. This is intended to stimulate business that will ultimately go to American companies, thus creating exports and jobs in the United States. The TDA is a small, independent agency led by a presidential appointee.

United States Trade Representative (USTR). The Office of the USTR is mentioned only because of its familiarity. Many trade-related agencies focus on activities other than export promotion. For the most part, this involves negotiation and monitoring international trade agreements. This is the primary responsibility of the United States Trade Representative, not export promotion. The Department of Commerce is also involved in this activity. The Office of the USTR is part of the Executive Office of the President.

Department of Agriculture. The agency with the largest budget by far in the field of export promotion is the Department of Agriculture. USDA essentially performs all the functions outlined above with respect to agricultural commodities. The orientation of the program is somewhat different, however, inasmuch as agricultural export programs are inextricably tied into domestic agricultural support programs. Thus the imperatives and expectations are quite different for this agency; it is judged primarily on its ability to assist American farmers, not its ability to increase agricultural exports per se (interviews 50, 51). Although USDA is part of the TPCC, it is by all accounts an independent player. Thus this study is concerned with non-agricultural export promotion (though the opportunity for interesting comparison is tremendous).

Small Business Administration. Under President Clinton, the Small Business Administration became more involved with export promotion. This also reflected congressional interest in small businesses (discussed in chapter 6). Some of the guarantee programs operated by ExIm and OPIC are carried out by SBA for small businesses. And, through the SBA working group on small business, the agency has worked with other trade-related entities.

Several other executive agencies are involved in trade activities, including the Agency for International Development, the Environmental Protection Agency (which tries to promote environmentally friendly exports) and the Department of Energy. However, the focus of this study is on the core export promotion organizations described in greater detail because these organizations are the primary agents responsible for satisfying principals' export-related preferences.

International market development

The United States government operates development programs around the world. Previously such efforts were associated with the Cold War and strategic containment of Soviet expansion. Today international development efforts are frequently justified on the basis of American economic self-interest or the increase in political stability that generally accompanies economic development. By developing market economies, the rationale holds, programs contribute to future American economic growth through increased exports and reduce the likelihood that military force will be required in the future. Thus this area is increasingly tied to the export promotion activities described above.

The United States Agency for International Development is the primary federal entity devoted to development. It funds educational, medical and economic development programs in countries around the world.

In recent years, government-backed venture capital funds have become popular as instruments to spur development of market economies in formerly Communist countries and other nations with limited market activity. This is a relatively new type of development in that it is often directed at countries that have a developed infrastructure and industrial capacity but lack experience with the institutions and practices of market economies.

The funds are intended to introduce Western business knowledge and experience into developing countries along with an infusion of much needed capital. Two American fund programs that fall into this category were considered: Enterprise Funds, created following the break-up of the Soviet Union, and OPIC investment funds, a set of 26 privately owned funds that target various developing countries and economic sectors. Table 2.3 (page 32) provides an overview of the organizations studied in this area.

United States Agency for International Development

The core mission of USAID is to encourage and assist the social, economic and political development of nations around the world. It pursues this objective through a diverse collection of programs that are designed to encourage economic growth, agricultural development, public health, environmental quality, democracy and education. USAID also plays a role in providing humanitarian assistance in moments of crisis, such as hurricane relief in Central America and assistance for earthquake victims in Turkey.

USAID is an independent federal government agency that receives overall foreign policy guidance from the Secretary of State. It is headed by an administrator who is appointed by the President with the advice and consent of the Senate. In recent years, there have been efforts to move USAID into the State Department. At present, the agency retains its independence.

A brief history. The Foreign Assistance Act of 1961 called for the creation of the new Agency for International Development. This was the culmination of a lengthy process in which the organization and philosophy of American foreign assistance was debated. The sentiment leading to the creation of USAID was that the diffuse array of American assistance programs was ill-equipped to accomplish long-term development projects.

USAID grew out of the American programs designed to rebuild Europe after World War II. Unlike ExIm, USAID was not created with the intention of assisting American businesses while encouraging development abroad. That is not to say USAID was purely altruistic; although USAID's origins predated the Cold War, development assistance was looked upon as a political tool that contributed to the containment of the Soviet Union.

Originally, USAID sent its staff into the field to carry out development assistance programs ranging from the establishment of medical clinics and schools to the creation of inoculation programs. Over the years USAID has evolved such that a large share of its programmatic activities are now carried out by contractors rather than USAID personnel. These contractors run a wide variety of programs in developing countries, including educational, medical and professional training.

With the collapse of the Soviet Union and increased public skepticism regarding development programs and foreign assistance generally, defenders of USAID now emphasize the benefits of foreign development to American companies and their employees. Development means expanded markets receptive to American goods and services.

Enterprise Funds

The fall of the Berlin Wall in 1989 posed an unprecedented foreign policy challenge for the United States. The desire to help Eastern Europeans establish democratic political regimes and market-based economies was universal but the strategy was uncertain. With industrial experience, skilled and educated workforces and physical infrastructure, these nations were already "developed" in the traditional sense of the term. American development agencies were not practiced in the transformation of state-controlled economies into vibrant free markets. Nor, for that matter, was there a standard approach to the transition from single-party Communist rule to competitive multi-party democracy.

Table A.1 *Enterprise Funds*[a]

Enterprise Fund	Created	Total commitment ($ millions)
Polish American Enterprise Fund	1990	240
Hungarian American Enterprise Fund	1990	60
Czech and Slovak American Enterprise Fund	1991	65
Bulgarian American Enterprise Fund	1992	55
Romanian American Enterprise Fund	1994	50
Albanian American Enterprise Fund	1995	30
Baltic American Enterprise Fund	1994	50
US Russia Investment Fund[b]	1995[b]	440
Central Asian American Enterprise Fund	1995	150
Western NIS American Enterprise Fund	1995	150

[a] There are two additional Enterprise Funds – the South African American Enterprise Fund and the Defense Enterprise Fund – that are overseen separately from the eleven Enterprise Funds operating in Eastern Europe and the Newly Independent States.

[b] This Fund was created with the consolidation of two separate funds, both operating in Russia.

The Support for Eastern European Democracy Act of 1989 provided American aid to Poland and Hungary and set the template for future programs (Public Law 101–179). In addition to extending several traditional aid programs to these countries, the SEED Act created Enterprise Funds to develop the private sector through "loans, grants, equity investments, feasibility studies, technical assistance, training, insurance, guarantees, and other measures" (22 USCA §5,421(a)). The Enterprise Funds were to be chartered as private corporations but funded by government appropriation: $240 million for the Polish American Enterprise Fund, $60 million for the Hungarian American Enterprise Fund (§5,421(b)(1), (2)). The first director was designated in 1990; the two Funds were incorporated and began operations shortly thereafter.

There are now eleven Enterprise Funds operating in Eastern Europe and the former republics of the Soviet Union. As table A.1 indicates, the size of the commitment to each Fund varies considerably.

Not surprisingly, the Funds have experienced uneven results. To date, the Polish Fund is the most successful. It has earned a significant return on the appropriated dollars, creating an unexpected dilemma: who gets the profits? After much debate, half the money was used to establish a foundation to support Polish democracy and the rest will be returned to the US Treasury. Other Enterprise Funds operating in less developed economies have struggled (e.g., the Western Newly Independent States Fund, which operates in Ukraine, Belarus and Moldova). The differences in performance can be attributed to the significant differences in economic and political conditions in each country. Variation in the skill of each Fund's managers and directors surely accounts for some differences as well.

How they work. Both Enterprise Funds and OPIC investment funds (described below) are modeled on traditional, private venture capital funds. Venture capital funds are essentially pools of money that have been entrusted to an investment team seeking out promising new businesses. Fund managers review scores of potential investments; they typically invest in fewer than 5 percent of proposals they consider. Many funds are organized to invest in a particular sector of the economy (e.g., high technology) or region (e.g., Latin America).

Most private venture capital funds hope to generate at least a 25 percent return on the invested capital in ten years or fewer. At that time, the fund sells its equity stake either to another investor or in a public stock offering. The overhead costs for the management of the fund are paid by fees charged as a percentage of the capital pool. The fund managers also earn a share of the profits generated by the fund investments (Fox 1996).

Enterprise Funds differ from this model in two critical respects. First, they are funded not by privately invested capital but federally appropriated dollars.[15] Second, Enterprise Funds were created not by investors seeking a 25 percent return on their capital but by the US government. The "investment" of appropriated dollars was made in an effort to assist the development of market institutions.

Members of Enterprise Funds' staff have established offices in the countries they were created to target. Although every Fund was originally led by Americans, the Funds have employed and trained large numbers of nationals in the countries where they operate. These individuals have, in some cases, assumed management of Enterprise Fund operations.

Enterprise Fund staff seek to identify potential investments and evaluate their prospects. If an Enterprise Fund invests in a particular company, the Fund monitors the behavior and performance of that firm and often attempts to provide assistance. Funds have experimented with a variety of approaches, including equity investment (the traditional venture capital model), debt and indirect micro-lending (through designated lending

---

[15] Some Enterprise Funds have raised private capital that is invested through parallel funds (interview 74).

institutions). Some Enterprise Funds have combined their venture capital function with the delivery of technical assistance and other aid not intended to generate economic return.

OPIC investment funds

At about the same time that the Enterprise Fund program was created, the Overseas Private Investment Corporation was confronting a challenge. Neither of OPIC's core programs (loan guarantees and political risk insurance) addressed the need for capital investment in developing markets, and OPIC is prohibited by statute from making direct equity investments.

A creative solution was implemented with the creation of the Africa Growth Fund – the first OPIC investment fund. OPIC guarantees bank loans to this private, profit-seeking venture capital fund. The loans are used to attract private investment. The private capital is effectively "leveraged" because the loan requires a relatively low fixed interest payment while the capital investment could generate high returns. The OPIC investment funds more closely resemble the traditional private venture capital model than the Enterprise Funds inasmuch as they seek typical venture capital returns on their capital.

The model proved appealing and was replicated in a somewhat ad hoc fashion. Eventually, the terms of the loan agreements were roughly standardized. As of January 2002, there were twenty-six active OPIC investment funds, serving countries all over the world (OPIC 2002). The outstanding OPIC commitment was to guarantee about $1.5 billion in loans to the funds (as of December 2000), of which about $600 million has been disbursed to cover approximately 250 investments (interview 28).

A brief history. The OPIC investment funds were structured to facilitate equity investment utilizing OPIC's statutory authority to provide loan guarantees. The creators of the fund program acknowledge that the development of oversight capacity trailed the creation of the funds. Only after personnel with both government and venture capital experience were brought in did the process for creating and overseeing the investment funds take on structure (interview 23).

Subsequent to the creation of the first investment funds, Congress included language in foreign assistance legislation instructing OPIC to create additional investment funds to serve particular regions, but the OPIC statute has not been altered to include explicit provision for the investment fund program (22 USCA §2,194, §2,194b).

The investment fund program grew rapidly after the model proved appealing. New funds could be created as a "deliverable" for political purposes (see table A.2 for a listing of OPIC investment funds). For example, the

Table A.2 *OPIC investment funds*

Fund name	Fund manager	Status (as of January 15, 2002)	Total size of fund ($ millions)
Africa Growth Fund	Equator Investment Services Limited	Fully invested	25.15
Africa Millennium Fund	Savage & Associates	Negotiating	350
Agribusiness Partners International	NIS Management Company	Fully invested	95
AIG Brunswick Millennium Fund	American International Group/Brunswick Capital Management	Fully invested	288.5
Allied Small Business Fund	Allied Capital Advisors	Fully invested	20
Aqua International Partners Fund	Texas Pacific Group	Investing	222.75
Asia Development Partners	Olympus Capital Holdings (Asia)	Investing	150
Asia Pacific Growth Fund	H&Q Asia Pacific GP	Fully invested	75.25
Bancroft Eastern Europe Fund	Bancroft Advisors, LLP	Fully invested	95.3
Caucasus Fund	Caucasus Advisors, LLC	Investing	92
Draper International India Fund	Draper International	Repaid	55
Emerging Europe Fund	TDA, Inc.	Fully invested	60
First NIS Regional Fund	Baring Asset Management	Repaid	200
Global Environment Emerging Markets Fund I	GEF Management	Fully invested	66.7
Global Environment Emerging Markets Fund II	GEF Management Corporation	Fully invested	120
Great Circle Fund, LP	Great Circle Capital	Raising capital	200

(cont.)

Table A.2 (*cont.*)

Fund name	Fund manager	Status (as of January 15, 2002)	Total size of fund ($ millions)
India Private Equity Fund	TIPEF Investment Management Ltd/Indocean Fund Advisors II, Ltd	Fully invested	140
Inter-Arab Investment Fund	PanArab Investments LLC	Investing	45
Israel Growth Fund	n.a.	Repaid	40
Modern Africa Growth and Investment Fund	Modern Africa Fund Managers LLC	Investing	112
New Century Capital Partners	NCH Fund Management, Inc.	Fully invested	250
Newbridge Andean Partners	ACON Investments	Investing	160
PBO Fund	n.a.	Closed	240
Poland Partners	Poland Partners Management Co.	Fully invested	63.5
Russia Partners A	Sigular Guff & Co.	Fully invested	105
Russia Partners B	Sigular Guff & Co.	Fully invested	50
South America Private Equity Growth	Baring Latin America Partners LLC	Fully invested	180
South-east Europe Equity Fund Ltd	SEEF Management LLC	Investing	150
West Bank / Gaza & Jordan Fund	Capital Investment Management Corporation	Negotiating	60
ZM Africa Investment Fund	Zephyr Southern Africa Management Company	Investing	120

Clinton Administration celebrated the creation of a new investment fund for Africa before a single investment had been made. Still, the pace of fund creation has slowed dramatically, at least in part as a result of criticism that the program is politicized. Journalists have argued that the managers of OPIC investment funds are profiting from their political connections (Burstein and Shields 1997).

How the program works. The earliest investment funds were created in a haphazard manner. OPIC approached private fund managers with ideas for new investment funds or entertained proposals. In response to criticism that the program was influenced by political considerations, the process for soliciting and evaluating new bids for investment funds has gradually been formalized. OPIC advertises its intention to start a fund for a particular country or sector to interest potential fund managers.

Proposals are judged on the fund manager's ability to attract private investment, identify and manage equity investments and apply substantive knowledge of the proposed target country, region or sector (interviews 23, 31). OPIC also utilizes policy-related criteria in evaluating competing bids for a proposed fund. For example, competing prospective fund managers have highlighted investment strategies targeting woman-owned businesses or labor-intensive businesses (interview 31). Thus the selection process provides an opportunity for OPIC to give substantive direction to the investment fund.

Once a fund manager is selected, the terms of the loan guarantee are hammered out in a process resembling the negotiation of the charter and by-laws of Enterprise Funds. There are numerous details to be determined and incorporated into the loan agreements, including length of payment grace periods, profit stages and interest rates. OPIC also gets a portion of the "management carry" – the profit earned by the fund manager.

The funds are subject to two sets of restrictions. There is a generic set of restrictions that are placed on all OPIC programs. OPIC cannot undertake programs that have harmful effects in the United States (i.e., that export jobs), that fund companies that violate worker rights or that contribute to the degradation of the environment (22 USCA §2,191(3)). Additionally, the programmatic purpose of a particular fund imposes restrictions (e.g., a small business fund is limited by the size of the potential investment company).

OPIC is guaranteed a pre-set return on its loan regardless of the profit (or lack thereof) generated by the investment fund. The loan is the primary financial obligation of the fund. That is, in the event of a fund's failure, all recovered assets must be dedicated to repaying the loan before equity investors are made whole (Stillman 1996).

Once an investment fund is up and running, its staff reviews potential investments. When the fund staff identifies an investment opportunity in which it is interested, it presents it to its designated overseer at OPIC. The OPIC fund overseers review proposed investments for compliance with the loan agreements. Each deal must be approved by OPIC before the money is released from the lender to the investment fund. This includes the three major restrictions applicable to all OPIC programs as well as any specific constraints incorporated into a particular fund's agreement. For example, a fund operating in multiple countries may have a distribution scheme stipulated. OPIC overseers will review investments to ensure that the fund is, in fact, allocated its investment according to the negotiated distribution.

After being reviewed by the fund manager, the proposed investment is considered by an internal committee of OPIC staff. Deals are rarely rejected at this stage because the fund managers infrequently propose investments with a significant chance of rejection. Fund managers and OPIC staff emphasize that the review *does not* pertain to the financial aspects of the deal. That is, OPIC does not review the fund's evaluation of the business in terms of the market for the company's product or its likelihood of good economic return. It is concerned only with the investment fund's compliance with the loan agreement.

The oversight function continues after OPIC approves the release of funds for investment. Fund managers review investments periodically to ensure continued compliance with standards on environmental pollution and child labor, for example. This includes review of company statements, occasional site visits and informal conversation with investment fund managers. Some critics have argued that the restrictions placed on the investment funds lower the quality of professionals willing to manage them (interview 79).

Interview subjects

Identification Number	Anonymous description	Subject organization(s)	Interview date
1	Senior USAID official for EFs	EFs, USAID	12/9/98
2	House majority appropriations staff	EFs	1/8/99
3	House minority appropriations staff	EFs	1/8/99
4	Counsel to EFs	EFs	1/19/99
5	Counsel to EFs; Fmr State Department EF staff	EFs	1/18/99
6	House Intl. Rel. Cmte. Majority staff	OPIC, USAID	1/25/99
7	EF evaluator	EFs, USAID	1/26/99
8	Fmr EF counsel	EFs	1/27/99
9	State Department EF oversight staff	EFs	1/27/99
10	Fmr EF counsel to USAID	EFs	2/3/99
11	Senior USAID staff for EFs	EFs	2/4/99
12	USAID EF oversight staff	EFs	2/4/99
13	USAID EF oversight staff	EFs	2/4/99
14	EF staff	EF	2/13/99
15	EF director	EF	2/17/99
16	House international relations majority staff	EFs, OPIC, IFs	2/17/99
17	Fmr senior USAID official	EFs, USAID	2/22/99

(*cont.*)

(*cont.*)

Identification Number	Anonymous description	Subject organization(s)	Interview date
18	EF staff	EF	3/22/99
19	Fmr EF senior official	EF	2/2/99
20	EF director	EF	3/8/99
21	EF director	EF	3/12/99
22	Senior OPIC official	OPIC	2/1/99
23	Fmr senior OPIC IF official	IFs	2/11/99
24	Fmr Senate majority appropriations staff	EFs, USAID, OPIC	2/17/99
25	Senior OPIC official	OPIC	2/18/99
26	Senior IF official	OPIC, IFs	2/22/99
27	Fmr OPIC IF staff; IF manager	OPIC, IFs	2/24/99
28	Senior OPIC staff	OPIC, IFs	2/26/99
29	Fmr OPIC IF staff	OPIC, IFs	3/1/99
30	Fmr senior OPIC staff	OPIC, IFs	3/4/99
31	Senior OPIC official	OPIC, IFs	2/26/99
32	Fmr senior OPIC official	OPIC	3/9/99
33	Senior USAID official	AID, EFs, OPIC	3/22/99
34	Senior OPIC staff	OPIC	2/9/99
35	Senior OPIC official	OPIC	1/15/99
36	Senior OPIC staff	OPIC	2/18/99
37	Senior ExIm staff	ExIm, environment	1/19/99
38	Senior ExIm staff	ExIm	12/4/98
39	Senior ExIm official	ExIm	1/19/99
40	Senior ExIm staff	ExIm	1/11/99
41	Senior ExIm official	ExIm	1/19/99
42	Senior ExIm staff	ExIm	1/15/99
43	Senior ExIm official	ExIm	1/15/99
44	Senior ExIm official	ExIm, ICRAS	1/11/99
45	Senior TDA staff	TDA	1/13/99
46	Senior Commerce Department staff	Commerce, environment coordination	2/12/99
47	Fmr senior Commerce Department official	Commerce Dept.	2/26/99
48	Senior Commerce Department staff	Commerce Dept., TPCC	12/7/98
49	Senior TPCC staff	TPCC	12/00/98
50	Senior USDA staff	USDA, Foreign Agricultural Service	12/11/98

(*cont.*)

Identification Number	Anonymous description	Subject organization(s)	Interview date
51	Senior USDA staff	USDA, Foreign Agricultural Service	12/11/98
52	Congressional staff	ExIm	1/25/99
53	House banking committee majority staff	ExIm	1/28/99
54	Senior agricultural lobbyist	agricultural exports	2/18/99
55	Senior trade lobbyist	OPIC, ExIm, Commerce Dept., TDA	1/5/99
56	Senior trade lobbyist	OPIC, ExIm, Commerce Dept.	1/12/99
57	Senate budget committee staff	Budget, credit reform	1/14/99
58	Fmr Farm Credit Administration staff	FCA	2/17/99
59	Senior trade lobbyist	ExIm, OPIC, trade	2/19/99
60	EF official	EFs	4/9/99
61	EF director	EFs	4/15/99
62	EF director	EFs	4/15/99
63	EF counsel	EFs	4/15/99
64	EF director	EFs	4/16/99
65	EF director	EFs	4/16/99
66	Senior IF officer	IFs	4/25/99
67	Senior EF official	EF	5/13/99
68	Senior EF official, board member	EF	5/13/99
69	USAID mission director	EF, USAID	5/14/99
70	Senior EF officer	EF	5/19/99
71	USAID field staff	EF, USAID	5/19/99
72	USAID mission director	EF, USAID	5/26/99
73	Senior EF official	EF	5/26/99
74	Senior EF officer	EF	4/23/99
75	Senior administration political appointee	Commerce Dept., OPIC	6/3/99
77	EF chairman	EF	5/13/99
78	Senior ExIm official	ExIm	6/23/99
79	Venture capital fund professional	IFs, EFs	7/6/99

(*cont.*)

(*cont.*)

Identification Number	Anonymous description	Subject organization(s)	Interview date
80	Senior USAID official	EFs, USAID	7/7/99
81	Senior GNMA official	Ginnie Mae	10/10/99
82	Fmr senior HUD official	HUD, Fannie Mae, Freddie Mac	9/28/99
83	Senior IF official	IFs	9/27/99
84	Senior IF official	IFs, OPIC	9/27/99
85	Fmr senior FHA official	HUD, Fannie Mae, Freddie Mac, FHFB	10/28/99
86	Venture capital professional	OPIC, IFs	10/29/99
87	Senior OPIC IF staff	OPIC, IFs	8/4/99
88	OPIC staff	OPIC, IFs	8/4/99
89	Senior OPIC official (IF)	OPIC, IFs	8/4/99
90	Senior Farm Credit system organization official	Farm Credit system, FCA	7/15/99
91	GSE expert/activist	Fannie Mae, Freddie Mac	6/3/97
92	Fmr senior FNMA official	Fannie Mae	6/6/97
93	Fmr House banking staff, Fannie Mae staff	Fannie Mae, Freddie Mac	5/5/97
94	Senior Fannie Mae staff	Fannie Mae	6/2/97
95	Fmr House banking staff; Freddie Mac staff	Freddie Mac, Fannie Mae	6/4/97
96	Senior Freddie Mac official	Freddie Mac	6/6/97
97	Fmr senior HUD official	HUD, Fannie Mae, Freddie Mac	6/5/97
98	Senior OMB official	Fannie Mae, Freddie Mac	6/2/97
99	Fmr senior OMB official	Fannie Mae, Freddie Mac	5/29/97
100	Senior House committee staff	Fannie Mae, Freddie Mac	6/5/97
101	Fmr senior HUD official	Fannie Mae, Freddie Mac, HUD	6/4/97
102	Fmr senior Treasury staff	Fannie Mae, Freddie Mac, OFHEO	6/3/97

(*cont.*)

Identification Number	Anonymous description	Subject organization(s)	Interview date
103	Fmr Senate committee staff	Fannie Mae, Freddie Mac, OFHEO	6/3/97
104	Fmr Senate Member staff	Fannie Mae, Freddie Mac	6/10/97
105	Housing finance industry press	Fannie Mae, Freddie Mac, HUD	6/3/97
106	Fmr senior Treasury official	Fannie Mae, Freddie Mac	6/5/97
107	Fmr senior HUD official	Fannie Mae, Freddie Mac, HUD	6/16/97
108	Senior CBO staff	Fannie Mae, Freddie Mac	6/5/97
109	OPIC fund overseer	OPIC, IFs	8/11/99
110	OPIC fund overseer	OPIC, IFs	8/11/99
111	Senior Farmer Mac official	FCA, Farmer Mac, FCS	4/20/99
112	Fmr OMB official; scholar	GSEs	6/4/97

References

Note: * indicates that the information was retrieved from *Lexis-Nexis Academic Universe* [electronic database]

Aberbach, Joel D., and Bert A. Rockman. 1988. "Mandates or mandarins: control and discretion in the modern administrative state." *Public Administration Review*, 48 (2): 606–612.

Abramowitz, Michael. 1988. "The big business of PACs." *The Washington Post*. February 8: E1.

Abruzzese, Leo. 1997. "D'Amato vows to halt ExIm funds for Gazprom." *Journal of Commerce*. October 23: 2A.

Agence France Press. 1993. "Five former Presidents urge Congress to pass NAFTA." November 17.*

Albanian-American Enterprise Fund. 1998. *Annual Report*.

Alchian, Armen, and Harold Demsetz. 1972. "Production, information costs, and economic organization." *American Economic Review*, 62: 777–795.

Allan, John R. (ed.). 1998. *Public enterprise in an era of chance*. Saskatchewan, Canada: Canadian Plains Research Center.

American Banker. 2002. "In brief: OFHEO amends rule on capital for GSEs." February 21: 12.*

Arrow, Kenneth J. 1985. "The economics of agency." In John W. Pratt and Richard J. Zeckhauser (eds.), *Principals and agents: the structure of business*. Boston: Harvard Business School Press.

Atwood, Brian. 1993. Letter to Hon. David Obey, Chairman, Subcommittee of Foreign Operations, Committee on Appropriations. September 21.

214

Axelrod, Donald. 1992. *Shadow government: the hidden world of public authorities – and how they control over $1 trillion of your money.* New York: John Wiley & Sons.

Bailey, Dawn. 2000. "Financial trade groups urge Congress to halt GSE 'mission creep'." *American Banker-Bond Buyer.* July 24. 24 (44): 8.

Balla, Steven. 2000. "Political and organizational determinants of bureaucratic responsiveness." *American Politics Quarterly,* 28 (2): 163–193.

Baltic-American Enterprise Fund. 1997. *Annual Report.*

Banking Report. 1990. "GSEs need more oversight, risk-based capital, GAO concludes in GSE report." Bureau of National Affairs, Inc. 55: 288.

Banks, Jeffrey S., and Barry R. Weingast. 1992. "The political control of bureaucracies under asymmetric information." *American Journal of Political Science,* 36 (2): 509–524.

Barnard, Chester I. 1938. *The functions of the executive.* Cambridge, MA: Harvard University Press.

Barta, Patrick. 2001. "Why big lenders are so frightened by Fannie and Freddie." *The Wall Street Journal.* April 5: A1.

Bawn, Kathleen. 1995. "Political control versus expertise: congressional choices about administrative procedures." *American Political Science Review,* 89 (1): 62–73.

____ 1997. "Choosing strategies to control the bureaucracy: statutory constraints, oversight and the committee system." *Journal of Law, Economics and Organization,* 13 (1): 101–128.

Beamish, Rita, and Polly Lane. 1993. "Environment of competition – US industry gets boost from Clinton to compete globally." *The Seattle Times.* November 26: E1.

Beck, Nathaniel. 1982. "Presidential influence on the Federal Reserve in the 1970s." *American Journal of Political Science,* 26 (3): 415–443.

Behn, Robert D. 2001. *Rethinking democratic accountability.* Washington: Brookings Institution Press.

Bendor, Jonathan. 1988. "Review article: formal models of bureaucracy." *British Journal of Political Science,* 18: 353–395.

Bennett, James T., and Thomas J. DiLorenzo. 1983. *Underground government: the off-budget public sector.* Washington: Cato Institute.

Bergquist, Erick. 2000. "Under pressures, Fannie doubles pledge to underserved." *American Banker.* March 16: Mortgages 8.

Bernstein, Marver H. 1955. *Regulating business by independent commission.* Princeton, NJ: Princeton University Press.

Betnun, Nathan S. 1976. *Housing finance agencies: a comparison between states and HUD.* New York: Praeger.

Blustein, Paul. 1996. "House coalition deals blow to overseas insurer OPIC." *The Washington Post.* Final edn. September 12: D11.

Bozeman, Barry. 1987. *All organizations are public: bridging public and private organizational theories.* 1st edn. San Francisco: Jossey-Bass.

Bradsher, Keith. 1992. "Vote near on regulation of Fannie and Freddie." *The New York Times.* June 30: D2.

1993. "Administration plans new export initiative." *The New York Times.* September 27: D1.

Brauer, Birgit. 2001. "US missteps wasted investments in Central Asian economies, critic say." *The New York Times.* September 1: Section A6.*

Brennglass, Alan C. 1983. *The Overseas Private Investment Corporation: a study in political risk.* New York: Praeger.

Breyer, Stephen. 1982. *Regulation and its reform.* Cambridge, MA: Harvard University Press.

Brigman, William. 1981. "The executive branch and the independent regulatory agencies." *Presidential Studies Quarterly,* 11 (2): 244–261.

Brilliant, Eleanor L. 1975. *The Urban Development Corporation: private interests and public authority.* Lexington, MA: Lexington Books.

Brockman, Joshua. 1999a. "Political and rate risks cited in Fannie, Freddie plunge." *American Banker.* January 13: 6.

1999b. "Proposed capital rule irks Fannie Mae." *American Banker.* March 29: 32.*

Bulgarian-American Enterprise Fund. 1997. *Annual Report.*

Bunce, Harold L., and Randall M. Scheessele. 1998. *The GSEs' funding of affordable loans: a 1996 update.* US Department of Housing and Urban Development, Office of Policy Development and Research, Working Paper, no. HF-005.

Burstein, Rachel, and Janice C. Shields. 1997. "A probe not taken: Congress take a look at OPIC's taxpayer-backed sweetheart deals. We did." *Mother Jones.* July: 44.

Calomiris, Charles W. 1999. "Are Fannie and Freddie 'optimal mechanisms'?" In Peter J. Wallison (ed.), 2000, *Fannie Mae and Freddie Mac Vol. II: Prospects for controlling growth and expansion.* Washington: American Enterprise Institute Press.

Caro, Robert A. 1974. *The power broker: Robert Moses and the fall of New York.* New York: Knopf.

Central Asian American Enterprise Fund. 1997. *Annual Report.*

Chandler, Ralph C., and Jack C. Plano. 1988. *The public administration dictionary.* 2nd edn. Santa Barbara, California: ABC-Clio.

Chrysler, Dick. 1995. "Q: is it time to close the Commerce Department? Yes: taxpayers and exporters will be the winners of a dismantling plan." *Insight on the News.* Final edn. November 20: 18.

Clark, Cheryl. 2000. "Labs rush to put genome in public domain to prevent gene patents." *The San Diego Union-Tribune.* February 2: E6.*

Collins, Brian. 1999. "OFHEO urged to move ahead on RBC." *National Mortgage News.* May 17.

  2001. "After eight years, RBC green light." *American Banker-Bond Buyer.* July 23. 25 (42): 1.

Congressional Budget Office. 1991. *Controlling the risks of government-sponsored enterprises.* Washington: Government Printing Office.

  1996. *Assessing the costs and benefits of Fannie Mae and Freddie Mac.* Washington: Government Printing Office.

Connolly, Ceci, and Mike Allen. 2000. "Gore opposes FEC choice; candidate splits with Clinton on GOP member." *The Washington Post.* February 17.*

Connor, John. 1999. "Regulator, seeking new rules, says Fannie Mae needs risk-based capital." *The Wall Street Journal.* March 29: B7E.

  2001. "CBO director's letter blasts Fannie Mae for attack on study of federal subsidies." *The Wall Street Journal.* July 6: A2.

Cornwell, Ted. 1993. "Cisneros: FHA needs help." *National Mortgage News.* January 18: 1.

Cotterman, Robert F., and James E. Pearce. 1996. "The effects of the Federal National Mortgage Association and the Federal Home Loan Mortgage Corporation on conventional fixed-rate mortgage yields." In *Studies on privatizing Fannie Mae and Freddie Mac.* Washington: US Department of Housing and Urban Development, Office of Policy Development and Research.

Cowan, Alison Leigh. 2002. "A bipartisan call in Congress for scrutiny of Farmer Mac." *The New York Times.* June 27.*

Cox, Douglas C. 1990. Letter to Howard M. Fry, General Counsel, Agency for International Development. United States Department of Justice, Office of Legal Counsel, April 13.

Crenshaw, Albert B. 1997. "Sallie Mae management ousted; shareholder group wins proxy fight; federal charter to end." *The Washington Post.* August 1: G01.*

Crutsinger, Martin. 1996. "Now who will speak for American capitalism in the administration?" *The Associated Press.* April 7.*

Cushman, Robert E. 1941. *The independent regulatory commissions.* London: Oxford University Press.

Czech and Slovak American Enterprise Fund. 1997. *Annual Report.*

Dahl, Robert. 1957. "The concept of power." *Behavioral Science,* 2: 201–215.

DAI, see Development Alternatives, Inc.

Day, Kathleen. 1999. "HUD proposes an increase in low-income loans." *The Washington Post.* July 3: E3.

  2000a. "HUD says mortgage policies hurt blacks; home loan giants cited." *The Washington Post.* March 2: A1.*

2000b. "Fannie Mae chief defends record." *The Washington Post*. March 3: E1.

Dean, Alan L., and Harold Seidman. 1988. *Considerations in establishing the Patent and Trademark Office as a government corporation*. Washington: National Academy of Public Administration.

DeBorger, Bruno. 1993. "The economic environment and public enterprise behaviour: Belgian railroads, 1950–86." *Economica*, 60 (240): 443–463.

Denton, Nicholas. 1993. "Hungarian funds suffer from Washington politics: a look at the background to congressional censure of an Enterprise Fund whose independence was seen to be excessive." *Financial Times* (London). August 11: 2

Development Alternatives, Inc. 1995. *Program evaluation of the Central and Eastern Europe Enterprise Funds*. Bethesda, MD: Development Alternatives, Inc.

DiIulio, John D., Jr. 1994. "Principled agents: the cultural bases of behavior in a federal government bureaucracy." *Journal of Public Administration Research and Theory*, 4 (3): 277–318.

Dimock, Marshall E. 1949. "Government corporations; a focus of policy and administration, I." *American Political Science Review*, 43 (5): 899–921. Available on the World Wide Web at http://www.jstor.org/.

Dodd, Lawrence C., and Richard L. Schott. 1979. *Congress and the administrative state*. New York: John Wiley & Sons.

Doherty, Carol J. 1996. "House refuses to re-authorize trade promotion agencies." *Congressional Quarterly Weekly Report*. September 14: 2,584.

Doig, Jameson W. 1993. "Expertise, politics, and technological change: the search for mission at the Port of New York Authority." *Journal of the American Planning Association*, 59 (1): 31–44.

2001. *Empire on the Hudson: entrepreneurial vision and political power at the Port of New York Authority*. New York: Columbia University Press.

Durant, Robert F. 1985. *When government regulates itself*. Knoxville: The University of Tennessee Press.

Economist, The [London]. 1989. "Hey Mac, spare a dollar?" June 17: 91.

Eisner, Marc Allen, and Kenneth J. Meier. 1990. "Presidential control versus bureaucratic power: explaining the Reagan revolution in antitrust." *American Journal of Political Science*, 34: 269–287.

Emery, James J., Norman A. Graham, Richard L. Kauffman and Michael C. Oppenheimer. 1984. *The US Export-Import Bank: policy dilemmas and choices*. Boulder, CO: Westview Press.

Environmental Business Journal. 2002. Data provided to the author.

Epstein, David, and Sharyn O'Halloran. 1994. "Administrative procedures, information, and agency discretion." *American Journal of Political Science*, 38 (3): 697–722.

1996. "Divided government and the design of administrative procedures: a formal model and empirical test." *Journal of Politics*, 58 (2):
373–377.

Feigenbaum, Randi. 2000. "HUD pushes for affordable lending." *Newsday*.
March 3. Business & Technology: A48.

Feldman, Ron, and Jonathan G. S. Koppell. 1999. "Congressional oversight of Fannie Mae and Freddie Mac: does their GSE structure matter?" Paper presented at American Enterprise Institute conference on
government-sponsored enterprises. Washington. September 8.

Feldman, Ron. 1999. "Estimating and managing the federal subsidy of Fannie Mae and Freddie Mac: is either task possible?" *Journal of Public
Budgeting, Accounting and Financial Management* 11 (1): 81–116.

Fenno, Richard. 1973. *Congressmen in committees*. 2nd edn. Boston: Little,
Brown.

1978. *Homestyle: congressmen in their districts*. Boston: Little, Brown.

Ferejohn, John, and Charles Shipan. 1990. "Congressional influence on
bureaucracy." *Journal of Law, Economics and Organization*, 6 (special
issue): 1–20.

Fernandez, Tommy. 2002a. "In brief: mortgage bankers back GSE exemptions." *American Banker*. May 10: 20.

2002b. "MBA split on GSE legislation a size matter." *American Banker*.
May 13.*

Finer, Herman. 1940. "Administrative responsibility in democratic government." *Public Administration Review*, 1: 335–350.

1944. *The TVA: lessons for international application*. International Labor
Office, Studies and Reports, Series B (Economic Conditions), no. 37.

Fiorina, Morris. 1981. "Congressional control of the bureaucracy: a mis-
match of incentives and capabilities." In Lawrence Dodd and Bruce
Oppenheimer (eds.), *Congress reconsidered*. 2nd edn. Washington:
Congressional Quarterly Press.

Fish, Gertrude S. 1979. *The story of housing*. New York: Macmillan.

Fleming, Marcus. 1950. "Production and price policy in public enterprise."
Economica. New Series, 17 (65): 1–22. Available on the World Wide
Web at http://links.jstor.org/.

Flinders, Matthew V. 1999. "Setting the scene: quangos in context." In
Matthew V. Flinders and Martin J. Smith (eds.), *Quangos, accountability and reform*. New York: St. Martin's Press, Inc.

Foreman-Peck, James, and Michael Waterson. 1985. "The comparative efficiency of public and private enterprise in Britain: electricity generation between the world wars." *The Economic Journal*, 95. Supplement: Conference Papers: 109–123. Available on the World Wide Web
at http://www.jstor.org/.

Fortune [magazine online]. 2002. "The 1999 Fortune 500." Available on the World Wide Web at http://www.pathfinder.com/fortune/fortune500/search.html.

Foster, Kathryn Ann. 1997. *The political economy of special-purpose government.* Washington: Georgetown University Press.

Fox, James W. 1996. *The venture capital mirage: assessing the USAID experience with equity investment.* USAID Center for Development Information and Evaluation. Report no. 17.

Friedmann, W., and J. F. Garner (eds.). 1970. *Government enterprise – a comparative study.* London: Stevens & Sons.

Friedrich, Carl J. 1940. "Public policy and the nature of administrative responsibility." *Public Policy,* 1: 3–24.

Froomkin, A. Michael. 1996. *Reinventing the government corporation.* Electronic document. Available on the World Wide Web at http://www.law.miami.edu/~froomkin/articles/reinvest.htm.

GAO, see General Accounting Office.

Garsson, Robert M., Jim McTague and Cheryl Zboril. 1988. "The selling of hostile takeover." *The Washington Post.* February 22: 13.

Garver, Rob. 2001. "Hearing finds scant interest in changing regulation of GSEs." *American Banker.* May 9: 6.

——— 2002. "In brief: OFHEO releases governance rule for Fannie, Freddie." *American Banker.* June 4: 4.*

General Accounting Office. 1991. *Government-sponsored enterprises: a framework for limiting the government's exposure to risks.* GAO/GGD-91-90. Washington: Government Printing Office.

——— 1994. *Enterprise Funds: evolving models for private sector development in Central and Eastern Europe.* GAO/NSIAD-94-77. Washington: Government Printing Office.

——— 1995. *Government corporations: profiles of existing government corporations.* GAO/GGD-96-14. Washington: Government Printing Office.

——— 1997. *Government-sponsored enterprises: advantages and disadvantages of creating a single housing GSE regulator.* GAO/GGD-97-139. Washington: Government Printing Office.

——— 2001. *Aviation Security: vulnerabilities in, and alternatives for, preboard screening security operations.* GAO-01-1171T. Washington: Government Printing Office.

Gilpin, Kenneth N. 2002. "The federal regulator of Fannie Mae and Freddie Mac, the two biggest mortgage finance companies, said yesterday that it would conduct a comprehensive review of their financial disclosures." *The New York Times.* April 9: C3.

Golden, Marissa Martino. 1992. "Exit, voice, loyalty, and neglect: bureaucratic responses to presidential control during the Reagan

Administration." *Journal of Public Administration Research and Theory*, 2 (1).

Goodnow, Frank J. 1900. *Politics and administration.* New York: Russell & Russell.

Goodrich, Carter. 1949. "The Virginia system of mixed enterprise." *Political Science Quarterly*, 64 (3): 355–387. Available on the World Wide Web at http://links.jstor.org/.

Gordon, Michael R. 1997. "Defying pressure over Iran deal, Russians spurn US loan pact." *The New York Times.* Late edn. – final. December 18: A5.

Grosh, Barbara, and Rwekaza S. Mukanda (eds.). 1994. *State-owned enterprises in Africa.* Boulder, CO: Lynne Rienner Publishers.

Gruber, Judith E. 1987. *Controlling bureaucracies.* Berkeley: University of California Press.

Gruber, Judith E., and Janet A. Weiss. 1984. "Using knowledge for control of fragmented policy areas." *Journal of Policy Analysis and Management*, 3: 225–247.

Guerrero, Kevin. 2000. "Bill to conglomerate regulatory agencies facing a tough fight." *American Banker.* March 13: 4.

Guild, Frederic H. 1920. "Special municipal corporation." *American Political Science Review*, 14 (2): 286–291. Available on the World Wide Web at http://www.jstor.org/.

Gulino, Denis G. 1985. "Reagan signs farm credit system bill; hope federal bailout won't be needed." *The Bond Buyer.* December 24: 3.*

Hamilton, Neil W., and Peter R. Hamilton. 1981. *Governance of public enterprise: a case study of urban mass transit.* Lexington, MA: Lexington Books.

Hammond, Thomas H., and Jack H. Knott. 1996. "Who controls the bureaucracy? Presidential power, congressional dominance, legal constraints and bureaucratic autonomy in a model of multi-institutional policymaking." *Journal of Law, Economics and Organization*, 12 (1): 119–165.

Hawkins, Robert B. 1976. *Self-government by district: myth and reality.* Stanford, CA: Hoover Institution Press.

Healy, Melissa. 1999. "State posts drop in births to single women; welfare: California leads the US in reducing unwed motherhood, which is linked to dependence on aid." *The Los Angeles Times.* Home edn. September 14: A3.

Heclo, Hugh. 1977. *Government of strangers.* Washington: Brookings Institution Press.

    1978. "Issue networks and the executive establishment." In Anthony King (ed.), *The new American political system.* Washington: American Enterprise Institute Press.

Heller, Michele. 2001. "Rep. Baker to scale back GSE overhaul legislation." *American Banker.* March 29: 1.

Hendrie, Paul. 1998. "Capital investments: OPIC's politically connected investors can't lose as US taxpayers shoulder the risks." *Capital Eye.* January 15: 1.

Henriques, Diana B. 1986. *The machinery of greed: public authority abuse and what to do about it.* Lexington, MA: Lexington Books.

Henry, Shannon. 2002. "In-Q-Tel, investing in intrigue; CIA unit scours country for useful technologies". *The Washington Post.* July 1.*

Hill, Jeffrey S., and James E. Brazier. 1991. "Constraining administrative decisions: a critical examination of the structure and process hypothesis." *Journal of Law, Economics and Organization,* 7 (2): 373–400.

Hill, L. B. 1991. "Who governs the American administrative state: a bureaucratic-centered image of governance." *Journal of Public Administration Research and Theory,* 1: 261–294.

Hofstadter, Richard. 1969. *The idea of a party system.* Berkeley: University of California Press.

Holmes, Steven A. 1990. "Senate votes economic sanctions against China." *The New York Times.* January 31: A8.

Horn, Murray J., and Kenneth A. Shepsle. 1989. "Symposium on the law and economics of bargaining: commentary on 'administrative arrangements and the political control of agencies': administrative process and organizational form as legislative responses to agency costs." *Virginia Law Review,* 75.*

Housing and Development Reporter Current Developments. 1991. "Quick action expected on GSE bills; extension of MRBs, tax credits appears uncertain." September 2: 297.

— 1992. "Trade groups urge regulatory restraint in Senate GSE bill." February 3: 744.

Howard, Frank. 1985. "Overseas risk agency mistakes girth for growth." *The Wall Street Journal.* September 19: A1.

Hummel, Ralph P. 1987. *The bureaucratic experience.* 3rd edn. New York: St Martin's Press.

Hungarian American Enterprise Fund. 1998. *Annual Report.*

International trade Administration. 1999. *Small and medium-sized exporting companies: a statistical profile.* Available on the World Wide Web at http://www.ita.doc.gov/td/industry/otea/doos/SMEseminar.PDF. ITA, see International Trade Administration.

Jackson, Kenneth T. 1985. *Crabgrass frontier: the suburbanization of the United States.* New York: Oxford University Press.

Jacoby, Mary. 2000. "Critics question Fannie Mae's influence." *The St Petersburg Times.* July 17: A1.

Julavits, Robert. 2000. "GSE regulator wants more control over budget." *American Banker*. January 28: 8.

2002. "OFHEO's momentum stalls as Senator slams budget plan." *American Banker*. March 27: 9.*

Kane, Edward J. 1989. *The S&L insurance mess: how did it happen?* Washington: Urban Institute Press.

1999. "Housing finance GSEs: who gets the subsidy?" In Peter J. Wallison (ed.), 2000, *Fannie Mae and Freddie Mac* Vol. II: *Prospects for controlling growth and expansion*. Washington: American Enterprise Institute Press.

Kaufman, Herbert. 1977. *Red Tape*. Washington: Brookings Institution Press.

Kearney, Richard C., and Chandan Sinha. 1988. "Professionalism and bureaucratic responsiveness: conflict or compatibility?" *Public Administration Review*, 48 (1): 571–579.

Kettl, Donald F. 1983. *The regulation of American federalism*. Baton Rouge: Louisiana State University Press.

1993. *Sharing power: public governance and private markets*. Washington: Brookings Institution Press.

Khademian, Anne M. 1995. "Reinventing a government corporation: professional priorities and a clear bottom line." *Public Administration Review*, 55 (1): 17–28.

Kopecki, Dawn. 2002. "Freddie Mac note sales rile banks." *The Wall Street Journal*. May 9: D2.

Kosterlitz, Julie. 2000a. "Siblings fat and sassy." *National Journal*, 32 (10): 1,498–1,507.

2000b. "Beltway money yes, Fannie PACs no." *National Journal*, 32 (20): 1,502.*

Krause, George A. 1994. "Federal Reserve policy decision making: political and bureaucratic influences." *American Journal of Political Science*, 38 (1): 124–144.

Krause, George A., and David B. Cohen. 1997. "Presidential use of executive orders." *American Politics Quarterly*, 25 (4): 458–482.

Krislov, Samuel, and David H. Rosenbloom. 1981. *Representative bureaucracy and the American political system*. New York: Praeger.

Kulish, Nicholas, and Jacob M. Schlesinger. 2001. "How Fannie Mae beat effort by adversaries to rein it in." *The Wall Street Journal*. July 5. Available on the World Wide Web at http://interactive.wsj.com/.

Kulish, Nicholas. 2001. "Effort to curb Fannie Mae, Freddie Mac in Congress will be watched closely." *The Wall Street Journal*. March 28.

Kupiec, Paul. 1995. "Techniques for verifying the accuracy of risk measurement models." *Federal Reserve Board Finance and Economics Discussion*, Series 95, no. 24.

Labaton, Stephen. 1991. "Power of the mortgage twins." *The New York Times.* November 12: B2.

Lawrence, Richard. 1989. "Congress votes to ban ExIm Bank China credits." *Journal of Commerce.* November 24: 1A.

1996. "Commerce Secretary lauded as strong business advocate; export promotion effort praised." *Journal of Commerce.* April 4: 2A.*

1997. "Export fund bill wins victory on Capitol Hill." *Journal of Commerce.* June 27: 2A.

Leazes, Francis J. 1987. *Accountability and the business state: the structure of federal corporations.* New York: Praeger.

Levine, Daniel S. "It's alive! ExIm Bank's reprieve." *World Trade,* 11: 38–40.

Lewis-Beck, Michael S., and John R. Alford. 1980. "Can government regulate safety? The coal mine example." *American Political Science Review,* 74 (3): 745–756.

Light, Paul. 1993. "An end to the war on waste (bureaucratic inefficiency)." *Brookings Review,* 11 (2): 48.

Lillienthal, David E. 1944. *TVA, democracy on the march.* New York: Pocket Books, Inc.

Lioukas, S., D. Bourantas and V. Papadakis. 1993. "Managerial autonomy of state-owned enterprises: determining factors." *Organization Science,* 4 (4): 645–666. Available on the World Wide Web at http://www.jstor.org/.

Lott, John R., Jr. 1995. "Are government or private enterprises more likely to engage in dumping? Some international evidence." *Managerial and Decision Economics,* 16 (3): 185–204. Available on the World Wide Web at http://links.jstor.org/.

2001. "Governmental structure, trustee selection, and public university prices and spending: multiple means to similar ends." *American Journal of Political Science,* 45 (4): 845–861.

Maass, Peter. 1993a. "US helps pay Hungary's chief of state industries." *The Washington Post.* May 13: D11.

1993b. "Congressman charges aid effort goes awry; Hungary Enterprise Fund pays fat salaries." *The Washington Post.* July 29: A15.

Macey, Jonathan R. 1992. "Organizational design and political control of administrative agencies." *Journal of Law, Economics and Organization,* 8 (1): 93–125.

Manchester, Paul B. 2002. *Goal performance and characteristics of mortgages purchased by Fannie Mae and Freddie Mac, 1998–2000.* US Department of Housing and Urban Development, Office of Policy Development and Research, Working Paper, no. HF-015.

March, James G. 1966. "The power of power." In David Easton (ed.), *Varieties of political theory.* Englewood Cliffs, NJ: Prentice Hall.

Markoff, John. 1999. "CIA to nurture companies dealing in high technology." *New York Times on the Web.* September 29. Electronic document. [No longer available at the original address.]

Mashaw, Jerry L. 1994. "Improving the environment of agency rule-making: an essay on management, games and accountability." *Law and Contemporary Problems,* 57 (2): 185–257.

Matlack, Carol. 1990. "Getting their way." *National Journal,* 22 (43): 2,584–2,588.

Mayer, Kenneth R. 1999. "Executive orders and presidential power." *Journal of Politics,* 61 (2): 445–467.

McCubbins, Matthew. 1985. "The legislative design of regulatory structure." *American Journal of Political Science,* 29 (4): 721–748.

McCubbins, Matthew, Roger G. Noll and Barry R. Weingast. 1987. *Administrative procedures as instruments of political control.* St. Louis, MO: Washington University Press.

    1989. "Structure and process, politics and policy: administrative arrangements and the political control of agencies." *Virginia Law Review,* 75: 431–482.

McCubbins, Matthew, and Thomas Schwartz. 1984. "Congressional oversight overlooked: police patrols versus fire alarms." *American Journal of Political Science,* 28: 165–179.

McDiarmid, John. 1940. "California uses the government corporation." *American Political Science Review,* 34 (2): 300–306. Available on the World Wide Web at http://www.jstor.org/.

McTague, Jim. 1996. "Embattled Bankroller." *Barron's.* September 16: 15.

Meade, J. E. 1944. "Price and output policy of state enterprise." *The Economic Journal,* 54 (215/216): 321–339. Available on the World Wide Web at http://links.jstor.org/.

Meier, Kenneth J., and John P. Plumlee. 1978. "Regulatory administration and organizational rigidity." *Western Political Quarterly,* 21: 80–95.

Meier, Kenneth J., Joseph Stewart, Jr., and Robert E. England. 1991. "The politics of bureaucratic discretion: educational access as an urban service." *American Journal of Political Science,* 35 (1): 155–177.

Meier, Kenneth J., Robert D. Wrinkle, and J. L. Polinard. 1999. "Politics, bureaucracy and farm credit." *Public Administration Review,* 59: 293–302.

Melnick, R. Shep. 1983. *Regulation and the courts: the case of the Clean Air Act.* Washington: Brookings Institution Press.

Meyers, Roy T. 1988. "Budgetary controls for federal public authorities." Tenth annual research conference of the Association for Public Policy Analysis and Management. October 27–29. Seattle.

Mihyo, Paschal B. 1994. *Non-market controls and the accountability of public enterprises in Tanzania.* Basingstoke: Macmillan.

Miller, Gary J. 1992. *Managerial dilemmas: the political economy of hierarchy.* New York: Cambridge University Press.

Mitchell, Jerry. 1999. *The American experiment with government corporations.* Armonk, NY: M. E. Sharpe.

Mitnick, Barry M. 1980. *The political economy of regulation: creating, designing and removing regulatory forms.* New York: Columbia University Press.

Mladenka, Kenneth R. 1980. "The urban bureaucracy and the Chicago political machine: who gets what and the limits to political control." *American Political Science Review,* 74: 991–998.

Modern Africa Fund. Undated. Company materials provided to the author.

Moe, Ronald C. 1983. *Administering public functions at the margin of government: the case of federal corporations.* Washington: Congressional Research Service.

Moe, Ronald C., and Robert S. Gilmour. 1995. "Rediscovering principles of public administration: the neglected foundation of public law." *Public Administration Review,* 55 (2): 135–146.

Moe, Ronald C., and Thomas H. Stanton. 1989. "Government-sponsored enterprises as federal instrumentalities: reconciling private management with public accountability." *Public Administration Review,* 49 (4): 321–329.

Moe, Terry M. 1982. "Regulatory performance and presidential administration." *American Journal of Political Science,* 26 (2): 197–224.

1985. "Control and feedback in economic regulation: the case of the NLRB." *American Political Science Review,* 79(4): 1,094–1,116.

1989. "The politics of bureaucratic structure." In John E. Chubb and Paul E. Peterson (eds.), *Can the government govern?* Washington: Brookings Institution Press.

1990. "Political institutions: the neglected side of the story." *Journal of Law, Economics and Organization,* 6 (special issue): 213–261.

Moe, Terry M., and Jonathan Bendor. 1985. "An adaptive model of bureaucratic politics." *American Political Science Review,* 79 (3): 755–774.

Moe, Terry M., and M. Caldwell. 1994. "The institutional foundations of democratic government: a comparison of presidential and parliamentary systems." *Journal of Institutional and Theoretical Economics,* 150 (1): 171–195.

Mortgage Marketplace. 1993. "Cisneros will rely on GSEs to achieve housing goals." January 18: 1.

Mortgage Servicing News. 2001. "Regulators clear GSE capital rule." 4 (9): 14.

Mosher, Frederick. 1979. *The GAO: the quest for accountability in American government.* Boulder, CO: Westview Press.

Musolf, Lloyd D. 1956. "Canadian public enterprise: a character study." *American Political Science Review,* 50 (2): 405–421. Available on the World Wide Web at httpl//:www.jstor.org/journals/.

—— 1963. "Public enterprise and development perspectives in South Vietnam." *Asian Survey,* 3 (8): 357–371. Available on the World Wide Web at http://www.jstor.org/journals/.

—— 1983. *Uncle Sam's private profit-seeking corporations: Comsat, Fannie Mae, Amtrak and Conrail.* Lexington, MA: Lexington Books.

—— 1984. *Employing US public enterprises as instruments of public policy: techniques and limitations.* Austin: University of Texas at Austin Press.

Musolf, Lloyd D., and Harold Seidman. 1980. "The blurred boundaries of public administration." *Public Administration Review,* 40 (2): 124–130.

Nakashima, Ellen. 2002. "For Bush's regulatory 'czar,' the equation is persuasion; Graham wields cost-benefit analysis for, against rules." *The Washington Post.* Final edn. May 10: A35.*

National Mortgage News. 1999. "GSE cap rule could hurt low-mod loans." February 15.*

—— 2002. "OFHEO will add staff to monitor GSE accounting." February 18. 26 (21): 8.

Neikirk, William. 1996. "Clinton readies tobacco crackdown; proposed rules take aim at teen smoking and could open the door to FDA regulation." *The Chicago Tribune.* North sports final edn. August 22: 1.

Nellis, John R. 1994. "Public enterprises in sub-Saharan Africa." In Barbara Grosh and Rwekaza S. Mukanda (eds.), *State-owned enterprises in Africa.* Boulder, CO: Lynne Rienner Publishers.

Newcomer, Kathryn E. 1998. "The changing nature of accountability: the role of the Inspector General in federal agencies." *Public Administration Review,* 58 (2): 129–136.

Niskanen, William A., Jr. 1971. *Bureaucracy and representative government.* Chicago: Aldine, Atherton.

Nitschke, Lori. 1998. "Private enterprises with official advantages." *Congressional Quarterly Weekly Report.* June 18: 1,569–1,648.

Noll, Roger G. 1971. *Reforming regulation; an evaluation of the Ash Council proposals.* Washington: Brookings Institution Press.

Office of Federal Housing Enterprise Oversight. 1994. *Annual Report to Congress.*

—— 1995. *Annual Report to Congress.*

—— 1997. *Annual Report to Congress.*

—— 2001. *Annual Report to Congress.*

2002. "Statement of OFHEO director Armando Falcon, Jr., regarding the President's budget recommendation to remove OFHEO from the appropriations process." February 4.

OFHEO, see Office of Federal Housing Enterprise Oversight.

O'Laughlin, Michael G. 1990. "What is bureaucratic accountability and how can we measure it?" *Administration & Society*, 22 (3): 275–302.

OPIC, see Overseas Private Investment Corporation.

Overseas Private Investment Corporation. 2001. *Annual Report.*

2002. *Annual Report.*

Osborne, David, and Ted Gaebler. 1992. *Reinventing government: how the entrepreneurial spirit is transforming the public sector.* Reading, MA: Addison-Wesley.

Ottaway, David B. 1996. "At US-sponsored Enterprise Funds, a question of authority." *The Washington Post.* February 14: A19.*

Pennock, J. Roland. 1941. *Administration and the rule of law.* New York: Farrar and Rinehart.

Perry, James, and H. G. Rainey. 1988. "The public-private distinction in organizational theory." *Academy of Management Review*, 13: 182–201.

Pickle, J. J., and Bill Gradison. 1992. "Dear colleague" letter (provided to the author). October 2.

Piven, Frances Fox, and Richard A. Cloward. 1971. *Regulating the poor: the functions of public welfare.* New York: Pantheon Books.

Polish-American Enterprise Fund. 1998. *Annual Report.*

Prakash, Snigdah. 1996. "With heat on, Fannie and Freddie press for relief." *American Banker.* June 5: 1–8.

Pritchett, C. Herman. 1943. *The Tennessee Valley Authority: a study in public administration.* Chapel Hill: University of North Carolina Press.

1946a. "The paradox of the government corporation." *Public Administration Review*, 1: 381–389.

1946b. "The Government Corporation Control Act of 1945." *American Political Science Review*, 40 (3): 495–509.

Raines, Franklin. 2000. "Fannie Mae's credit history." *The Washington Post.* Final edn. March 10: A21.

Rauch, Jonathan. 1989. "Treating S&Ls with farm credit tonic." *National Journal*, 21 (9): 529.

1991. "You lose, we all pay." *National Journal*, 23 (14): 784–788.

Rees, Ray. 1984. "The public enterprise game." *The Economic Journal*, 94. Supplement: Conference Papers: 83–95. Available on the World Wide Web at http://www.jstor.org/.

Rehm, Barbara. 2001. "Put-up time for White House on supervision of the GSEs." *American Banker.* July 16 mortgage 1.

Riley, Dennis D. 1987. *Controlling the federal bureaucracy.* Philadelphia: Temple University Press.

Ripley, Randall B., and Grace A. Franklin, 1980. *Congress, the bureaucracy and public policy.* Georgetown, Ontario: Irwin-Dorsey.

Robinson, Glen O. 1989. "Symposium on the law and economics of bargaining: commentary on 'administrative arrangements and the political control of agencies': administrative process and organizational form as legislative responses to agency costs." *Virginia Law Review,* 75.*

Romanian-American Enterprise Fund. 1997. *Annual Report.*

Romzek, Barbara S. 1996. "Enhancing accountability." In James L. Perry (ed.), *Handbook of Public Administration.* San Francisco: Jossey-Bass.

Romzek, Barbara S., and Melvin J. Dubnick. 1987. "Accountability in the public sector: lessons from the Challenger tragedy." *Public Administration Review,* 47 (3): 227–238.

Rosen, Bernard. 1989. "Revitalizing the federal civil service." *Public Administration Review,* 49 (5): 501–506.

Rourke, Francis E. 1984. *Bureaucracy, politics and public policy.* 3rd edn. Boston: Little, Brown.

    1990. "Executive responsiveness to presidential policies: the Reagan Presidency." *Congress & the Presidency,* 17 (1): 1–11.

Sacks, Oliver W. 1987. *The man who mistook his wife for a hat and other clinical tales.* New York: Perennial Library.

Salkowski, Joe. 2000. "Is granting of net patents out of synch with reality?" *Los Angeles Business Journal,* 22: 19.

Sanghera, Sathnam. 2000. "Fannie Mae and Freddie Mac come up against their lobbying match: the companies may face an overhaul in regulation." *Financial Times* (London). June 15: 4.

Savage, J. A. 1997. "Privatization, political insurrection, and corporate welfare." *Business and Society Review,* 97: 39–40.

Scales, Ann. 1999. "Bush raps rivals, own party on education; urges accountability for schools; rues Democrats' 'despair.'" *The Boston Globe.* City edn. October 6: A29.

Schaefer, Brett. 1996. "Test of corporate welfare durability." *The Washington Times.* September 10: 28.

Schattschneider, Elmer Eric. 1942. *Party government.* New York: Holt, Rinehart and Winston.

Scher, Seymour. 1961. "Regulatory agency control through appointment: the case of the Eisenhower Administration and the NLRB." *Journal of Politics,* 23 (4): 667–688.

Scherer, Ron. 1999. "Want to start a day care? Help is on the way." *Christian Science Monitor.* December 22: 18.

Schneider, Greg. 2002. "Airport checkpoint control shifts today; with changes ahead, US security agency begins to step in at commercial sites." *The Washington Post.* February 17.*

Schneider, Greg, and Ellen Nakashima. 2001. "Bush air safety plan stops short of federal takeover." *The Washington Post.* September 17.*

Schneider, Keith. 1985. "Farm credit overhaul is approved by Senate." *The New York Times.* December 3: D1.*

Scholz, John T., Jim Twombly and Barbara Headrick. 1991. "Street-level political controls over federal bureaucracy." *American Political Science Review,* 85 (3): 829–850.

Schroeder, Michael. 1999. "Critics of Fannie Mae finally gain a powerful voice." *The Wall Street Journal.* June 17: A28.

Seidman, Harold. 1952. "The theory of the autonomous government corporation: a critical appraisal." *Public Administration Review,* 12 (2): 89–96.

1954. "The government corporation: organization and controls." *Public Administration Review,* 14 (3): 183–192.

1975. "Government-sponsored enterprise in the United States." In Bruce L. R. Smith (ed.), *The new political economy: the public use of the private sector.* New York: John Wiley & Sons.

1988. "The quasi world of the federal government." *Brookings Review.* Summer: 23.

Seidman, Harold, and Robert Gilmour. 1986. *Politics, position, and power: from the positive to the regulatory state.* 4th edn. New York: Oxford University Press.

Seiler Jr., Robert S. 1999. "Fannie Mae and Freddie Mac as investor-owned public utilities." *Journal of Public Budgeting, Accounting & Financial Management,* 11 (1): 117–154.

Selznick, Philip. 1953. *TVA and the grass roots: a study in the sociology of formal organization.* Berkeley: University of California Press.

1957. *Leadership in administration: a sociological interpretation.* New York: Harper & Row.

Sensenbrenner, Joseph. 1991. "Quality comes to city hall." *Harvard Business Review,* 69 (2): 64–70.

Shapiro, Martin. 1997. "The problem of independent agencies in the United States and the European Union." *Journal of European Public Policy,* 4 (2): 276–291.

Sharkansky, Ira. 1979. *Whither the state? Politics and public enterprise in three countries.* Chatham, NJ: Chatham House Publishers.

Shrivastava, M. P. 1992. *Parliamentary accountability and supervision over public enterprises.* New Delhi: Deep & Deep Publications.

Sinclair, Ward. 1987. "Administration backs $5 billion farm credit; support conditioned on reforms." *The Washington Post.* June 10: A4.*

Skelcher, Chris. 1988. *The appointed state.* Philadelphia: Open University Press.

Smith, Bruce L. R. (ed.). 1975. *The new political economy: the public use of the private sector.* New York: John Wiley and Sons.

Stanton, Thomas H. 1991. *A state of risk: will government-sponsored enterprises be the next financial crisis?* New York: HarperBusiness.

——— 1994. "Nonquantifiable risks and financial institutions: the mercantilist legal framework of banks, thrifts, and government-sponsored enterprises." In Charles A. Stone and Anne Zissu (eds.), *Global Risk Based Capital Regulations,* vol. 1. Burr Ridge, IL: Irwin Professional Publishing.

——— 1999. "Devising an effective legal framework for supervising the public benefits and public costs of government-sponsored enterprises." Paper presented at American Enterprise Institute conference on government-sponsored enterprises. Washington September 1.

——— 2002. *Government-sponsored enterprises.* Washington: American Enterprise Institute Press.

Stevens, Douglas F. 1993. *Corporate autonomy and institutional control.* Montreal & Kingston: McGill-Queen's University Press.

Stevenson, Richard W. 2000. "Defending home turf from attack; Fannie Mae is facing assault by House panel and business rivals." *The New York Times.* April 22: C1.

Stillman, Robert D. 1996. "To the editor." *Barron's.* September 23.

Surrey, Stanley. 1976. *The federal tax legislative process.* New York: Association of the Bar of the City of New York.

Tangri, Roger. 1999. *The politics of patronage in Africa.* Trenton, NJ: Africa World Press.

Taub, Stephen and Jackey Gold. 1989. "Twilight zone." *Financial World.* December 12: 42–46.

Taylor, Andrew. 1992. "Bill establishing new overseer for Fannie, Freddie clears." *Congressional Quarterly Weekly Report.* October 10: 3,138.

Thompson, James D. 1967. *Organizations in action: social science bases of administrative theory.* New York: McGraw-Hill.

Thynne, Ian. 1998. "Government companies as instruments of state action." *Public Administration and Development.* New York: John Wiley & Sons.

Tierney, John T. 1984. "Government corporations and managing the public's business." *Political Science Quarterly,* 99 (1): 73–92. Available on the World Wide Web at http://www.jstor.org/.

TPCC, see Trade Promotion Coordinating Committee.

Trade Promotion Coordinating Committee. 1997. *The National Export Strategy.*

Treves, Giussepino. 1970. "The public corporation in Italy." In W. Friedmann and J. F. Garner (eds.), *Government enterprise – a comparative study.* London: Stevens & Sons.

Truman, David B. 1993. *The governmental process.* 2nd edn. Berkeley: Institute of Governmental Studies Press.

Tullock, Gordon. 1965. *The politics of bureaucracy.* Washington: Public Affairs Press.

US Agency for International Development. 1998. Internal documents describing the Enterprise Fund program (provided to the author).

US Department of State. 2000. *West Bank and Gaza: overview of assistance program.* Internal memorandum (provided to the author).

US Department the Treasury. 1991. *Report of the Secretary of the Treasury on government-sponsored enterprises.* Washington: Government Printing Office.

　　1996. *Government sponsorship of the Federal National Mortgage Association and the Federal Home Loan Mortgage Corporation.* Washington: Government Printing Office.

US House of Representatives. Committee on Banking, Finance and Urban Affairs. 1991. *Government-sponsored housing enterprises financial safety and soundness act of 1991: report together with additional and dissenting views (to accompany H. R. 2,900).* House Report 102–206. Washington: Government Printing Office.

US House of Representatives. Committee on Banking, Finance and Urban Affairs. Subcommittee on Housing and Community Development. 1991. *Government-sponsored housing enterprises financial safety and soundness act of 1991: hearings before the subcommittee on housing and community development of the Committee on Banking, Finance and Urban Affairs.* Washington: Government Printing Office.

US House of Representatives. 1991. *Government-sponsored housing enterprises financial safety and soundness act of 1991.* 102nd Congress, 1st session, H. R. 2,900. Washington: Government Printing Office.

US Russia Investment Fund. 1997. *Annual Report.*

US Senate. 1992. Senator Levin of Michigan commenting on the FHEFSSA. 102nd Congress, 2nd session. *Congressional Record,* 138 (91).

US Senate: Committee on Banking, Housing and Urban Affairs. 1991. *Legislative proposals to ensure the safety and soundness of government-sponsored enterprises.* 102nd Congress, 1st session, May 10 and July 11. Washington: Government Printing Office.

　　1994. "Testimony April 13, 1994, Henry Cisneros, Secretary of Housing and Urban Development, Senate Banking: GSE Housing Goals." *Federal Document Clearing House Congressional Testimony.* April 13.*

Vogelsang, Ingo. 1990. *Public enterprise in monopolistic and oligopolistic industries.* Chur, Switzerland: Harwood Academic Publishers.

Wachter, Susan, James Follain, Peter Linneman, Roberto G. Quercia and George McCarthy. 1996. "Implications of privatization: the attainment of social goals." In *Studies on privatizing Fannie Mae and Freddie Mac.* Washington: US Department of Housing and Urban Development, Office of Policy Development and Research.

Wald, Matthew L. 1996a. "Board resigns at US Fund for Czechs and Slovaks." *The New York Times.* March 3: 9.

1996b. "Pushing for a new FAA focus." *The New York Times on the Web.* June 24. Electronic document. [No longer available at the original address.]

Wallison, Peter J. 2001. "Rein in Fannie Mae – before it's too late." *Wall Street Journal.* March 3: A14.

Walsh, Annmarie Hauck. 1978. *The public's business: the politics and practices of government corporations.* Cambridge, MA: MIT Press.

Ware, Roger. 1986. "A model of public enterprise with entry." *Canadian Journal of Economics,* 19 (4): 642–655. Available on the World Wide Web at http://links.jstor.org/.

Waterman, Richard W. 1989. *Presidential influence and the administrative state.* Knoxville: University of Tennessee Press.

Weicher, John. 1999. "The development of housing GSEs." Paper presented at American Enterprise Institute conference on Fannie Mae and Freddie Mac: "Public purposes and private interests." Washington. March 24.

Weidenbaum, Murray L. 1984. "US sticklers for safety extras jack up your auto sticker prices." *Christian Science Monitor.* October 30.*

Weingast, Barry R. 1981. "Regulation, reregulation and deregulation: the political foundations of agency clientele relationships." *Law and Contemporary Problems,* 44: 147–177.

Weingast, Barry R., and Mark J. Moran. 1983. "Bureaucratic discretion or Congressional control? Regulatory policy-making by the Federal Trade Commission." *Journal of Political Economy,* 91 (5): 765–800.

Weiss, Janet A., and Judith E. Gruber. 1984. "Using knowledge for control of fragmented policy areas." *Journal of Policy Analysis and Management,* 3: 225–247.

Weiss, Janet A., Judith E. Gruber and R. H. Carver. 1989. "Two cheers for paperwork: the value and burden of federal reporting." *Publius: The Journal of Federalism,* 19 (2): 161–174.

West, William F. 1995. *Controlling the bureaucracy: institutional constraints in theory and practice.* Armonk, NY: M. E. Sharpe.

Western NIS American Enterprise Fund. 1997. *Annual Report.*

Wettenhall, Roger L. 1987. *Public enterprise and national development: selected essays.* Canberra: Royal Australian Institute of Public

Administration (ACT Division) in association with the National Council, Royal Australian Institute of Public Administration.

Wildavsky, Aaron B. 1992. *The new politics of the budgetary process.* 2nd edn. New York: HarperCollins Publishers.

Wilke, John R., and Patrick Barta. 2001. "Firms report Fannie Mae, Freddie Mac threats." *The Wall Street Journal.* March 8: A3.

Willoughby, W. F. 1917. "The national government as a holding corporation: the question of subsidiary budgets." *Political Science Quarterly*, 32 (4): 505–521. Available on the World Wide Web at http://links.jstor.org/.

Wilson, David. 1995. "Quangos in the skeletal state." In F. F. Ridley and David Wilson (eds.), *The quango debate.* Oxford: Oxford University Press.

Wilson, James Q. 1980. "The politics of regulation." In James Q. Wilson (ed.), *The politics of regulation.* New York: Basic Books.

1989. *Bureaucracy: what government agencies do and why they do it.* New York: Basic Books.

Wilson, James Q., and Patricia Rachal. 1977. "Can the government regulate itself?" *The Public Interest*, 46: 3–14.

Wilson, Woodrow. 1887. "The study of administration." *Political Science Quarterly*, 2: 197–222.

Wood, B. Dan. 1990. "Does politics make a difference at the EEOC?" *American Journal of Political Science*, 34 (2): 503–530.

Wood, B. Dan, and Richard W. Waterman. 1991. "The dynamics of political control of the bureaucracy." *American Political Science Review*, 85 (3): 801–850.

1994. *Bureaucratic dynamics: the role of bureaucracy in a democracy.* Boulder, CO: Westview Press.

Woodward, Calvin. 1997. "Union deal averts passenger rail strike." *The Chattanooga Times.* November 3: A10.

Zuckman, Jill. 1991a. "Banking panel approves bill to oversee Fannie, Freddie." *Congressional Quarterly Weekly Report.* July 27: 2,059.

1991b. "The $50,000 question." *Congressional Quarterly Weekly Report.* August 3: 2,140.

Index

9 780521 819565